Welcome to the
World of
Computers,
5th Edition

D1298744

RUSSEL STOLINS
Institute of American Indian Arts

LABYRINTH
LEARNING™

Product Manager:
Brian Favro

Development Manager:
Laura Popelka

Senior Instructional Designer:
Arl Nadel

Senior Editor:
Susan Scharf

Editorial Assistant:
Alexandria Henderson

Production Manager:
Rad Proctor

Production Assistant:
Andrew Kenower

Cover Concept:
Huckdesign

LABYRINTH
LEARNING™

Welcome to the World of Computers, 5th Edition
Russel Stolins

Labyrinth Learning
2560 9th Street, Suite 320
Berkeley, California 94710
800.522.9746
On the web at lablearning.com

Screenshots reprinted with permission.

ITEM: 1-59136-652-6
ISBN-13: 978-1-59136-652-2

Manufactured in the United States of America.

10 9 8 7 6 5 4 3 2

Table of Contents

Quick Reference Table Summary . . . . *vii*
Behind the Screen Summary . . . . *viii*
Preface . . . . *ix*

U N I T   1

Windows Basics

L E S S O N   1

Exploring the Start Screen . . . 3

Starting Windows 5
   Starting a Session 5
   Signing On 5
Comparing the Two Desktops 7
   Using the Tablet Desktop 8
   Using the Traditional Desktop 8
Using a Mouse and Touchpad 9
   Using a Mouse 11
   Performing Basic Mouse Motions 11
   Using a Touchpad 11
   Using Touchscreen Gestures 12
Using the Start screen 14
   Display Live Tiles 14
   Configuring Tiles 15
   Using the Apps Screen 15
Changing Use Modes 18
   Signing Out 19
   Windows 8.1 Charms 19
Shutting Down and Restarting Windows 24
   Restarting Windows 24
Concepts Review 26
Skill Builders 27
Try This at Home 31

L E S S O N   2

Using Programs 33

Using the Traditional Desktop 35
   The Windows Taskbar 35
   Pinning Programs to the Taskbar 35
Searching for Programs 37
   Search Charm 37
Controlling Application Windows 39
   Using Quick-Sizing Buttons 39
   Aero Window Commands 42
Multitasking 45
   Switching Between Programs 45
Drawing with Paint 48
   Paint's Ribbon 48
   How Ribbon Commands Are Organized 48
Saving Your Work 52
   Where Your Work Takes Place 53
   Save Locations 53
   File-naming Rules 54
Writing with WordPad 55
   WordPad's Ribbon 55
Using Copy and Paste 58
   The Clipboard 59
Removing Flash Drives Safely 61
   Safely Remove Hardware Command 61
Concepts Review 63
Skill Builders 64

LESSON 3

Using a Word Processor 71

Knowing Your Writing Instrument 73
Creating a New Document 73
   Templates 74
Typing in Programs 75
   Word's Ribbon 75
   Changing the View 76
Using Tab Settings 79
   Tab Leaders 79
Formatting with Styles and Themes 83
   Styles 83
   Themes 83
Using Bullets and Symbols 88
   About Symbol Fonts 88
Using Cut, Copy, and Paste 91
   Cut Compared to Copy 91
   Selecting Text 91
   Cursor Keys 91
Printing Documents 95
   The Default Printer 95
   Saving as a PDF 95
   Opening Recent Documents 97
Concepts Review 100
Skill Builders 101

LESSON 4

Working with Files 109

Using the Control Panel 111
   Common Control Panel Tasks 111
   Opening the Control Panel 112
   Setting Mouse Properties 113
   Double-Clicking 113
Browsing Files 115
   File Explorer 115
   Changing the View 116
   Sorting Files 116
   The File Storage Hierarchy 118
   Folders Compared to Files 119
   Opening Files 119
   Default Programs 119
Using Folders 122
   Creating New Folders 122
   Opening Folders 122
   The Back Button 123
Moving and Copying Files 124
   Cut, Copy, and Paste for Files 124
   The Undo Command 124
   Modifying the Quick Access Toolbar 125
   Moving and Copying Multiple Files 127
   Using Select All 127
   Copying Files with the Copy Command . . . 127
Backing Up Flash Drives 128
   Storing Backups 129
Deleting Files and Folders 131
   What Happens to Deleted Files
     and Folders? 131
   Restoring Files from the Recycle Bin 131
   Emptying Files from the Recycle Bin 132
Using the Save As Command 134
Concepts Review 139
Skill Builders 140

UNIT 2

The Internet

LESSON 5

Browsing Web Pages 147

Defining the Internet 149
Using Internet Explorer. 150
   Two Versions 150
   Other Browsers 151
   The Homepage 151
   Internet Explorer Window Features. 152
Navigating with the Address/Search Bar 152
   Typing Web Addresses. 152
   URLs 153
   The Refresh Button 153
   The Smart Address Bar 156
   Recently Viewed Pages. 157
Navigating with Links. 158
   Varieties of Links 159
   About WebSims 159
Browsing Controls. 161
   Basic Navigation Buttons. 161
   Making Multipage Jumps 162
   The Home Button 163
   Setting a Custom Homepage 163
Viewing Web Pages 166
   The Mouse Scroll Wheel 166
   Full-screen View. 166
   Zooming the View 167
Concepts Review. 170
Skill Builders 171

LESSON 6

Searching for Websites . . .175

Searching from the Address Bar. 177
   About Search Engines 177
   Choosing a Search Engine 177
   Adding Search Providers 178
   Setting a Default Search Provider. 178
Performing Basic Keyword Searches 182
   Selecting Search Words 182
   Search Suggestions. 183
   Interpreting Search Results 186
   Searching for Specific Types of Results. 187
   Narrowing a Search 188
Using Tabbed Browsing. 189
   Opening Links in a New Tab 189
   Navigating Tabs. 191
Bookmarking Favorite Websites 194
   The Favorites Bar 194
   Creating Favorites 195
   Hidden Controls 195
   The Favorites Center 199
   Organizing Favorites into Folders 199
   Deleting Favorites 200
Using the History View 200
   Changing the History View 201
Printing Web Pages 202
   Selecting What to Print 202
Concepts Review. 206
Skill Builders 207

LESSON 7

Using Cloud File Storage . .213

Defining the Cloud 215
   Using Servers 215
   Services 215
   Cloud Storage Options 216
   Technology Moves Forward. 216
Using Web Access to Cloud Storage. 216
   Navigating Cloud Storage 217
Downloading and Uploading 220
   Downloading Files. 223
   Changing the View 223
Using Synchronized Storage 226
   Watched Folders 226
Saving to Watched Folders 229
   OneDrive and Office 2013. 229
   Dropbox Example 229
Deleting Files from Cloud Storage. 231
   Deleted Online Files and the Recycle Bin . . 231
Viewing Files Offline 233
   Setting Files for Offline Viewing 233
Creating a File in the Cloud. 235
   OneDrive Web Apps 235
   Web App Capabilities 235
   Missing Save Button 236
Concepts Review. 240
Skill Builders 241

LESSON 8

Sharing Files 249

Using the Outlook Web App 251
   Composing a Message 251
   Using Email Addresses. 252
Sharing Files Overview 254
Sending Email Attachments 254
   Attachment Size 255
Saving Email Attachments 256
   Attachment Security Risks. 257
Sharing Cloud Storage Files 260
   Sharing Compared to Attachments. 260
   Types of Sharing 261
   Online Editing of Shared Files 261
Sharing Cloud Folders. 266
   Shared Folders and Subscriptions 266
   Shared Folder Display 267
Concepts Review. 271
Skill Builders 272

APPENDIX A

Units of Measure 277

Glossary 279
Index 283

Quick Reference Table Summary

Folder and File Tasks

Creating a New Folder 122

Backing Up Flash Drive Files 129

Internet and Email Tasks

Starting Internet Explorer 150

Setting Homepages in Internet Explorer 164

Adjusting the View of a Web Page 167

Searching with the Address Bar 179

Using Tabbed Browsing 191

Creating and Using Favorites 200

Printing Web Pages 203

OneDrive: Setting Files for Offline Viewing 233

Sending and Receiving Attachments with Outlook.com .257

Sharing Files in Cloud Storage 261

Windows Tasks

Editing Tiles 16

Switching Between Modes and Shutting Down 20

Pinning Applications to the Taskbar 35

Searching for Programs 37

Using Snap to Resize Windows 43

Switching Programs with Windows 45

Word Tasks

Setting Tabs and Tab Leaders 79

Using Styles and Themes 84

Applying Bullets 88

Behind the Screen Summary

Internet and Email

Internet Domains 154
How Internet Search Engines Work. 184
Online Storage Privacy 219
Avoiding Security Risks. 255
Phishing Scams 259

The Physical Computer

Basic Computer Components. 40
Computer Displays 58
About Computer Keyboards 78
About Printers 96

Windows

Power and Privacy. 6
We've Been Here Before. 10
About Operating Systems 20

Working with Programs

How Programs Run 52
Software Standards and Ease of Use. 87
Drive Letter ABCs 120
Organizing Digital Photos. 138

Preface

In today's digital world, knowing how to use the most popular suite of Desktop software applications is critical. Our goal is to teach new users how to take advantage of this technology and to help experienced users understand how the applications have changed from previous versions. We begin with fundamental concepts and take learners through a systematic progression of exercises, resulting in skill mastery.

An online student resource center accompanies this book. It contains Concepts Review quizzes, any student exercise files needed, and other learning tools. The URL for the student resource center is printed on the inside cover of this textbook.

Visual Conventions

This book uses visual and typographic cues to guide students through the lessons. Some of the cues are described below.

`Type this text`	Text you type at the keyboard is printed in this typeface.
Start screen	The important words in exercise steps are presented like this.
Windows	Glossary terms are presented like this.
Ribbon Tab → Command Group → Command	Commands to execute from the Ribbon are presented like this.
FROM THE KEYBOARD `Ctrl`+`S` to save	These margin notes present shortcut keys for executing certain tasks.
	Tips, notes, and warnings are called out with special icons.
	This icon indicates the availability of a web-based simulation for an exercise. You may need to use a WebSim if your computer lab is not set up to support particular exercises.

Hands-On exercises appear after concepts discussions. They provide detailed, step-by-step tutorials so you can master the skills presented.

 The Concepts Review Quizzes appear in the book as well at the online student resource center.

 Skill Builder exercise provide additional skills practice with moderate assistance.

 Try This at Home exercises are challenging exercises that you are encouraged to try outside of class and on your own.

Acknowledgements

This textbook has benefited greatly from the reviews and suggestions of the following instructors.

Anita Jones, *West Central Technical College*

Gordon Pike, *Haywood Community College*

Susan Swanson, *Nicolet Area Technical College*

Clay Teague, *Central Georgia Technical College*

Jacob Walker, *Grant Adult Education*

Kathy Yeomans, *Ventura Adult & Continuing Education*

Windows Basics

This unit focuses on Windows, word-processing, and file organization. In Lesson 1, you will log on to the computer and explore the Windows 8.1 Start screen, as well as the Traditional Desktop and the Tablet Desktop. You will also start programs, set the computer to different modes, and properly sign off Windows and shut down the computer. In Lesson 2, you will get busy working in the Paint and the WordPad applications. You will size program windows, create and save files, and copy and paste between applications. In Lesson 3, you will explore the Word window and learn about the Ribbon, the Quick Access toolbar, and the Mini toolbar. This unit closes out with a discussion of file management. You will browse for and open files, create folders for file organization, delete and restore files, and create a backup of your important work.

Windows Basics

Lesson 1: Exploring the Start Screen 3

Lesson 2: Using Programs 33

Lesson 3: Using a Word Processor 71

Lesson 4: Working with Files 109

Exploring the Start Screen

When you start Windows 8.1 and sign in, the first thing you'll see is the Start screen. With its distinctive tiles based on the Windows Phone interface, Windows 8.1 takes some getting used to when you've worked with previous versions. Windows 8.1 also features two Desktops, rather than the single Desktop of previous Windows versions. In this lesson, you get started signing on and off of Windows, switching between the two Desktops, and logging off or shutting down Windows properly.

LESSON OBJECTIVES

- Sign on and log off from Windows
- Identify the significant features of the Windows Start screen and Desktops
- Start any installed Windows program
- Switch between the tablet and Traditional Desktops
- Use Lock, Sleep, and Switch Users modes
- Sign off and shut down Windows

Case Study: Starting Over

Destiny felt a familiar uncertainty as she first started using Windows 8.1. She remembered her tentative first steps using Windows XP on an old computer. In some ways, Windows 8.1 was like starting over again. For example, the Start menu was missing. Some programs filled the entire screen, without a Taskbar or window-sizing buttons.

Destiny decided to try an old-tech approach to learning this new tech. She bought a stack of index cards. Whenever she learned a new command, she created a card about it, with a brief title at the top, and a few notes about it below. Then whenever she felt stuck, she'd flip through her cards. Oftentimes, just seeing the name of a command jogged her memory and she was back on track. Even the process of writing a card helped fix the new feature in her memory.

Search Charm

Searches for programs, web pages, etc.

- Point at top-right corner of screen
- [Windows key] + C — charms
- [Windows key] + S — search

After a couple of weeks, Destiny felt more comfortable with the basic commands. She rarely needed her cards anymore.

Starting Windows

The first thing your computer does when it "wakes up" is locate and load an operating system, such as Windows, into its RAM. This book covers the latest version of Windows: 8.1.

Starting a Session

Once Windows loads, it indicates that it's ready to work by displaying a Lock screen. Depending on how Windows is configured, you may also see status information, such as email or the local weather.

Signing On

Windows 8.1 renames the "log on" command to "sign on." It's similar to the Windows 7 logon command, with one exception: Signing on with a Microsoft account sends data to Microsoft from your work sessions. Microsoft uses this data to perform tasks, such as synching your personal settings between devices. It may also use such data to target personal ads in some programs or web browsing sessions. Signing on with a local (non-Microsoft) account does not send out data.

 HANDS-ON 1.1 **Sign On to Windows 8.1**

In this exercise, you will sign on to Windows 8.1 and view the Start screen.

1. If necessary, switch on the power to the computer and monitor.
   The computer goes through its startup routine, ending with a Windows Welcome screen.

2. Write your sign-on information below. Your instructor will give you this.

   Username: _____

   Password: _____
   After a pause, Windows displays the lock screen.

3. Click once anywhere on the **Lock screen**.
   A sign-on screen appears, displaying the available user names.

4. Click the **username** you've been assigned for the course.

5. Sign on:

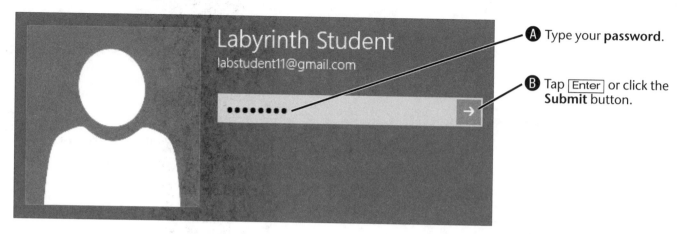

Labyrinth Student
labstudent11@gmail.com

Ⓐ Type your **password**.

Ⓑ Tap [Enter] or click the **Submit** button.

The Start screen appears, displaying tiles for various activities and programs.

Behind the Screen

Power and Privacy

Windows 8.1 introduces some convenient features, such as easy access to email, and OneDrive cloud storage. You can arrange to synchronize multiple Windows devices to use the same Start screen, passwords, and other settings. Most of these convenience features are associated with a Microsoft account. In fact, there are parts of Windows 8.1, such as the Microsoft Store, Photos, and Skype that you can't access at all without signing on using a Microsoft account. A Microsoft account is simply a sign-on ID that gives access to various Microsoft services. It can be linked to any email account, not just one hosted by Microsoft.

There are privacy trade-offs you should be aware of when you use a Microsoft account with Windows 8.1. Your account gives Microsoft the capability to track many of your activities without your being aware of it. For example, when you perform a search via Windows Help, Microsoft may record and use it. Microsoft may also transmit this data to third parties, enabling them to send ads targeted to some of your activities.

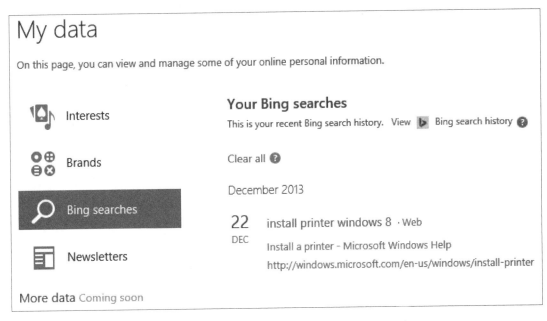

A search in Windows 8.1 Help that was recorded by Microsoft.

Comparing the Two Desktops

Windows 8.1 has two Desktops: Tablet and Traditional. You can run programs on both Desktops simultaneously and easily switch between them. Each Desktop has specific capabilities. With Windows 8.1, you can even view both Desktops at the same time.

The Internet Explorer app version on the Tablet Desktop

The Internet Explorer program version on the Traditional desktop

Using the Tablet Desktop

The Tablet Desktop runs new apps designed for Windows 8.1 and optimized to run on tablet touchscreens. These apps usually fill the screen completely. Windows 8.1 added the capability to split the Tablet Desktop between two and sometimes three apps.

!NOTE! Microsoft calls the Tablet Desktop the Modern Interface.

Using the Traditional Desktop

The Traditional Desktop is similar to that used in previous versions of Windows. It runs traditional Windows programs, such as Word, Excel, iTunes and others, that can't run in the Tablet Desktop. This Desktop retains program windows you can size flexibly, as you will learn in the next lesson.

!NOTE! Windows 8.1 allows you to display Traditional Desktop programs alongside tablet apps.

 HANDS-ON 1.2 **View the Two Desktops**

In this exercise, you will launch a tablet app and view the Traditional Desktop.

!NOTE! If Internet Explorer is not set as your default web browser, it may not open on the Tablet Desktop in the first step. Your instructor can tell you if you should try a different browser.

1. Click the **Internet Explorer** tile.

   Windows launches the Internet Explorer tablet app. Notice how it fills the entire screen.

2. Tap the **Windows** ⊞ key.

   You return to the Start screen.

Internet Explorer

3. Click the **Desktop** tile, which may appear different from the figure below.

Windows displays the Traditional Desktop.

4. Click **Internet Explorer**.

Windows launches the Desktop version of Internet Explorer. You can see the window-sizing buttons at the top-right corner.

5. Close the **Internet Explorer** window.

The window disappears.

6. Tap the **Windows** key.

You return to the Start screen.

Using a Mouse and Touchpad

Regardless of the device used, a computer or tablet lets you give commands by pointing and clicking or tapping items on the screen. There are three primary devices used to control the computer.

- **Touchpad** – A touch-sensitive pad on laptop computers
- **Mouse** – An external pointing device
- **Touchscreen** – A touch-sensitive screen that lets you give commands with your hand or a stylus

We've Been Here Before

The release of Windows 8.1 brought plenty of headaches for many users. Familiar features such as the Start button and Start menu suddenly disappeared, and it wasn't always obvious where they'd gone. Adjusting to significant changes in a computer we use daily is always a challenge. This is especially so if the "improvements" aren't really.

18 Years Ago... In 1995, Microsoft introduced Windows 95. This was the first version of Windows to feature the Start button. Prior to Windows 95, you'd have started programs from a screen like this:

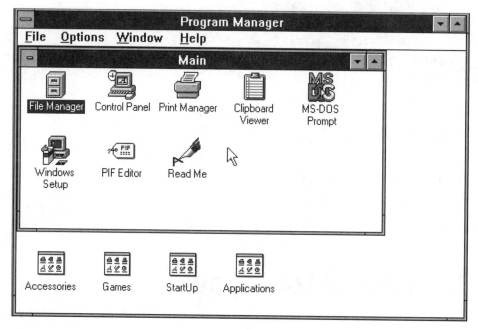

A screen from Windows 3.1 circa 1992

!NOTE! Want to learn more about the evolution of computer interfaces? Check out the links on the student resource center.

Using a Mouse

Even on new touchscreen computers, the mouse remains a significant pointing device. It often offers greater precision than the touchscreen. It can also be tiring to repeatedly raise your hand up to the touchscreen. The mouse has a primary (left) button and secondary (right) button. Most mice have a scroll wheel.

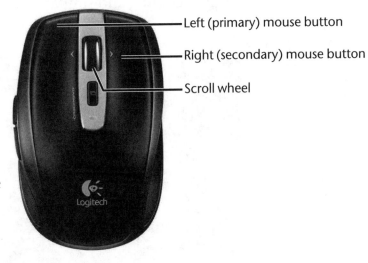

Left (primary) mouse button

Right (secondary) mouse button

Scroll wheel

Performing Basic Mouse Motions

There are five basic motions you can perform with the mouse. If your computer has a touchscreen, there are additional motions (called gestures) you can use.

Mouse Motions

Command Name		Description
point		Point at a spot on the screen without clicking.
click		Tap and release the primary (left) mouse button.
double-click		Quickly tap and release the primary mouse button twice.
right-click		Tap and release the secondary (right) mouse button.
drag		Hold down the primary mouse button as you move the mouse.

Using a Touchpad

Virtually all laptop computers have a built-in touchpad. A touchpad translates your finger location into a command to move the mouse pointer on the screen. A tap on most touchpads translates into a click with the mouse. Many touchpads also detect whether more than one finger is in use. This allows you to give scrolling and similar commands without moving the mouse pointer to a scrollbar.

A laptop computer touchpad

Using Touchscreen Gestures

All tablet computers use a touchscreen. This allows you to give commands by touching items on the screen directly, rather than pointing at them with a mouse or touchpad. An increasing number of laptop and Desktop computers feature this, too. However, they tend to be $100 or so more expensive than non-touchscreen computers.

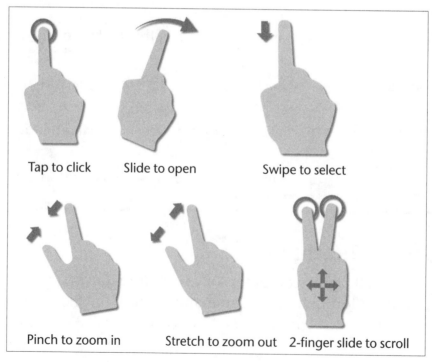

| Tap to click | Slide to open | Swipe to select |

| Pinch to zoom in | Stretch to zoom out | 2-finger slide to scroll |

Some examples of gestures used with a touchscreen.

NOTE! Because so few computer labs feature touchscreens, these commands are not given in any exercise instructions.

HANDS-ON 1.3 Practice Mouse Motions

In this exercise, you will practice using the five basic mouse motions.

1. Click the **Desktop** tile.

2. Practice mouse motions with the Recycle Bin:

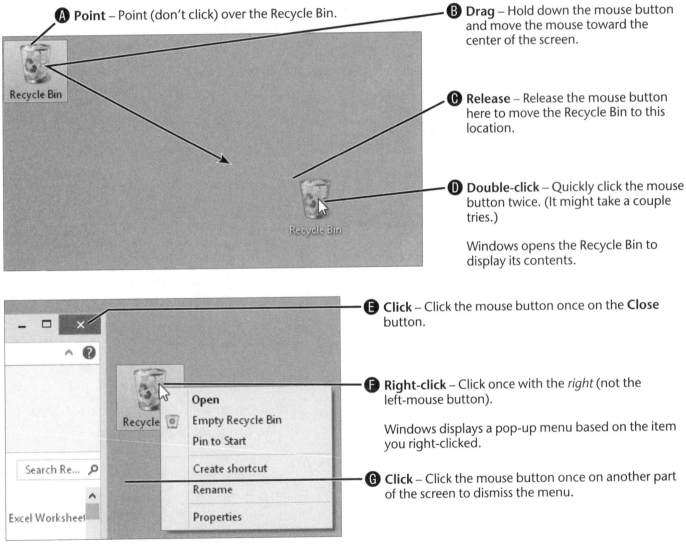

Ⓐ **Point** – Point (don't click) over the Recycle Bin.

Ⓑ **Drag** – Hold down the mouse button and move the mouse toward the center of the screen.

Ⓒ **Release** – Release the mouse button here to move the Recycle Bin to this location.

Ⓓ **Double-click** – Quickly click the mouse button twice. (It might take a couple tries.)

Windows opens the Recycle Bin to display its contents.

Ⓔ **Click** – Click the mouse button once on the **Close** button.

Ⓕ **Right-click** – Click once with the *right* (not the left-mouse button).

Windows displays a pop-up menu based on the item you right-clicked.

Ⓖ **Click** – Click the mouse button once on another part of the screen to dismiss the menu.

3. Tap the **Windows** ⊞ key.

You return to the Start screen.

Using the Start screen

The Windows 8.1 Start screen performs functions similar to the Start menu on Windows 7. Start screen tiles let you start programs and see the latest information from some programs. The following figure displays features typical of the Windows 8.1 Start screen.

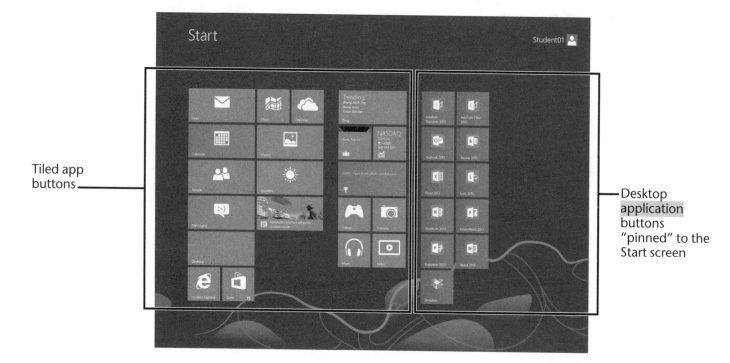

Tiled app buttons

Desktop application buttons "pinned" to the Start screen

NOTE! Depending on your Windows sign-on ID, the locations of tiles can change. The image displayed on some tiles (live tiles) may also change.

Display Live Tiles

Some Windows 8.1 app (programs) display changing information. For example, the Weather tile can display the current weather of a location you choose. Some users find this distracting. Fortunately, you can turn off the animation, making the tile static.

HANDS-ON 1.4 **Use the Start screen**

In this exercise, you will use the Start screen to launch a tablet app.

1. Click the **Weather** tile. It should be on the left side of the screen.

   Windows launches the Weather tablet app. You may see a prompt to use your location.

2. Click **Allow** if you are asked to use your location. Otherwise skip to step 4.

Weather displays the city you are in, or nearby.

3. Click **Confirm**.

Weather displays the current weather.

4. Use the **scroll wheel** on top of the mouse or the scroll bar at the bottom of the screen to scroll toward the right.

Various additional features and information displays appear.

5. Tap the **Windows** key.

The Start screen reappears, a very convenient shortcut we'll use a lot. Notice that the weather tile displays your local weather, unless it wasn't doing so before.

Configuring Tiles

You can move tiles around on the Start screen. For example, you can put more frequently used tiles into more convenient spots.

- **Resize** – You can change the size of individual tiles
- **Move** – You can move tiles around on the Start screen
- **Remove** – You can send unneeded tiles to the Apps screen
- **Add** – You can add tiles from the Apps screen to the Start screen

Using the Apps Screen

The Apps screen contains all available program tiles. Even if you remove a tile from the Start screen, it will remain in the Apps screen unless you uninstall it.

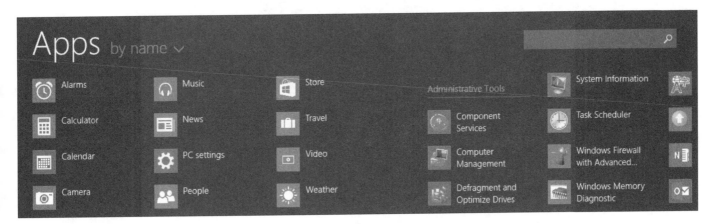

Task	Procedure
Start Customize Tiles Mode	• Right-click a clear (non-tile) area of the Start screen. • Choose Customize.
Edit a tile	• Right-click any tile. • Choose the desired customization (unpin, resize, etc.).
Switch off a live tile	• Right-click the live tile. • Choose Turn Live Tile Off.
Add a new tile to Start screen	• Point near the bottom-left of the Start screen. • Click the Apps ⊙ button. • Right-click the desired app, then choose Pin to Start.

HANDS-ON 1.5 Customize Start screen Tiles

In this exercise, you will customize tiles on the Start screen.

⚠️ **NOTE!** If you accidentally left-click rather than right-click a tile, tap the Windows key on the keyboard to return to the Start screen.

1. Change the size of the Mail tile:

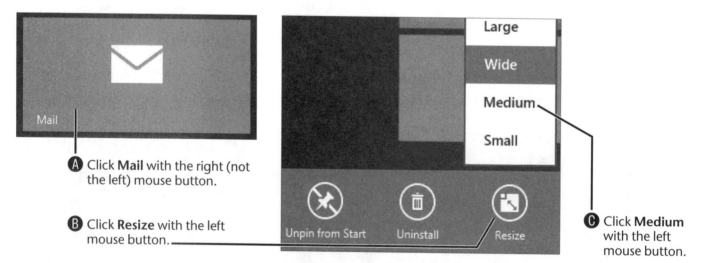

Ⓐ Click **Mail** with the right (not the left) mouse button.

Ⓑ Click **Resize** with the left mouse button.

Ⓒ Click **Medium** with the left mouse button.

Windows resizes the tile.

2. Right-click (don't left-click) the **Mail** tile again.

3. Choose **Resize→Wide** from the bottom of the screen.

The tile becomes as wide as the column.

4. Move the Mail tile:

Ⓐ Right-click (don't left-click) on a blank area of the screen.

Ⓑ Click once on **Customize** at the bottom-right corner of the screen.

Windows shifts into editing mode.

Ⓒ Hold down the mouse button, then drag the **Mail** tile below the **Calendar**; release the mouse button.

The Calendar tile jumps above the Mail tile.

Ⓓ Drag the **Calendar** back below the **Mail** tile.

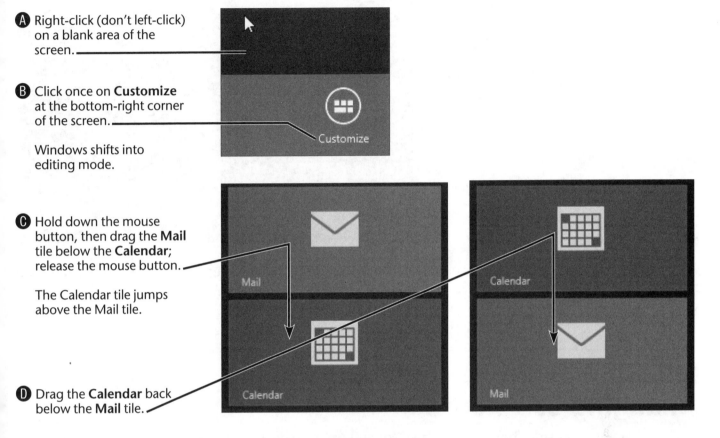

5. Remove a tile from the Start screen:

Ⓐ Right-click (don't left-click) on the **Skype** tile (or another tile near the bottom-left corner of the screen).

Ⓑ Click once on **Unpin from Start**.

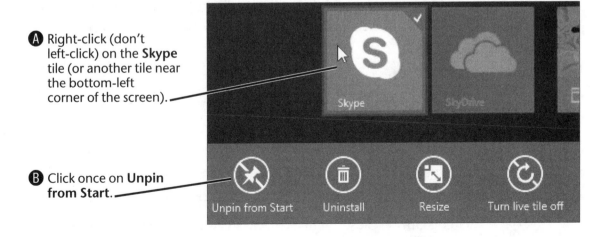

The tile disappears. Other tiles may change position to fill in the gap.

6. Return the tile to the Start screen:

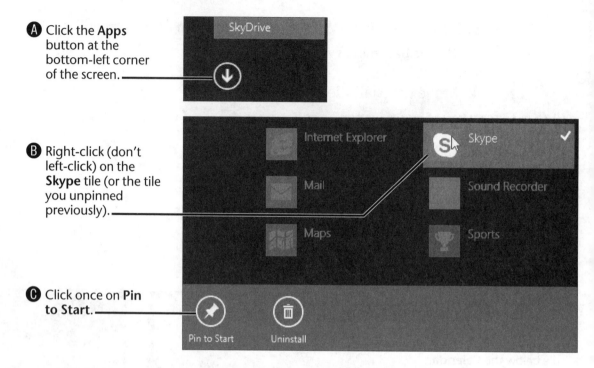

(A) Click the **Apps** button at the bottom-left corner of the screen.

(B) Right-click (don't left-click) on the **Skype** tile (or the tile you unpinned previously).

(C) Click once on **Pin to Start**.

The tile reappears on the Start screen. It probably won't reappear in the same location you removed it from. It may even appear in a new column.

7. Drag the tile to any new location on the Start screen.

Changing Use Modes

Besides being active and logged on, you can put the computer into other modes of operation. The most useful mode is Sleep, which puts the computer into a low-power state until you "wake" it. Lock mode keeps the computer running normally, but won't display the screen again until your password is entered.

Windows Modes of Operation

Mode	Description/Use
Sleep	Puts the computer into a low-power mode until a key is tapped or the mouse is moved.
Lock	Blocks any view of the Desktop until you reenter your password.
Log Off/ Sign Out	Closes your Windows session, which shuts down all running programs and windows.

Signing Out

Signing out in Windows 8.1 is identical to logging off in previous versions of Windows. Your program windows close and Windows signs you out of any active services.

Windows 8.1 Charms

Charms are a set of basic commands available via the Charms corner. You can access charms from both Windows 8.1 Desktops. You'll learn more about charms in later lessons. The following figure explains the basic function of each charm.

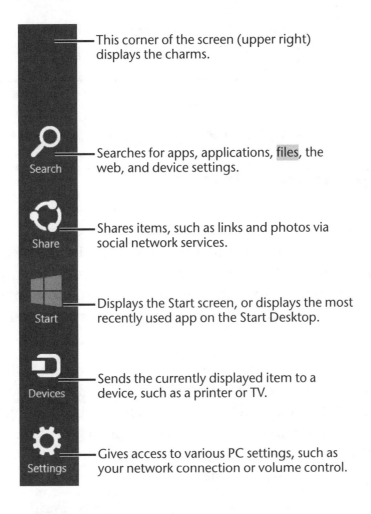

This corner of the screen (upper right) displays the charms.

Search — Searches for apps, applications, files, the web, and device settings.

Share — Shares items, such as links and photos via social network services.

Start — Displays the Start screen, or displays the most recently used app on the Start Desktop.

Devices — Sends the currently displayed item to a device, such as a printer or TV.

Settings — Gives access to various PC settings, such as your network connection or volume control.

FROM THE KEYBOARD

Use Windows 🏴+C to display charms

Task	Procedure
Sign out	• Display the Start screen, and then click your username and choose Sign Out.
Switch to a different user	• Display the Start screen, and then click your username and choose a new user from the list.
Sleep	• Display the charms (top-right screen corner), and then choose Settings. Click the Power button, and then choose Sleep.
Lock	• Display the Start screen, click your account name, and choose Lock.
Shut down or restart	• Display the charms (top-right screen corner), and then choose Settings. Click the Power button, and then choose Shut Down or Restart.

Behind the Screen

About Operating Systems

An operating system (OS) is the most basic software your computer needs to function. When you first switch on the computer, it does a check of its hardware. Next, it searches for and loads an OS into RAM so it can begin doing work for you. Until the OS loads, a computer can recognize only the most rudimentary keyboard commands. After the operating system loads, the computer or tablet is ready to interact with you normally via the mouse and touchscreen gestures.

Varieties of Operating System　There are many operating systems available to run personal computers. This book is based on Microsoft Windows, the world's most widely used OS. Other computers run different operating systems. For example, Apple® Macintosh® computers run Mac OS X. Linux is an open source OS; its source code is widely available and any programmer can contribute improvements to it.

Behind the Screen *(continued)*

Versions of Windows   Over the years, there have been numerous versions of Windows. This book supports the latest version: 8.1. There are multiple Windows versions in common use:

- **Windows XP** (released 2002)
- **Windows Vista** (released 2007)
- **Windows 7** (released 2009)
- **Windows 8** (released 2012)
- **Windows 8.1** (released 2013)

The primary reason to use an operating system is to run one or more specific programs. Every program is designed to run with one or more versions of an OS. Some programs need a more recent version of the OS in order to function. You can see these details under System Requirements on the program's web page.

Roles of an Operating System   An operating system performs many roles.

- **Interpreting commands:** The OS is the interface between you and all of the computer's hardware and software. When you point and click with the mouse or type on the keyboard, the OS receives the input and decides what to do with it.

- **Controlling hardware:** The OS controls all hardware in the computer system. When you need to load a program or a user data file from a hard drive, the OS locates it and sends it to RAM for processing. When you give a print command, the OS tells the printer how to print the desired document.

- **Keeping track of files:** All computer software resides on one (or more) storage drives as files. The OS sets the rules for naming and storing these files. A hard drive can only think in terms of bits and bytes stored on various tracks and sectors of its storage system. Fortunately, the OS allows you to give files easy-to-recall names and keeps track of how and where each file is stored. When you need a file or program, you tell the OS what you want and it then tells the hard drive how to get it.

- **Running application programs:** Application programs are software that let you get work done. Most software is written and coded to run on a specific OS. The OS controls loading software into RAM and switching from one application program to another.

HANDS-ON 1.6 Change Modes

In this exercise, you will view other users who could log in on your computer, then put the computer into lock and sleep mode.

1. Sign out:

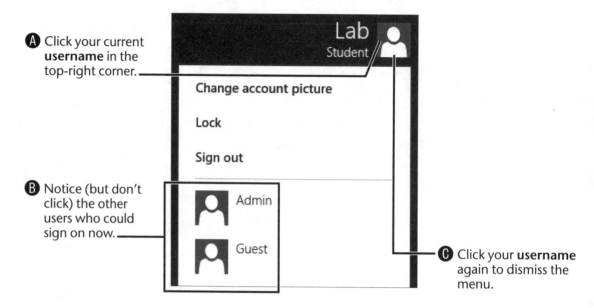

🅐 Click your current **username** in the top-right corner.

Lab
Student

Change account picture

Lock

Sign out

🅑 Notice (but don't click) the other users who could sign on now.

Admin

Guest

🅒 Click your **username** again to dismiss the menu.

2. Give the Lock command:

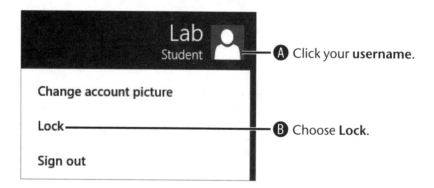

Lab
Student

Change account picture

Lock

Sign out

🅐 Click your **username**.

🅑 Choose **Lock**.

Windows displays its startup screen.

3. Click the **Startup screen**.

Windows displays a password box.

4. Type your **password** and tap Enter.

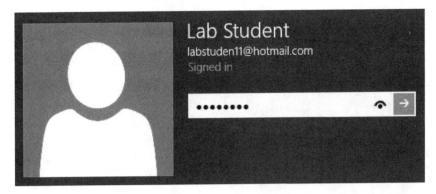

5. Give the Sleep command:

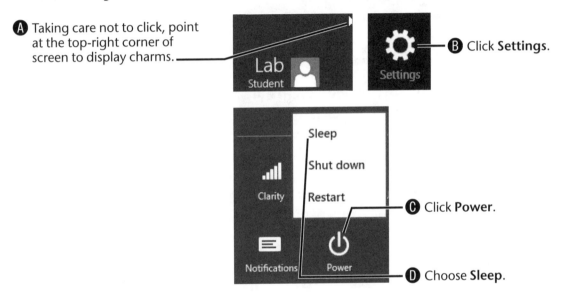

Ⓐ Taking care not to click, point at the top-right corner of screen to display charms.

Ⓑ Click **Settings**.

Ⓒ Click **Power**.

Ⓓ Choose **Sleep**.

Windows turns off the screen and goes into a low-power state.

6. Tap any keyboard key or move the mouse to exit Sleep mode.

Windows "wakes up" and the startup screen or a password prompt appears.

7. Click the startup screen if it appeared.

8. Type your **password** and tap Enter.

You are back at your Windows session. All previously running programs are in the same state they were in when you put the computer to sleep.

Shutting Down and Restarting Windows

You always want to shut down the computer properly. Don't press or hold down the power button. The Shut Down command tells Windows to close any open application windows, save your work, then shut off power to the computer. If your computer needs to install some updates to its software, the Shut Down or Restart command can also perform this task.

Windows Update

Restart your PC to finish installing updates. Automatic restart will occur in 1 day.

Windows displays a notification when it needs to restart in order to install software updates.

Restarting Windows

Sometimes when you install or uninstall software, you need to restart the computer. The restart command essentially shuts down, then immediately restarts the computer.

!TIP! If the computer seems especially sluggish, a restart will often clear unnecessary program code and help it run more efficiently.

 HANDS-ON 1.7 **Use Shut Down and Restart**

In this exercise, you will shut down and then restart the computer.

1. Restart the computer:

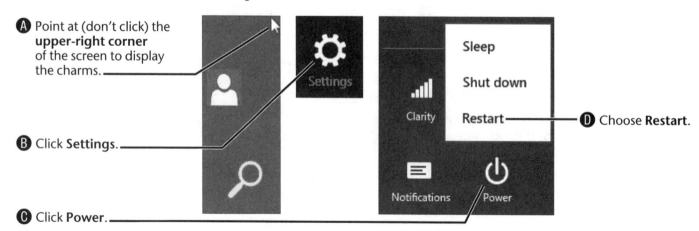

A Point at (don't click) the **upper-right corner** of the screen to display the charms.

B Click **Settings.**

C Click **Power.**

Sleep

Shut down

Restart ——— **D** Choose **Restart.**

Windows goes through its shutdown routine then restarts the computer. When it finishes, the lock screen appears again.

2. Click the lock screen, then **Sign on**.

3. Shut down the computer:

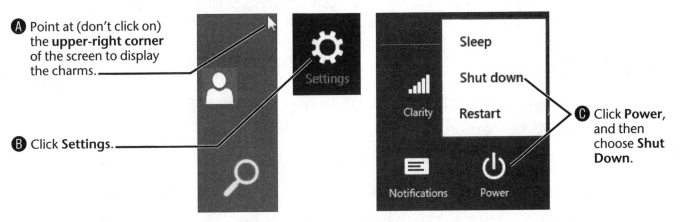

Ⓐ Point at (don't click on) the **upper-right corner** of the screen to display the charms.

Ⓑ Click **Settings**.

Ⓒ Click **Power**, and then choose **Shut Down**.

Windows goes through its shutdown routine, then powers off the computer.

Concepts Review

To check your knowledge of the key concepts introduced in this lesson, complete the Concepts Review quiz here or on the student resource center.

True/False Questions

Page Number

1. A screen where you run programs is called a Desktop. **True** **False** _____

2. You can't change the location of Start screen tiles. **True** **False** _____

3. The Start screen allows you to launch programs. **True** **False** _____

4. The primary mouse button is the right button. **True** **False** _____

5. The dragging motion requires you to hold down the mouse button while moving the mouse. **True** **False** _____

6. A right-click usually displays a pop-up or other type of menu. **True** **False** _____

Multiple Choice Questions

7. Which of the following is not a mouse motion?

   Page Number: _____

   a. Tap
   b. Drag
   c. Right-click
   d. Point

8. How many Desktops does Windows 8.1 feature?

   Page Number: _____

   a. 1
   b. 2
   c. 3
   d. None

9. Which mode puts Windows into a low-power state but keeps it running?

   Page Number: _____

   a. Sign Out
   b. Shut Down
   c. Sleep
   d. Restart

10. What can you do with tiles on the Start screen?

    Page Number: _____

    a. Resize
    b. Move
    c. Unpin
    d. Pin
    e. All of the above

Skill Builders

Use Lock and Sleep Modes

In this exercise, you will practice locking the computer and putting it to sleep.

1. Sign on to Windows on your own computer or laptop.

2. Display the **Start screen** if it's not already visible.

3. Click your username, then **Lock** the computer.

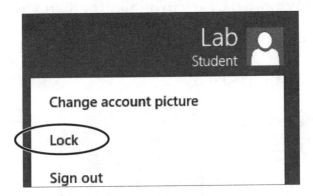

The computer displays the lock screen and remains running. This mode is useful if you must leave the computer for a short time.

4. Click the **Lock** screen, then type your **password**, and tap the [Enter] key on the keyboard.

5. Hold down the **Windows** ⊞ key, then tap the [C] key.
   Windows displays charms on the right side of the screen.

6. Put the computer to sleep:

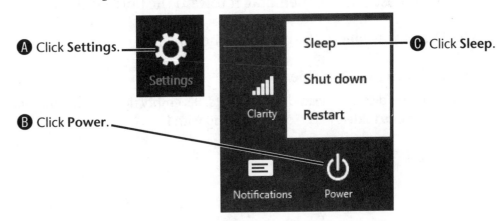

After a pause, Windows goes into a state with just a trickle of electricity. It's watching for any sign of activity with the mouse or keyboard.

7. Tap a key on the keyboard or move the mouse.

Windows starts running again and prompts for your password.

8. Type your **password**, then tap ⟨Enter⟩.

The Start screen reappears and you are ready to continue working. This mode is energy efficient when you will be away from the computer for five minutes or more.

SKILL BUILDER 1.2 **Practice Mouse Motions**

In this exercise, you will practice the basic mouse motions using a mouse or touchpad.

1. If necessary, tap the **Windows** ⊞ key to display the Start screen.

2. Click the **Desktop** tile.

3. Create a folder icon on the Desktop:

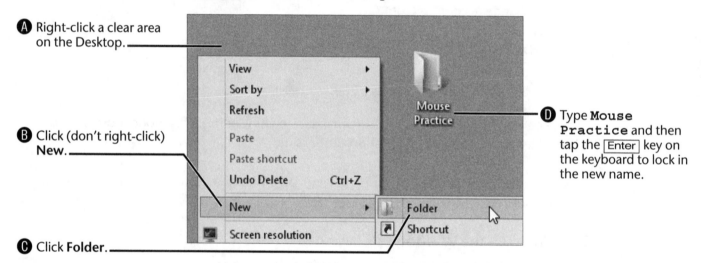

Ⓐ Right-click a clear area on the Desktop.

Ⓑ Click (don't right-click) **New**.

Ⓒ Click **Folder**.

Ⓓ Type **Mouse Practice** and then tap the ⟨Enter⟩ key on the keyboard to lock in the new name.

4. Point (don't click) at the **new folder icon** (not the folder name), hold down the mouse button, then drag it toward the bottom-left corner of the screen.

5. Drag the folder to the center of the screen.

6. Double-click the folder.

Windows displays the folder's contents. It's empty right now. (You'll learn how to put things into folders in Lesson 4, Working with Files.)

7. **Close** ▬✕▬ the folder.

8. Right-click (don't left-click) the folder, then choose **Properties** from the pop-up menu.

   Windows displays basic details about the folder.

9. **Close**  the Properties window.

10. Tap the **Windows** ⊞ key to return to the Start screen.

SKILL BUILDER 1.3 **Practice Editing Tiles**

In this exercise, you will edit the appearance of tiles on the Start screen.

1. If necessary, tap the **Windows** ⊞ key to display the Start screen.

2. Right-click (don't left-click) the **People** tile, then click **Unpin from Start** at the bottom-left corner of the screen.

3. Click the **Apps screen** ⊙ button.

4. Click **By Name**, then choose **By Most Used**.

5. Click **By Most Used**, then choose **By Name**.

6. Find the **People** tile on the left side of the screen, then right-click and choose **Pin to Start**.

7. Look for the **People** tile on the right side of the screen.

8. Drag the **People** tile back to its previous location on the left side of the screen.

Pin a Tile to the Taskbar

9. Click the **Apps screen** ⊙ button.

10. Under **Windows Accessories**, look for the **Calculator** program.

11. Right-click the **Calculator**, then choose **Pin to Taskbar**.

12. Tap **Windows** ⊞, then click the **Desktop** tile.

13. Click the **Calculator** on the Taskbar.

14. **Close** ⊠ the Calculator.

    The program's icon remains on the Taskbar.

15. Right-click the **Calculator** on the Taskbar, then unpin it.

16. Tap **Windows** ⊞ to return to the Start screen.

Try This at Home

Switch Users

In this exercise, you will practice switching from one user login to another.

> **⚠ NOTE!** Skip this exercise if there is only one user listed on the Windows signon screen. You need at least two user accounts to switch between users.

1. Sign On to Windows on your own computer or laptop.

2. Display the **Start screen** if it's not already visible.

3. Switch users:

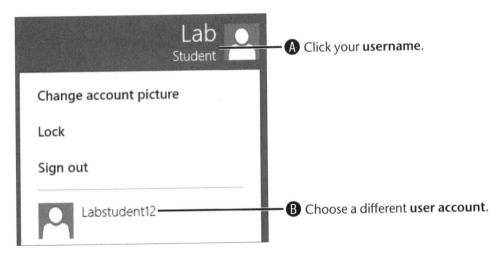

4. Type the **password** and tap the ⌷Enter⌷ key on the keyboard.
   Windows signs on the new user. If he or she customized the Start screen, the layout of tiles will be different.

5. Click the **username** at the top-right corner of the Start screen.

6. Choose **your own username** from the menu, then type **your password** and tap ⌷Enter⌷.
   Notice that your Start screen tiles are as they were before. If you were running any programs, those are still active too.

7. Click **your username** at the top-right corner of the Start screen, then choose the **other user** from the menu, type **their password**, and tap ⌷Enter⌷.

8. Click the **username** at the top-right corner of the Start screen, then choose **Sign Out** from the menu (rather than your own username).

Windows displays the Lock screen.

9. Click the **Lock** screen.

Notice that "Signed in" appears under your username.

10. Choose **your own username**, type your **password**, then tap $\boxed{\text{Enter}}$.

Using Programs

Programs are the way you get things done on every computer or tablet. One key to making the most of a computer is to use programs that work best for each task. This often works best by running more than one program at a time. Using copy and paste, you can combine items created with different programs into a single file. You'll also want to regularly save your work to locations where you can find and open the files later.

LESSON OBJECTIVES

After studying this lesson, you will be able to:

- Run multiple programs at the same time (multitask)
- Search for an application
- Size program windows on the screen
- Create and save a drawing with Paint
- Create and save a document with WordPad
- Copy and paste between applications

Case Study: Movie Night Flyer

Owen is a member of a movie club on campus. They show movies every Saturday night on a big screen. At the start of a new term, they want to get the word out. So Owen offers to create a flyer. Everyone agrees that a map will help potential new members find the showings, so Owen will include a map, too. He decides to use two programs to create the flyer: a word processor for the text and a drawing program for the map.

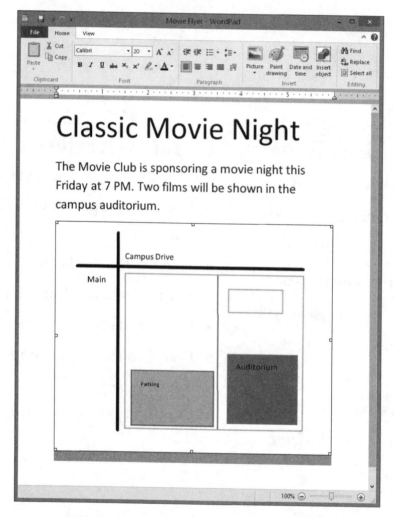

A WordPad document, with a map created with Paint placed on the page.

Using the Traditional Desktop

The Traditional Desktop continues to be the place where you run the most powerful applications, such as Word, Excel, PowerPoint, Photoshop Elements, and others. This Desktop also has the most powerful multitasking capabilities. Multitasking is running multiple programs at once. This allows you to use the best programs for each task.

The Windows Taskbar

The Windows Taskbar along the bottom of the screen displays buttons for each active application. Use these buttons to switch among applications. Taskbar buttons also allow you to minimize application windows.

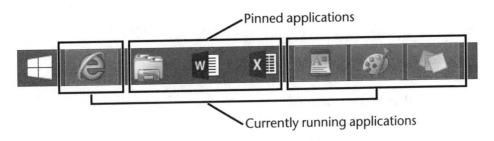

Pinned applications

Currently running applications

Pinning Programs to the Taskbar

You can "pin" frequently used programs directly to a spot on the Taskbar. This keeps their buttons in a stable location that's easy to find. Not only can you start programs from the Taskbar buttons, you can also quickly view and select open program windows. You can pin a program that's currently running on the Traditional Desktop, or you can pin it from the Start and All Apps screens. Whichever method you use, pinning programs makes them easier to start.

QUICK REFERENCE: Pinning Applications to the Taskbar

Task	Procedure
Pin a running application	• Right-click the application's icon on the Taskbar. • Choose Pin this Program to Taskbar.
Pin from the Start or Apps screen	• Display the Start or Apps screen. • Right-click the application you wish to pin. (Commands will appear at the bottom of the screen.) • Choose Pin to Taskbar.

HANDS-ON 2.1 Pin a Program to the Taskbar

In this exercise, you will start a program, then pin it to the Taskbar.

1. If necessary, start the computer and sign on to Windows.

2. Look for the **Word 2013** button on the Start screen, or click the **Apps screen** button near the bottom-left corner of the screen, then find **Word 2013** in the Microsoft Office 2013 application group.

3. Click the tile to start **Word**.

   Windows starts Word. Word asks what type of document to create.

4. Click **Blank Document**.

5. Pin Word to the Taskbar:

Ⓐ Right-click (don't left-click) **Word** on the Taskbar.

Ⓑ Left-click **Pin This Program to Taskbar.**

6. **Close** ☒ Word.

   The application's button remains on the Taskbar, even though it isn't running.

7. Click **Word's** Taskbar button.

   The application starts again. Without the pinned button, you would have to go back to the Start screen and look for the application. You might even have to open the Apps screen, then scroll to find the application.

8. Choose **Blank Document**.

9. **Minimize** ⎯ Word.

   Word disappears from the screen but continues running in the background, ready for use when you need it.

Searching for Programs

You don't want to pin too many programs to the Taskbar. And, if you have numerous programs installed, it might become difficult to find an application you don't use very often. Windows has a search feature to help you locate applications.

Search Charm

The Windows 8.1 Search charm allows you to search for programs, files and devices, and to perform web searches. Depending on your search type selection, the Search charm may give you a choice of items to open. A click on a result can open a program, app, or file directly.

Searches start with Everywhere.

You can narrow the search to specific types of items.

The Windows 8.1 Search charm displays a search box.

QUICK REFERENCE: Searching for Programs

Task	Procedure
Search with the Search charm	• Point to the top-right corner of the screen, or use `Windows`+`S` from the keyboard. • Click the Search charm. • Type the name of the program in the Search box.
Search from the Start screen	• Start typing a search word (a Search box appears).
Search via the Apps screen Search box	• Display the Start or Apps screen. • Type the name of the program in the Search box at the top-right corner of the screen.

HANDS-ON 2.2 Search for an Application

In this exercise, you will search for and start an application.

1. Search for an application:

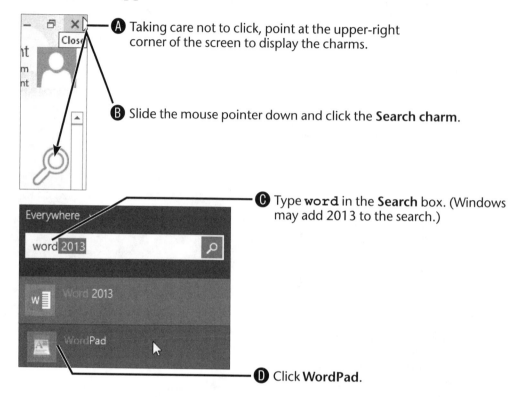

A Taking care not to click, point at the upper-right corner of the screen to display the charms.

B Slide the mouse pointer down and click the **Search charm**.

C Type **word** in the **Search** box. (Windows may add 2013 to the search.)

D Click **WordPad**.

Windows opens WordPad, a very basic word processor built into Windows.

2. Pin WordPad 2013 to the Taskbar:

A Right-click (don't left-click) **WordPad**.

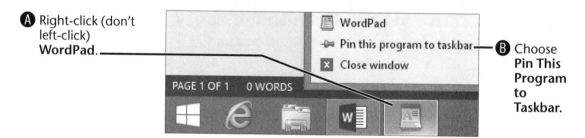

B Choose **Pin This Program to Taskbar**.

Windows pins the WordPad button to the Taskbar. It will now appear whether WordPad is running or not so you can start WordPad without navigating back to the Start screen.

3. Minimize — WordPad.

Now the screen should be clear of program windows.

Controlling Application Windows

Every application running on the Desktop has one or more program windows. You can position windows on the Desktop as you see fit. Many beginning Windows users forget that they can instantly size a window to fill the entire screen, which reduces the amount of scrolling you might have to do to view your work. Program windows open with quick-sizing buttons that help you change their placement on the Desktop.

NOTE! Tablet Desktop windows don't have quick-sizing buttons. You'll learn how to control the Tablet Desktop later in the lesson.

Using Quick-Sizing Buttons

Most program windows have three quick-sizing buttons that allow you to instantly give a commonly used window command. The center button changes depending on how the window is currently sized.

When you click the Maximize button... the middle button changes to Restore. When you click the Restore button... the middle button changes to Maximize.

Quick Sizing Buttons

Command Name	Icon	Description
Close	☒	Closes the program window and exits the program
Maximize	▢	Makes the program window instantly fill the entire screen
Restore	◱	Restores a maximized program window back to filling only part of the screen
Minimize	▬	Removes the program window from the screen but leaves it running in the background
Ribbon Display Options	▣	Controls options for displaying the Ribbon in Office 2013 programs

Basic Computer Components

Your computer is a collection of hardware working with Windows and other applications. Knowing a few details about these components helps you make better purchasing decisions when you buy your next computer or tablet.

Processor   The processor is the "brain" of the computer that helps you get work done, or play. The speed of your computer depends a great deal on the design of the processor. Most processors contain multiple computers (cores) on a single chip. A typical basic computer or tablet processor has two (dual) cores. This means it can work on two tasks

Photo courtesy of Intel Corporation

Intel's latest Core i5 processor contains the circuitry of four computers on a single chip.

simultaneously. This is enough to efficiently browse the web, access email, word process, and perform other basic tasks. Most business and gaming computers have four or more cores, giving them even greater processing power to display high-resolution game screens and run multiple programs at once.

ARM Processors   ARM is a class of processors that is especially popular on smartphones and tablets. They use a less-complex architecture to place a premium on low-energy use and heat generation. However, these processors can't run the types of software used with the Traditional Desktop. Windows 8.1 RT is a version of Windows designed to run on ARM processors.

Random Access Memory   The computer's random access memory (RAM) is where the work actually gets done. Think of RAM as the computer's "workbench." Everything you see onscreen takes place in RAM. More RAM allows you to run more programs efficiently (multitask), or to run very complex programs or games. Most computers allow you to add more RAM, which is easily installed via snap-in modules. Tablets and smartphones have a fixed amount of RAM.

Photo courtesy of Micron Technology, Inc.

RAM comes with snap-in modules of varying capacities.

Storage Hardware   Your computer can use a variety of storage devices and services.

Network Hardware   Virtually all computers have hardware to access a network, particularly the Internet. For example, every notebook computer has a built-in wireless receiver. This can detect and connect to wireless access in the home or in public places such as libraries, cafes, and schools. Many computers have a port into which you can plug a network cable for wired access.

Universal Serial Bus (USB) Port   A USB port is the small rectangular connector now common on all computers. USB ports let connect various pieces of equipment to your computer using a single standardized cord and plug. Once a device is connected via the USB port, Windows recognizes the equipment and helps with its configuration. USB ports come in two primary versions: USB 2 and USB 3. New computers have USB 3 ports, which are also compatible with USB 2 devices. USB 3 ports communicate about three to four times faster than USB 2s.

HANDS-ON 2.3 Use Quick-Sizing Buttons

In this exercise, you will use the quick-sizing buttons to change the appearance of an application window.

1. Click **Word** on the Taskbar.

   The program reappears from its minimized state.

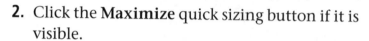

2. Click the **Maximize** quick sizing button if it is visible.

   Continue to the next step if the window is already maximized.

   The Word program window now fills the entire screen.

3. Click **Restore** 🗗.

   Now the window only fills a portion of the screen.

4. **Minimize** ➖ the window.

   The program window disappears, but Word is still running. Any work being done in the program is still there.

5. Click **Word** on the Taskbar.

   The Word window reappears in whichever shape it was when minimized. Leave Word open.

Aero Window Commands

The Aero window commands make many common program window arrangements automatic. For example, you can instantly make a program window fill just half of the screen. The Aero window commands also make the Maximize and Restore commands even more intuitive.

Aero Window Commands

Aero Command	Description/Use
Aero Snap	Dragging snaps program windows to fill the right or left half of the screen, or maximizes the window.
Aero Peek	Briefly makes all program windows transparent so you can view the Desktop.
Aero Shake	Causes all but one program window to minimize.

QUICK REFERENCE: Using Snap to Resize Windows

Task	Procedure
Maximize a window	• Drag the title bar to the top edge of the Desktop.
Restore down a window	• Drag the title bar of a maximized window away from the top edge of the Desktop.
Display two windows side by side	• Drag one window's title bar to the left or right edge of the Desktop.

 HANDS-ON 2.4 Use Aero Desktop Features

In this exercise, you will use Aero Desktop shortcuts to control program windows.

1. Make sure **Word** is the active program window and that it is not maximized.

2. Drag the **Word window title bar** to the top of the screen.

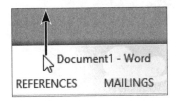

The Word window snaps to maximized.

3. Drag the **Word window title bar** away from the top of the screen.

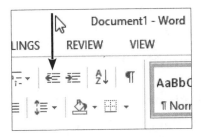

The Word window snaps back to its restored shape.

⚠ **NOTE!** If you have trouble with the next step, or want a preview, a video about using this feature of Aero Snap is available on the student resource center.

4. Use Aero Snap:

Ⓐ Drag while holding down the mouse button to move the Word window title bar to the **left side** of the screen.

Ⓑ Release the mouse button when the mouse pointer touches the edge of the screen and an outline displays on half of the screen. (Drag the left side of the window off the edge of the screen to get the tip of the mouse pointer all the way to the edge.)

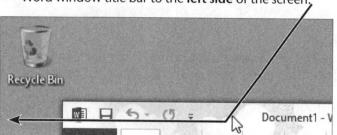

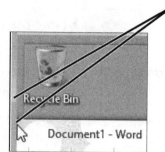

Windows shapes the Word window to fill half the screen. This can be a useful shortcut when you want to split the screen between two program windows.

5. Click the **File Explorer** button.

Windows opens a new window.

6. Drag to make File Explorer fill the **right half** of the screen.

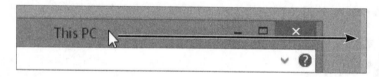

7. Restore Word:

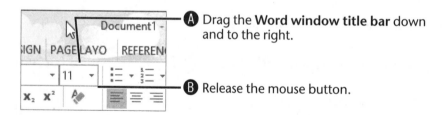

Ⓐ Drag the **Word window title bar** down and to the right.

Ⓑ Release the mouse button.

Windows restores the Word window to its previous shape.

8. **Use Aero Shake:** Point at the **Word window title bar**, then hold down the mouse button and shake the window back and forth for a couple seconds.

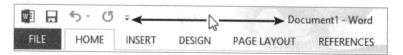

The File Explorer window minimizes, leaving Word the only window visible on the Desktop.

9. Click the **Show Desktop** corner.

All open windows are immediately minimized.

10. Click the **Show Desktop** corner again.

Word reappears.

Multitasking

Running more than one program at the same time is called multitasking. Multitasking can definitely enhance your productivity. For example, you can view a web page in one window while you are writing about a related topic in your word processor. Or you might enter data in an Excel spreadsheet while you prepare a PowerPoint presentation. Although only one window at a time is active, you can view the inactive windows. You can switch active windows instantly to change tasks.

Switching Between Programs

There are two primary methods for switching between programs:

- **The Taskbar** – The Windows Taskbar lets you see which programs are running and choose a new one to be active.

- **The Keyboard** – A pair of keys on the keyboard lets you switch programs without reaching for the mouse, track pad, or touchscreen.

QUICK REFERENCE: Switching Programs with Windows

Task	Procedure
Switch between Desktop programs with the keyboard	• Hold down the Alt key and tap the Tab key. • Continue tapping Tab until the desired program is chosen. • Release the Alt key.
Switch between tablet apps and the Desktop	• Hold down the Windows ⊞ key and tap the Tab key. Release Tab when the Desktop or desired app is chosen.
Clear the Desktop of open windows	• Click the Desktop bottom-right corner. Windows 8.1 does not display a visible button.

HANDS-ON 2.5 Flip Between Program Windows

In this exercise, you will flip between Desktop programs using the keyboard.

!NOTE! Word, WordPad, and File Explorer should be running.

1. Tap the **Windows** ⊞ key to display the Start screen.

2. Click the **Apps screen** ⊕ button.

3. Search for Paint:

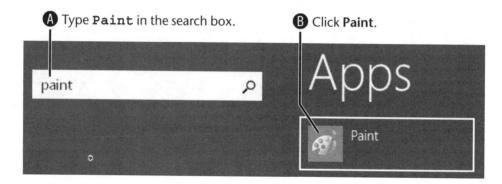

A Type **Paint** in the search box.　　**B** Click **Paint**.

Paint opens on the Traditional Desktop.

Practice Flipping via the Keyboard

4. Use the keyboard to flip between Desktop programs:

A Using your thumb, hold down the Alt key on the keyboard and keep it held down.

B Using your index finger, tap the Tab key.

A window displaying icons for currently running programs appears in the middle of the screen.

!NOTE! A keystroke combination like this will often be shown as Alt + Tab .

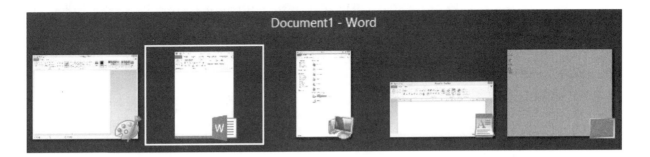

5. Taking care to continue holding down the Alt key, tap Tab again.

   The highlight in the program icon display moves to the next program.

6. Still holding down the Alt key, tap Tab a few more times until the highlight gets to **WordPad**, and then release the Alt key.

   WordPad becomes the active program.

7. Use Alt + Tab to switch to **Paint**.

Flip Between Desktops

You can also use the keyboard to flip between tablet apps and the Traditional Desktop.

8. Tap the **Windows** ⊞ key.

9. Click the **Internet Explorer** tile.

   The Internet Explorer tablet app starts.

10. Hold down the **Windows** ⊞ key and tap Tab .

    Windows displays apps and the Traditional Desktop at the upper-left corner.

11. Release the **Windows** ⊞ key.

    The Traditional Desktop becomes active.

12. Hold down **Windows** ⊞ , tap Tab , and then release Windows ⊞ .

    The Internet Explorer app reappears.

13. Use **Windows** ⊞ + Tab to return to the Traditional Desktop.

    The Desktop and Paint reappear.

Drawing with Paint

Paint is a drawing program that comes bundled with Windows. This basic program has many tools to create quick drawings on the screen. Once you've created a drawing, you can save it and/or copy and paste it into a document.

Paint's Ribbon

Similar to WordPad, Paint contains application commands on a Ribbon. Paint's Ribbon is filled with various drawing tools. It also contains a section where you can select and edit colors.

How Ribbon Commands Are Organized

Commands on the Ribbon are grouped at three levels. Paint has a fairly simple Ribbon. On more complex Ribbons, you'll want to find commands by looking at each level of the hierarchy to locate the ones you need.

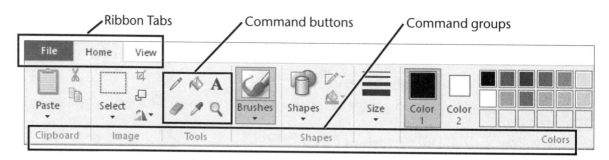

TIP! Use this order to search efficiently for a Ribbon command: Ribbon Tab→Command Group→Command.

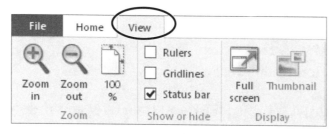

The View tab contains a different set of command groups and commands.

HANDS-ON 2.6 **Create a Drawing with Paint**

In this exercise, you will create a simple map.

1. **Maximize** ▫ Paint.

2. Choose a drawing tool, width, and color:

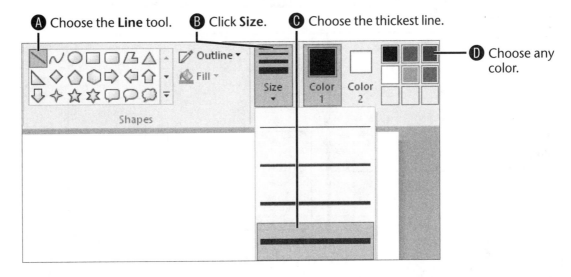

Ⓐ Choose the **Line** tool.   Ⓑ Click **Size**.   Ⓒ Choose the thickest line.

Ⓓ Choose any color.

⚠ TIP! If a step doesn't work as you create the drawing, click the Undo button.

3. Draw two streets, then draw two rectangles:

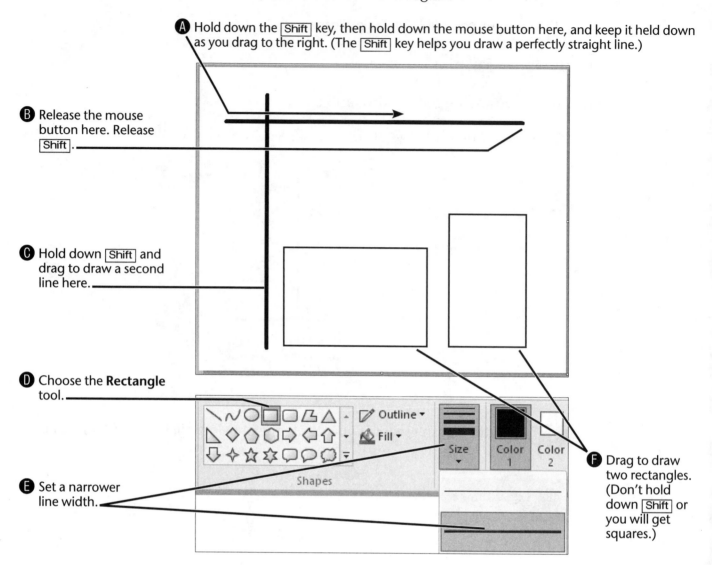

A Hold down the Shift key, then hold down the mouse button here, and keep it held down as you drag to the right. (The Shift key helps you draw a perfectly straight line.)

B Release the mouse button here. Release Shift.

C Hold down Shift and drag to draw a second line here.

D Choose the **Rectangle** tool.

Outline ▾

Fill ▾

Size ▾

Color 1

Color 2

Shapes

E Set a narrower line width.

F Drag to draw two rectangles. (Don't hold down Shift or you will get squares.)

4. Label a street:

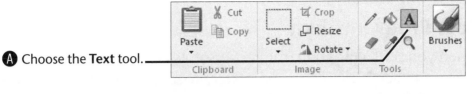

Ⓐ Choose the **Text** tool.

Ⓑ Click where the name will start.　Ⓒ Choose a font size of **24**.　Ⓓ Choose any font color.

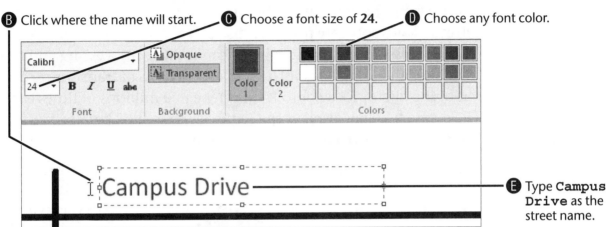

Ⓔ Type **Campus Drive** as the street name.

5. Click outside the text box.

The normal Paint tools reappear.

6. Add color and a text label:

Ⓐ Choose the **Paint Bucket** tool and a dark color.

Ⓑ Click with the paint bucket within the right rectangle.

Ⓒ Choose the **Text** tool and a light color.　Ⓓ Click inside the colored rectangle.

Ⓔ If necessary, drag the text box boundary inside the rectangle.

Ⓕ Change the font size to **18**.

Ⓖ Type **Auditorium**.

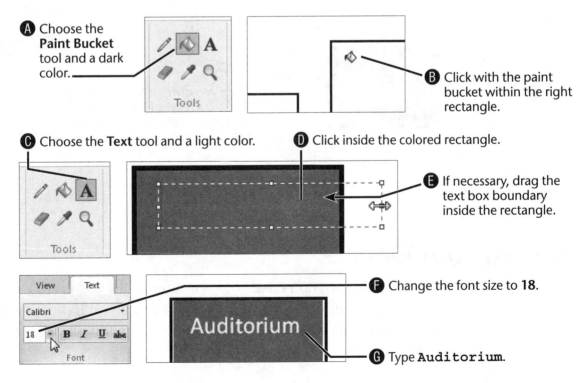

Before doing anything else, it's a good idea to save what you have done so far.

How Programs Run

When you start a program, the processor, RAM, and storage drive work together to get things done. The microprocessor never accesses software directly from the computer's disk drives. Instead, the operating system software loads software from the disk drives into RAM. Then the microprocessor reads the software from RAM for processing and places the results of processing back into RAM. The process of transferring data in and out of the microprocessor to RAM is repeated millions of times each second. The diagram below displays the sequence that one operating system, Windows, follows to run programs and process data as you work.

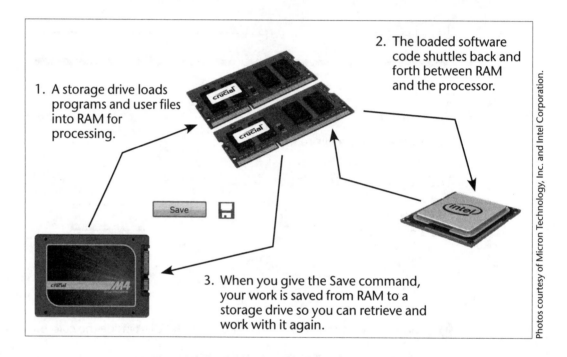

1. A storage drive loads programs and user files into RAM for processing.

2. The loaded software code shuttles back and forth between RAM and the processor.

Save

3. When you give the Save command, your work is saved from RAM to a storage drive so you can retrieve and work with it again.

Photos courtesy of Micron Technology, Inc. and Intel Corporation.

Saving Your Work

Saving from a program creates a computer file of whatever you've created. Creating, storing, and finding files is a key skill you'll practice a lot in this book. Every time you finish a key piece of work, it's always a good idea to give the Save command.

Where Your Work Takes Place

Everything you see on the computer screen is actually taking place in the computer's random access memory (RAM). Many computer users think the work takes place on the computer's disk drive or their USB flash drive. But the work doesn't get to either of these places until you save it.

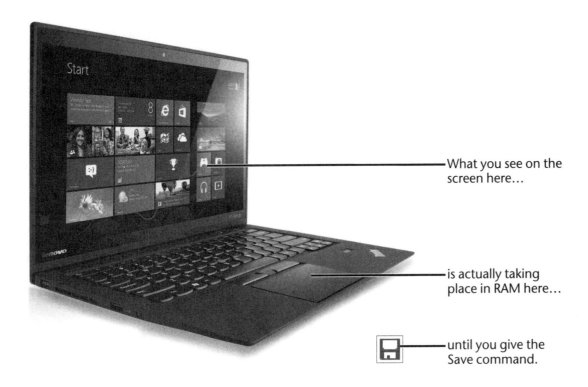

What you see on the screen here…

is actually taking place in RAM here…

until you give the Save command.

Save Locations

The computer has more than one place where you can save your work. Some locations are on the computer's local disk drive. Other locations include removable storage, such as a USB flash drive, and cloud-based locations, such as Dropbox, Google Drive, or OneDrive. It's critical to know exactly where you save each file, especially when you're not working at your own computer.

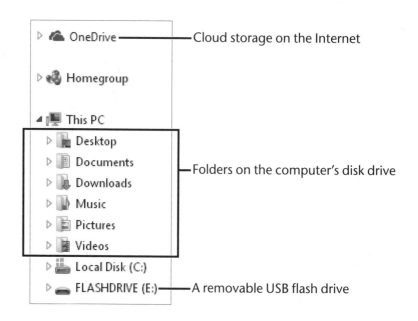

OneDrive — Cloud storage on the Internet

Homegroup

This PC

Desktop
Documents
Downloads — Folders on the computer's disk drive
Music
Pictures
Videos

Local Disk (C:)

FLASHDRIVE (E:) — A removable USB flash drive

File-naming Rules

There are specific rules for naming Windows files. If you create a filename that's too long or contains characters that aren't allowed, Word will prompt you to fix this before it saves the file.

Naming Files

Rule	Description
Filename length	Filenames can contain up to 255 characters.
Characters allowed in filenames	A filename may contain alphabetic characters, numbers, spaces, periods, commas, semicolons, dashes, apostrophes, and parentheses. Examples: ( ) & + -
Characters not allowed in filenames	A filename *cannot* contain the following characters: \ / : * ? " < > |

HANDS-ON 2.7 **Save the Map**

In this exercise, you will save the map for future use.

NOTE! Your instructor will tell you where to save your work for this lesson. It could be on a USB flash drive, the Documents folder, or cloud storage such as OneDrive, Google Drive, or Dropbox.

1. If you use a **USB flash drive**, carefully plug it into a USB port on the computer. Ask your instructor if you aren't sure where to find a USB port.

2. Ignore any prompt for an action to take if you inserted a flash drive.

3. Save the drawing:

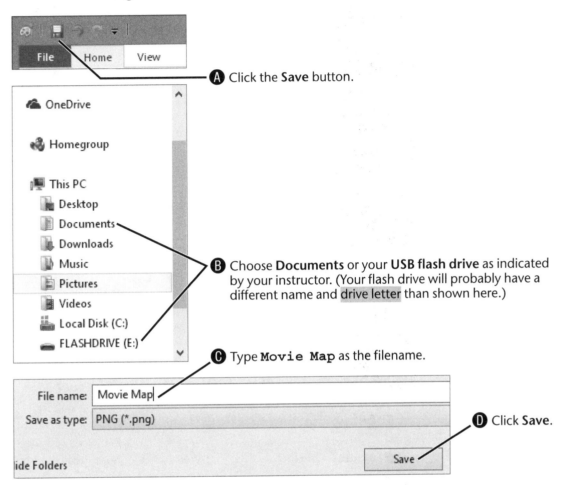

A Click the **Save** button.

B Choose **Documents** or your **USB flash drive** as indicated by your instructor. (Your flash drive will probably have a different name and drive letter than shown here.)

C Type **Movie Map** as the filename.

D Click **Save**.

Windows saves the map to the Documents folder or your flash drive.

Writing with WordPad

WordPad is a basic word processing program built into every copy of Windows. It features a simpler set of commands than a full-featured program like Word. You'll create a simple flyer with WordPad in the next exercise. In the next lesson, you'll create a more complex document using Word.

WordPad's Ribbon

WordPad arranges its commands on a Ribbon, much like Paint. Because WordPad is designed for a different purpose, its commands differ from Paint a great deal, but the organization is similar.

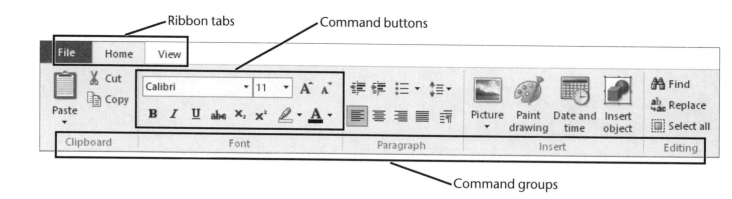

Ribbon tabs　　　Command buttons

Command groups

 HANDS-ON 2.8　Create a Flyer

In this exercise, you will create a simple flyer for a campus club movie night.

1. Click **WordPad** on the Taskbar.

WordPad becomes the active program.

2. If necessary, **Maximize** ☐ WordPad so it fills the screen.

3. Format and type the flyer heading:

Ⓐ Choose **Arial Black** as the font type.　　Ⓑ Choose **48** as the font size.

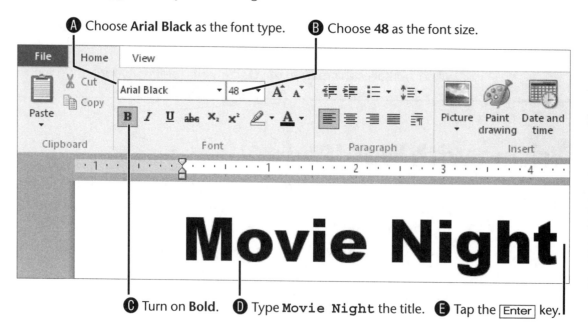

Ⓒ Turn on **Bold**.　Ⓓ Type `Movie Night` the title.　Ⓔ Tap the Enter key.

4. Change the font settings for the flyer body:

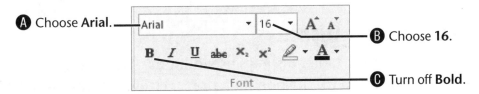

Ⓐ Choose **Arial**.

Ⓑ Choose **16**.

Ⓒ Turn off **Bold**.

5. Type the flyer body:

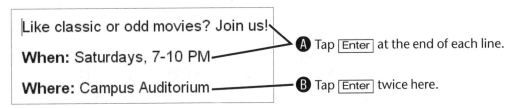

Like classic or odd movies? Join us!

When: Saturdays, 7-10 PM

Where: Campus Auditorium

Ⓐ Tap Enter at the end of each line.

Ⓑ Tap Enter twice here.

6. Save the flyer:

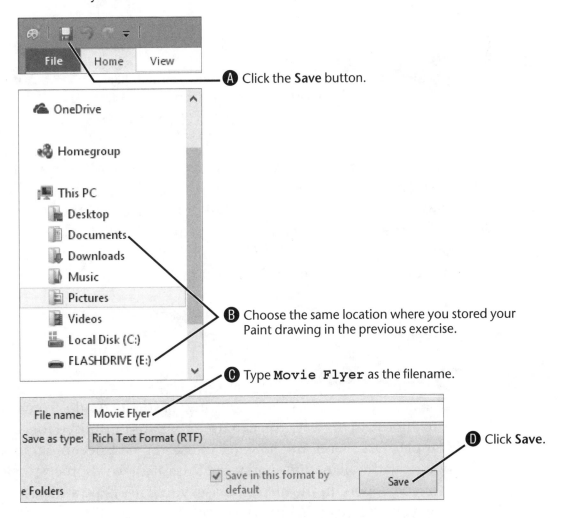

Ⓐ Click the **Save** button.

OneDrive

Homegroup

This PC
- Desktop
- Documents
- Downloads
- Music
- Pictures
- Videos
- Local Disk (C:)
- FLASHDRIVE (E:)

Ⓑ Choose the same location where you stored your Paint drawing in the previous exercise.

Ⓒ Type **Movie Flyer** as the filename.

File name: Movie Flyer

Save as type: Rich Text Format (RTF)

☑ Save in this format by default

Save

e Folders

Ⓓ Click **Save**.

Windows saves the flyer.

Computer Displays

Computer and tablet displays use millions of tiny points of light (pixels) to form images. With the popularity of HD (high definition) television, most computer displays use the same wide-screen proportion of 16:9. Tablets and a growing number of Desktop computers also have touchscreen capabilities, allowing you to give commands by touching and sliding your fingers across the screen.

How Computers Display Video   The more pixels the screen of a computer monitor has, the sharper the image it can display. Displays are therefore rated for the number of pixels they display horizontally and vertically. For example, a 24" display may be rated to display 1920 pixels across by 1080 pixels high (usually abbreviated as 1920x1080). A popular screen resolution for notebook computers is 1366x768.

Illustration courtesy of Ed 2gs.

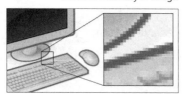

The images you see on a computer screen are composed of thousands of tiny points of light (pixels).

Native Resolution   Every display has a native resolution at which it displays best. This is the highest resolution it's capable of. Many displays can be set to a lower resolution, which may make small objects on the screen appear larger. Many computers and tablets have settings to help those with vision problems see the display more easily. For example, it may be possible to change the size of icons on the screen, or the size of text.

Using Copy and Paste

One reason to multitask is to copy and paste the results from one program into another. This way, you can use programs optimized for each part of a complex task. For example, you can use a spreadsheet program to create a budget with calculations and paste this into a word-processing document for a monthly report. In the next exercise, you'll use copy and paste to place the map you created earlier into the flyer.

The Clipboard

Whenever you give the Copy or Cut command, Windows places your current selection into a special place in memory called the Clipboard. Your most recent cut or copied selection remains in the Clipboard until you give the command again. So you can paste the same item over and over again.

 HANDS-ON 2.9 **Copy and Paste Between Programs**

In this exercise, you will copy the map you just created to a different program.

Before You Begin: The Paint program and map should be open.

1. Click its Taskbar button to make **Paint** the active program.

2. Select and copy the entire map:

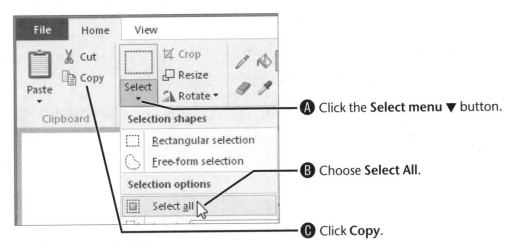

Ⓐ Click the **Select menu ▼** button.

Ⓑ Choose **Select All**.

Ⓒ Click **Copy**.

Windows copies the map to the Clipboard.

3. Make **WordPad** active.

4. Paste content into WordPad:

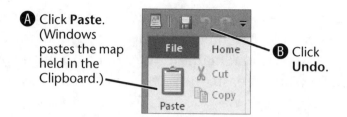

Ⓐ Click **Paste**. (Windows pastes the map held in the Clipboard.)

Ⓑ Click **Undo**.

The Paste command is undone. This button is handy whenever you see something unexpected after you give a command.

5. Click **Paste** again.

Because it's still in the Clipboard, Windows pastes the same map again.

6. Save the document.

Close Program Windows

7. Close x Paint and WordPad. Choose **Save** if you are asked to save your work when you close a program.

8. Click **Word** on the Taskbar, then **close** ☒ it.

The program reappears from its minimized state.

Removing Flash Drives Safely

USB drives require extra care for removal from a USB port. If the drive is active when you remove the device, you could lose one or more files on it. For example, if a file stored on a flash drive is open in an application. In an extreme case, the USB flash drive itself could be corrupted and most of the files on it lost.

WARNING! Always take care removing a USB flash drive. Never remove it if it is showing activity (usually via a flashing light on the drive).

Safely Remove Hardware Command

Window's Safely Remove Hardware command ensures that a drive or device is inactive and can be removed without risk. The command checks for any open files or other activity, then signals you when it's safe to remove the device. The command also signals when it's not safe to remove a device.

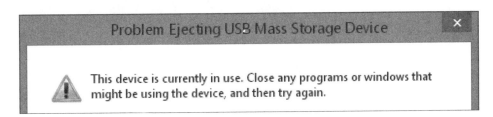

Notification Area   The Notification Area is on the Taskbar just left of the date/time display. It may contain hidden icons.

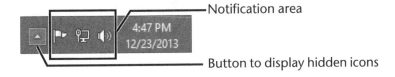

HANDS-ON 2.10 **Remove a Flash Drive**

In this exercise, you will safely eject your USB flash drive.

⚠️**NOTE!** Skip this exercise if you are not using a USB flash drive.

1. Give the Safely Remove Hardware command:

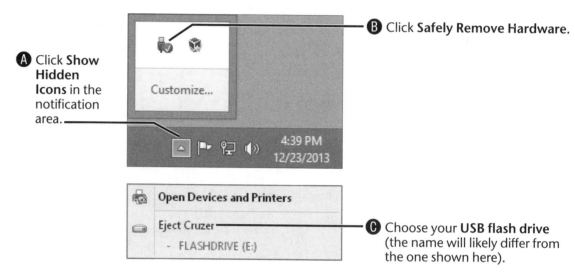

Ⓐ Click **Show Hidden Icons** in the notification area.

Ⓑ Click **Safely Remove Hardware.**

Ⓒ Choose your **USB flash drive** (the name will likely differ from the one shown here).

Windows determines if your USB flash drive is still in use. You'll see a prompt when it can be safely removed.

2. Remove the USB flash drive if the Safely Remove Hardware prompt appears and skip the rest of this exercise. Otherwise, continue to the next step.

3. Check to see if you have any open files in an application if a problem is signaled, then repeat step 1 to safely remove the USB flash drive.

4. Tap **Windows** ⊞ to return to the Start screen.

Concepts Review

To check your knowledge of the key concepts introduced in this lesson, complete the Concepts Review quiz here or on the student resource center.

True/False Questions

Page Number

1. Multitasking is running more than one program at the same time. **True** **False** _____

2. Pinning a program to the Windows Taskbar makes it easier to start the next time. **True** **False** _____

3. Before you save it, your work on the screen exists only in RAM. **True** **False** _____

4. Whatever you copy is placed in a place in RAM called the Clipboard. **True** **False** _____

5. You can paste the same copied item more than once. **True** **False** _____

6. The space for command buttons in WordPad and Paint is called the Ribbon. **True** **False** _____

Multiple Choice Questions

7. Which of the following *is not* a window-sizing button?

   Page Number: _____

   a. Minimize
   b. Maximize
   c. Restore
   d. Close
   e. None of the above

8. Multitasking is _____.

   Page Number: _____

   a. using one program to accomplish more than one task
   b. running two or more programs at the same time
   c. using a computer or tablet along with another device
   d. None of the above

9. A Ribbon contains _____.

   Page Number: _____

   a. commands
   b. command groups
   c. tabs
   d. All of the above

10. In which order should you search for commands?

    Page Number: _____

    a. Command→Command Group→Tab
    b. Command Group→Command Group→Tab
    c. Command→Tab→Command Group
    d. Tab→Command Group→Command
    e. All of the above

Skill Builders

SKILL BUILDER 2.1 Multitask, Save, Copy, and Paste

In this exercise, you will practice running multiple programs and using copy and paste between them.

1. Sign on to **Windows** or display the **Start screen** if it's not already visible.

2. Create a sticky note:

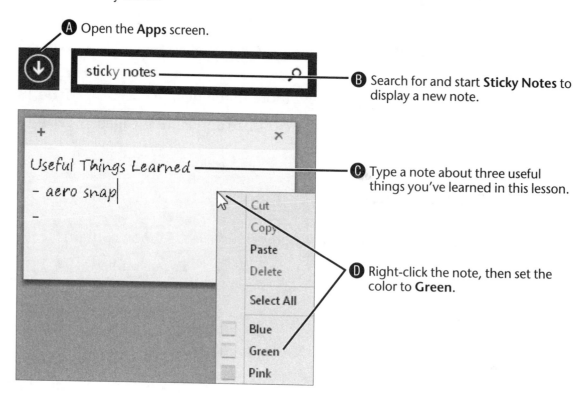

Ⓐ Open the **Apps** screen.

Ⓑ Search for and start **Sticky Notes** to display a new note.

Ⓒ Type a note about three useful things you've learned in this lesson.

Ⓓ Right-click the note, then set the color to **Green**.

3. Copy the note:

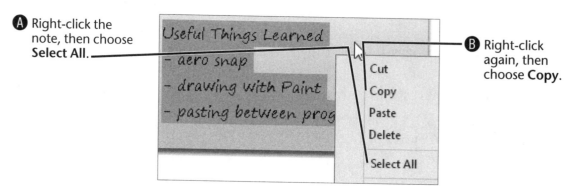

Ⓐ Right-click the note, then choose **Select All**.

Ⓑ Right-click again, then choose **Copy**.

The contents of the note are copied to the Clipboard, ready to paste into another application.

4. Hold down the **Windows** ⊞ key, and then tap ⑤. Or, point at the top-right corner of the screen and choose the **Search charm**.

5. Search for and open **WordPad**.

6. Click **Paste**.

   The text from your sticky note appears in WordPad. The pasted text is still in the Clipboard until you copy something else, so you can paste it again.

7. Paste into another note:

Ⓐ Make **Sticky Notes** the active application.

Ⓑ Create a **New Note**.

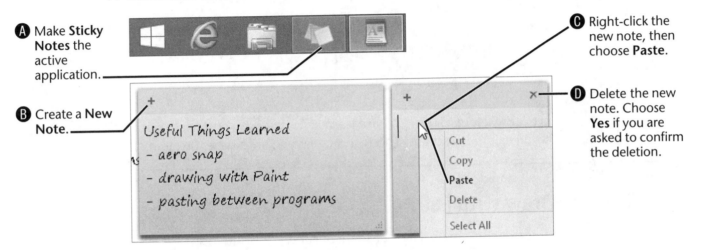

Ⓒ Right-click the new note, then choose **Paste**.

Ⓓ Delete the new note. Choose **Yes** if you are asked to confirm the deletion.

8. Click **Sticky Notes** on the taskbar.

   Windows minimizes the program. Now only WordPad should appear on the screen.

Save the WordPad Document

9. Save the document:

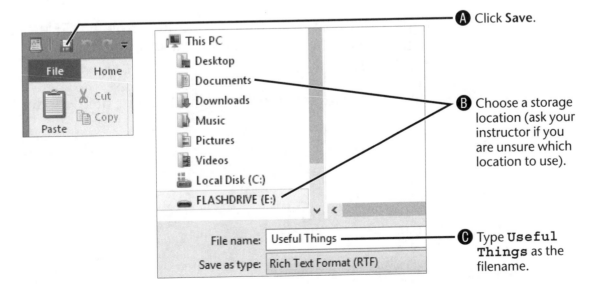

Ⓐ Click **Save**.

Ⓑ Choose a storage location (ask your instructor if you are unsure which location to use).

Ⓒ Type **Useful Things** as the filename.

10. Click **Save** or tap the ⎡Enter⎤ key.

The document is saved with the name you assigned. Notice the document name in the WordPad title bar.

11. **Close** ❎ WordPad.

12. Right-click **Sticky Notes**, then choose **Close Window**.

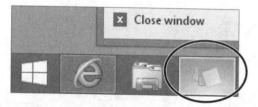

Since Sticky Notes doesn't have a normal Close ❎ button, the right-click technique lets you exit the program. This technique works with other programs, too.

SKILL BUILDER 2.2 **Draw with Paint**

In this exercise, you will try out some of Paint's drawing tools.

1. Sign On to **Windows**, or display the **Start screen** if it's not already visible.

2. Search for and open **Paint**.

3. Review the bulleted tips below and use Paint's drawing tools to create a picture of anything you want (for example, an abstract design, a floor plan, a flower, etc.).

   - If something goes wrong, use the Undo button or ⎡Ctrl⎤+⎡Z⎤ from the keyboard. Or you can use File→New from the Ribbon to start over.

   - Experiment with different shapes and outline or fill modes.

- Try different brush shapes for some interesting effects. Point over a shape to see its name.

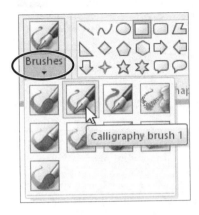
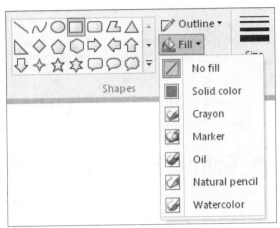

- Select a part of the drawing, then use Copy and Paste to repeat it.

- Save 🖫 the drawing (see steps 4–8 below) from time to time until you are finished.

Save the Drawing

4. Click the **Save** button.

5. Click your storage location, such as a **USB flash drive**, **OneDrive**, or **Documents**. If the one you need isn't visible, use the scroll bar to move the view up or down.

6. Type **Paint Drawing** for the filename.

7. Click **Save** or tap the ⸢Enter⸣ key.
   Your drawing is stored as a new file.

8. Simply click **Save** 🖫 to save your drawing from time to time. (After the first Save in step 4, you won't be asked for the location again. The latest version of the drawing is saved to the same file.)

Finish and Close

9. Click **Save** 🖫 one more time when you finish with the drawing.

10. **Close** ▮x▮ Paint.

11. Safely eject your flash drive if you use one as your storage location.

12. Tap **Windows** ⊞ to return to the Start screen.

Control Program Windows

In this exercise, you will manipulate program windows on the screen.

1. Sign on to **Windows** or display the **Start screen** if it's not already visible.

2. Click the **Desktop tile**.

3. Start **Internet Explorer** or a different web browser that's pinned to the taskbar.

4. If necessary, **Restore** ❐ the Internet Explorer window (so it's not maximized).

5. Use Aero Snap:

Ⓐ Drag the **Internet Explorer** title bar to the very **top** of the screen. (The window snaps to maximized.)

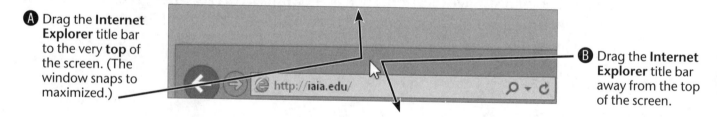

Ⓑ Drag the **Internet Explorer** title bar away from the top of the screen.

The window snaps to restored size.

6. Drag the **Internet Explorer** title bar to the **right side** of the screen. Make sure the tip of the arrow reaches the right side of the screen.
   The window fills the right half of the screen.

7. Drag the **Internet Explorer** title bar toward the **center** of the screen.
   The window is restored to its previous size.

Switch Programs

8. Tap **Windows** ⊞ to return to the Start screen; open the **Word** program and choose **Blank Document** after the program starts.

9. Tap **Windows** ⊞ to return to the Start screen; open **PowerPoint** and choose **Blank Presentation** after the program starts.

10. **Maximize** ☐ PowerPoint if it doesn't already fill the screen.

11. Hold down the ⎡Alt⎤ key on the keyboard and keep it held down, then tap the ⎡Tab⎤ key.

12. Still holding down ⎡Alt⎤, tap ⎡Tab⎤ one or more times until **Internet Explorer** shows as the active program, then release ⎡Alt⎤.
    Internet Explorer becomes the active program.

13. Use ⎡Alt⎤+⎡Tab⎤ to make **Word** the active program.

14. Drag **Word's title bar** to the **left side** of the screen.

15. Click its taskbar button to make **PowerPoint** the active program, then drag its title bar to make **PowerPoint** fill the **right half** of the screen.

16. Click the **Show Desktop** corner. (The tail of the mouse will be off the edge of the screen.)
    Windows minimizes all open windows.

17. Click the **Show Desktop** corner again.
    The Desktop items reappear.

Close the Programs

18. **Close** ☒ Word and PowerPoint. Choose **No** if you are asked to save.

19. **Close** ☒ Internet Explorer.

20. Tap **Windows** ⊞ to return to the Start screen.

Using a Word Processor

A word processor is an application optimized to help you work with words. Modern word processors have sophisticated editing and proofreading tools. If you're like most students, there's a lot about your word processor you don't know about; features that can save you time and brainpower, and that also make your pages look slick. In this lesson, you will be introduced to some features that place a word processor a cut above the simple typing capabilities in webmail and social media.

LESSON OBJECTIVES

After studying this lesson, you will be able to:

- Create and save a new document using Word 2013 or 2010

- Edit a document by inserting and deleting text

- Use the Copy and Paste commands

- Find commands on the Ribbon

- Describe time-saving formatting features of word processors

- Print a document

Case Study: Recruiting Club Members

Brooke has joined the student movie club on campus. The club sponsors showings of famous and obscure films twice a month in the auditorium; the sort of films that aren't available on Netflix. The club is always looking to recruit new members at each showing. As club secretary, Brooke tackles the task of creating a new member form. In addition to the usual contact information, the club wants ideas for films to show and how to raise funds to rent them.

Brooke starts up Word 2013 and sets up a basic form. She uses tab settings to make things easy to line up. She's also learned a few tricks that make creating a slick form much easier than it appears.

Join the Movie Club

Contact Information

Name: _____

Email: _____

Phone: _____

☐ I am willing to pay dues of $3/month

☐ I am willing to help with setup or cleanup after showings

Movie Recommendations

Movie 1: _____

Movie 2: _____

Join the Movie Club

Contact Information

Name: _____

Email: _____

Phone: _____

☐ I am willing to pay dues of $3/month

☐ I am willing to help with setup or cleanup after showings

Movie Recommendations

Movie 1: _____

Movie 2: _____

Word displays a print preview of the completed form.

Knowing Your Writing Instrument

If you are in college, you are necessarily a writer. In some courses, all of your work is writing and in others, at least part of it is. Online classes usually require even more writing, and every writer needs a writing instrument. But these days, most students don't know their writing instrument very well. This lesson offers a chance to work with powerful features you may not have tried yet. It suggests ways you can save time and brainpower to focus on the writing itself rather than the details of formatting to get pages to look the way you want.

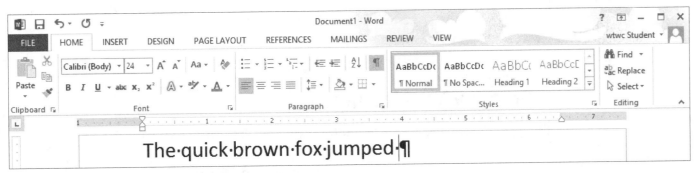

Your word processor is the latest model in a long line.

Creating a New Document

All your work in a word processor is performed within a document. When you start Word 2013, it asks which type of document you would like to create. Word 2010 simply creates a new blank document. In addition to blank documents, Word has a variety of predesigned documents you can start out with.

Templates

A template is document containing the design for some type of writing. For example, a calendar template can contain the design of a weekly or monthly calendar. There are letter, report, memo and many other types of templates. Even a blank document starts out with format settings in a template. Some templates are created by Microsoft, the company that produces Word. Others might be from third parties. The selection of templates can change over time. Word can search online through thousands of templates.

Searching with a keyword displays templates for a specific type of document.

HANDS-ON 3.1 **Create a New Document**

In this exercise, you will create a monthly calendar via a Word template.

1. If necessary, start the computer and sign on to **Windows**.

2. Look for the **Word 2013** button on the **Start screen**. Or, click the **Apps screen** button near the bottom-left corner of the screen, then find **Word 2013** in the Microsoft Office 2013 application group.

Windows starts Word. Word asks what type of document to create.

3. Click **Blank document**.

The new document appears. This contains settings from Word's blank document template. Later in this lesson, you'll use a template to create a calendar that has quite a bit of its content already set up in the template.

4. Make sure the **Word** window is maximized (fills the screen).

Typing in Programs

Typing is something you most likely do daily on your phone, in webmail, and perhaps some other programs. This topic points out a few basic features of typing in programs.

- **Cursor** – The blinking line that appears in text you are typing. This is also called the insertion point.

- **Text pointer** – The I-beam shaped pointer that appears over text area.

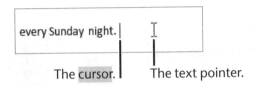

The cursor.   The text pointer.

Word's Ribbon

Compared to WordPad, Word's Ribbon has many more tabs and commands. However, the basic organization is the same. Tabs display major types of commands, command groups contain closely related commands, and buttons activate individual commands.

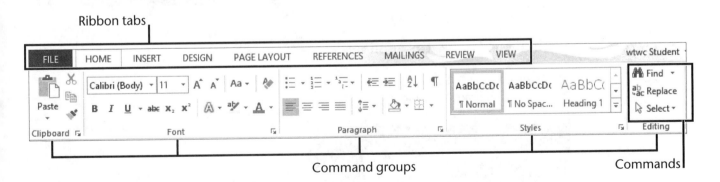

Changing the View

Word contains numerous view options. Most of these are organized under the View tab on the Ribbon. For example, you can switch on display of the ruler along the top and sides of the document. Or, you can choose to zoom in to a closer view. You can even view the same document in more than one window. Word also displays handy view shortcuts at the bottom-right corner of the document.

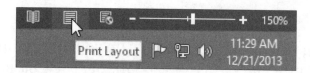

Word's view shortcuts. Pointing at a shortcut icon displays its name or function.

 HANDS-ON 3.2 Start Typing a Form

In this exercise, you will type the first lines of the membership form.

1. Type the first three lines of the form:

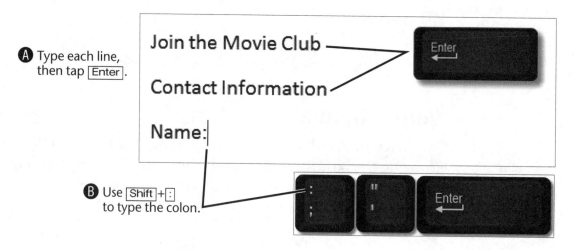

Ⓐ Type each line, then tap Enter.

Join the Movie Club

Contact Information

Name:

Ⓑ Use Shift + : to type the colon.

2. Zoom in and out with the slider:

Ⓐ Click the plus (+) sign three times to gradually zoom in.

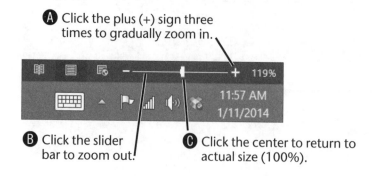

Ⓑ Click the slider bar to zoom out.

Ⓒ Click the center to return to actual size (100%).

3. Zoom the page to fit the screen:

Ⓐ Click **View**.

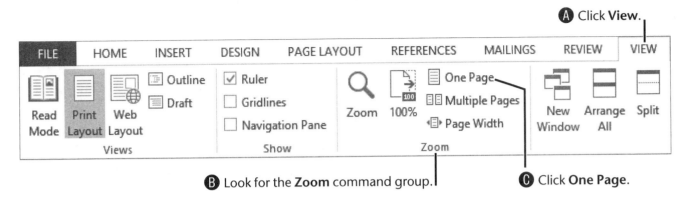

Ⓑ Look for the **Zoom** command group.

Ⓒ Click **One Page**.

!NOTE! This command can be written in shorthand like this:
Choose View→Zoom→One Page from the Ribbon.

Word shrinks the view so the entire page fits the window.

4. Choose **View**→**Zoom**→**Page Width** from the Ribbon.

Word zooms in again.

About Computer Keyboards

Although computer keyboards have a layout of keys similar to typewriters (the QWERTY layout), they also feature several special keys. For example, some computer keyboards add functionality with keys that help you start an email program or a program to play music. There are also keys that modify other keys that you tap. The following illustration displays a typical computer keyboard and points out the location of some types of keys. However, there are many designs for computer keyboards, and this is just one example.

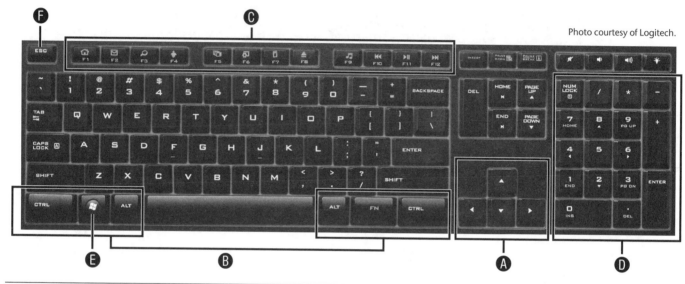

Photo courtesy of Logitech.

	Key Names	Description
A	Cursor keys	These keys allow you to move the blinking cursor without using the mouse.
B	Ctrl and Alt keys	You hold down one of these keys to modify the next key you tap. For example, hold down Ctrl and tap C to issue the Copy command. This is the same command you could issue using the Copy command on the Ribbon. Many computer users find these keyboard shortcuts quite handy.
C	Function keys	These keys change function depending on the program you are running.
D	Numeric keypad	When you press the Num Lock key at the top of the keypad, these keys function like a 10-key calculator.
E	Windows Key	Tapping this key opens the Start menu.
F	Esc key	You can use this key to switch off some functions. For example, if a program is in full-screen mode, this key will return the view to normal.

Using Tab Settings

Tab settings tell Word where to advance the cursor when you tap the [Tab] key. There are lots of things you can do with tab settings and this lesson will only touch on placing new settings and creating a tab leader.

Word displays tab settings on the ruler.

Tab Leaders

A tab leader tells Word to type a specific pattern between tab settings. There are three available patterns. It's a great way to create straight lines on a form; much better than using the underscore key.

The line tab leader on the 4" tab created a line between two tab settings.

QUICK REFERENCE: Setting Tabs and Tab Leaders

Task	Procedure
Display the ruler	• Choose View→Show→Ruler from the Ribbon.
Set a new tab	• Make sure the ruler is visible.
	• Click on the ruler where you wish to set a new tab.
	• Drag a tab setting to move it.
Set a tab leader	• Double-click on any tab setting in the ruler.
	• Select the tab location for the leader, then choose a leader type and click Set.

HANDS-ON 3.3 Use Tabs and Leaders

In this exercise, you will use tab settings and leaders to create lines on the form.

1. Make sure the ruler is displayed:

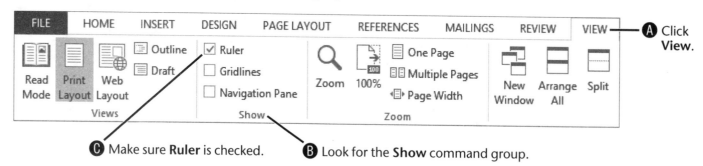

A Click **View.**

C Make sure **Ruler** is checked.

B Look for the **Show** command group.

⚠NOTE! If you have trouble with the next step, or want a preview, a video about creating tabs and setting tab leaders is located on the student resource center.

2. Create tabs:

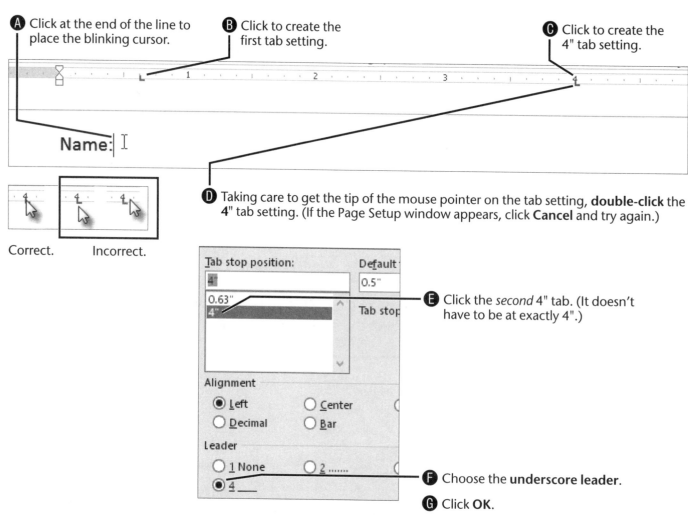

A Click at the end of the line to place the blinking cursor.

B Click to create the first tab setting.

C Click to create the 4" tab setting.

Correct.   Incorrect.

D Taking care to get the tip of the mouse pointer on the tab setting, **double-click** the 4" tab setting. (If the Page Setup window appears, click **Cancel** and try again.)

E Click the *second* 4" tab. (It doesn't have to be at exactly 4".)

F Choose the **underscore leader.**

G Click **OK.**

3. Tap the ⌐Tab⌐ key on the left side of the keyboard.

The cursor jumps to the first tab position.

4. Tap ⌐Tab⌐ again.

The cursor jumps to the 4" tab position and a leader line appears.

5. Tap ⌐Enter⌐.

Word starts the next line. Your special tab settings are automatically applied to the next line, so you can use them again.

6. Add more lines:

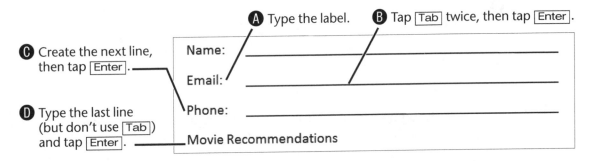

Ⓐ Type the label. Ⓑ Tap ⌐Tab⌐ twice, then tap ⌐Enter⌐.

Ⓒ Create the next line, then tap ⌐Enter⌐.

Ⓓ Type the last line (but don't use ⌐Tab⌐) and tap ⌐Enter⌐.

Name: _____

Email: _____

Phone: _____

Movie Recommendations

The form takes shape. There's not much formatting here, but you'll change that in the next exercise.

Save the Document

With this chunk of work completed, it's a good time to save the document. Notice that the title bar shows that the document is untitled; this means it hasn't been saved yet. The document only exists in RAM. So next you'll save the document to give it a name and storage location.

7. Insert your USB flash drive if you use one to store your coursework.

8. Save the form.

⚠**NOTE!** Skip step 9 if you use Word 2010 for this exercise.

9. Start the save command with Word 2013:

Since this is the first save command for this document, Word asks where you want to store it.

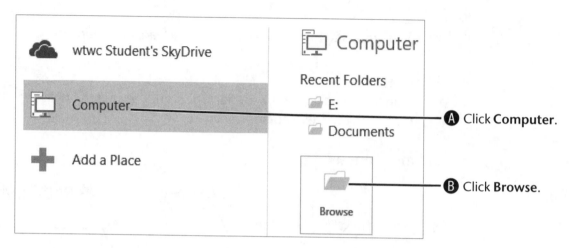

A dialog box appears similar to what you used with WordPad in Lesson 2, Using Programs.

10. Choose a specific storage location and save the document:

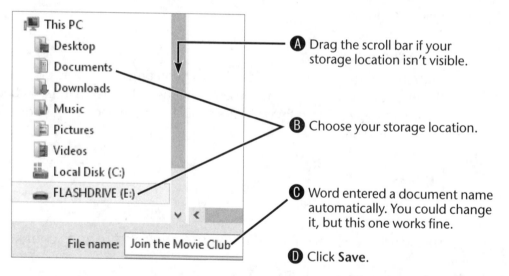

Word names the document and saves it to the new location. The title bar displays the name.

Formatting with Styles and Themes

Microsoft Word has two features that make formatting easier. Using themes and styles, you can change the appearance of a document with just a few clicks. When you work on long documents, styles help you keep consistent formatting from one page to the next.

Styles

A *style* is predesigned formatting you can apply to text with a single click. Styles instantly apply font- and paragraph-level formatting. This can save you several clicks applying bold or italics, changing the font color and size, etc. What's just as useful is that you don't need to remember the settings and reapply them manually. You just apply the style and Word takes care of the details.

The Styles commands in a typical Word document.

Themes

A *theme* is a coordinated set of styles. Style names are consistent from one theme to the next, but the settings for the styles can be quite different. For example, the color for headings might change from one theme to the next. A theme might use some additional formatting for some of its styles.

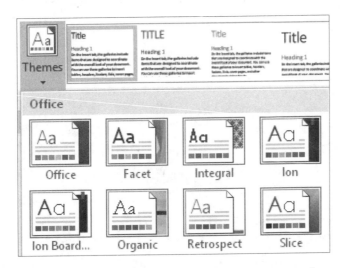

Word displays available themes.

Task	Procedure
Apply a style	• Select the paragraph(s) to receive the style setting. • Choose Home→Styles→[Style Name] from the Ribbon. • Click the Gallery button to expand the view of Styles.

Apply a theme	• Choose Design→Themes→[Theme] from the Ribbon.

HANDS-ON 3.4 Apply Styles and Themes

In this exercise, you will use styles and themes to change the formatting of the document.

1. Click the **Home** tab for your version of Word.

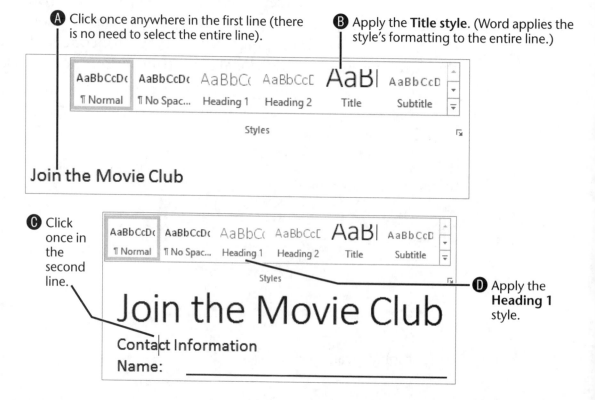

2. Format the flyer title:

A Click once anywhere in the first line (there is no need to select the entire line).

B Apply the **Title style**. (Word applies the style's formatting to the entire line.)

Join the Movie Club

C Click once in the second line.

D Apply the **Heading 1** style.

Join the Movie Club

Contact Information

Name: _____

These styles affect an entire paragraph, without the need to manually select all the text. There are styles that can apply to selected words only but for this lesson you'll focus on paragraph styles like Title and Heading 1.

3. Click the **Movie Recommendations** line and apply the **Heading 1** style.

So styles make it easy to apply format settings with two quick clicks. Changes that might have taken many clicks can instead be applied with one.

Apply Themes (Word 2013)

!NOTE! Skip to step 7 if you are using Word 2010.

4. Change the theme:

Ⓐ Choose the **Design** tab.

Ⓑ Click **Themes**.

Ⓒ Choose **Ion Board**. (The fonts and color scheme change to the new theme.)

Ⓓ Click **Themes**, then choose **Integral**.

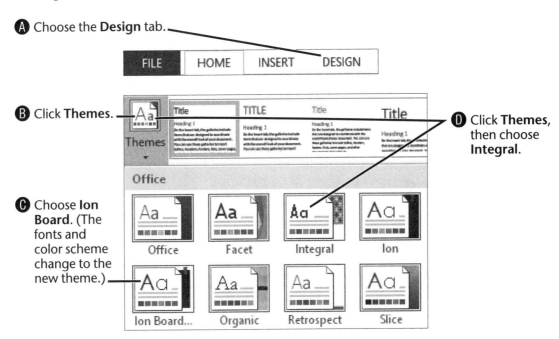

5. Click **Themes**, then choose any theme.

Each selection alters the fonts and color scheme. Sometimes the difference between themes is minor, sometimes it's radical.

6. Choose **Design→Document Formatting→Themes→Main Event** from the Ribbon.

!NOTE! Skip to step 10 if you are using Word 2013.

Apply Themes (Word 2010)

7. Practice changing the theme:

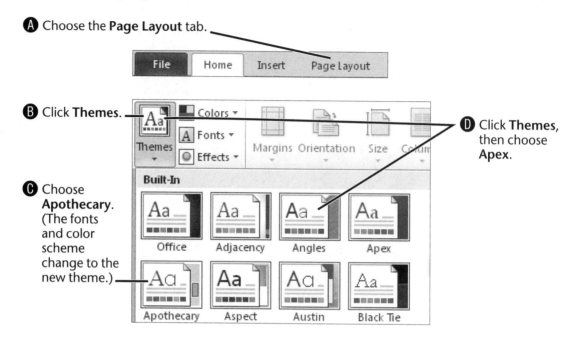

Ⓐ Choose the **Page Layout** tab.

Ⓑ Click **Themes**.

Ⓒ Choose **Apothecary**. (The fonts and color scheme change to the new theme.)

Ⓓ Click **Themes**, then choose **Apex**.

8. Click **Themes**, then choose any theme.

Each selection alters the fonts and color scheme. Sometimes the difference between themes is minor, sometimes it's radical.

9. Choose **Page Layout→Themes→Themes→Essential** from the Ribbon.

Save Your Work

All of these theme and style changes have taken place in RAM. They aren't yet saved to the document file in your storage location.

10. **Save** 🖫 the document.

It's a good habit to click Save after you make significant changes to a document.

Behind the Screen

Software Standards and Ease of Use

In the early days of personal computers, there was a great deal of innovation. Software companies would come up with all sorts of clever ways to make their programs useful and powerful. Unfortunately, what you learned with one program usually had nothing to do with another program. Learning a new program was so difficult that many people used the one or two programs they knew well for tasks the software was never designed for. These days, the situation is quite different. Now, what you learn as you use one program usually works with the next program. The reason for this enhanced ease of learning is standards: commonly used conventions that work similarly from one program to the next. The following examples illustrate how standards make it much easier for beginners to learn basic tasks.

Example 1: Cut, Copy, and Paste   The Cut, Copy, and Paste commands work in virtually all Windows programs. These commands work in a similar fashion to help you move and copy files too, not just text. Let's take a closer look at the similarities.

Example 2: Saving Your Work   The Save command is another example of software standards. With few exceptions, Windows programs feature File→Save and File→Save As commands. The first command always replaces the previously saved version of your file with the version that's currently on the screen. The second always allows you to name a file for the first time or to give the file a new name.

Example 3: Styles   The use of styles for formatting text is an easy-to-use feature that can save you time and tedium. Once you learn about a powerful feature like this, the next stage is to look for it in other programs. Excel is a spreadsheet program optimized to work with numbers. But it too has a styles feature.

Conclusion: It Gets Easier from Here   Your first sessions on the computer will be the most difficult; then it starts getting easier—I promise. Go ahead and try using common commands, such as Cut, Copy, and Paste when you use a new program. In nearly every case, common commands such as these will work just like they did when you first learned them. And with practice and repetition, these common commands will become second nature to you, just like numerous other everyday activities.

Using Bullets and Symbols

The Bullet command automatically inserts a bullet character and indents text. You can substitute various symbols for the standard round bullet character. In this case, we'll use a checkbox for the form.

About Symbol Fonts

Word lets you insert symbols into your writing. Windows and Office come with symbol fonts that don't contain alphabetic characters at all. The Symbol menu displays available symbols for easy insertion into the document.

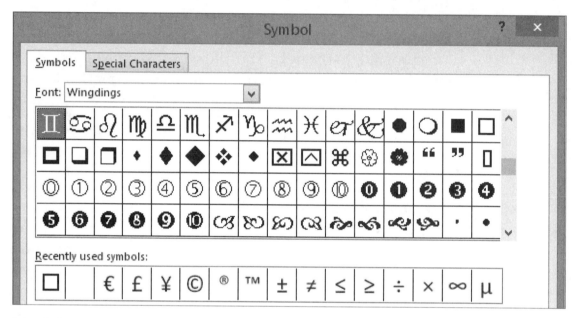

Word displays symbols available in the Wingdings font.

QUICK REFERENCE: Applying Bullets

Task	Procedure
Apply a bullet	• Choose Home→Paragraph→Bullet ⟐ from the Ribbon.
Apply a symbol to a bullet	• Choose Home→Paragraph→Bullet Menu ⟐ ▾ from the Ribbon.
	• Choose from the Bullet Library or click Define New Bullet to apply a new symbol.

HANDS-ON 3.5 **Insert Bullets with Symbols**

In this exercise, you will insert checkbox bullets onto the form, then you'll switch hidden formatting symbols on and off.

1. Click once below **Movie Recommendations**.

2. Define a symbol bullet:

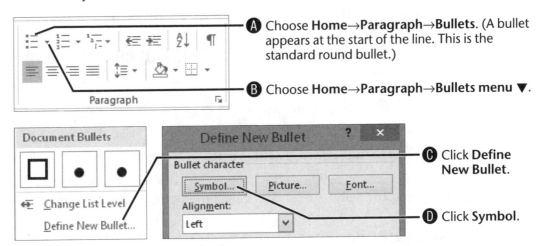

Ⓐ Choose **Home→Paragraph→Bullets**. (A bullet appears at the start of the line. This is the standard round bullet.)

Ⓑ Choose **Home→Paragraph→Bullets menu ▼**.

Ⓒ Click **Define New Bullet**.

Ⓓ Click **Symbol**.

3. Find and set the symbol:

Ⓐ Type **W** and then choose **Wingdings**.

Ⓑ Drag up toward the top of the list.

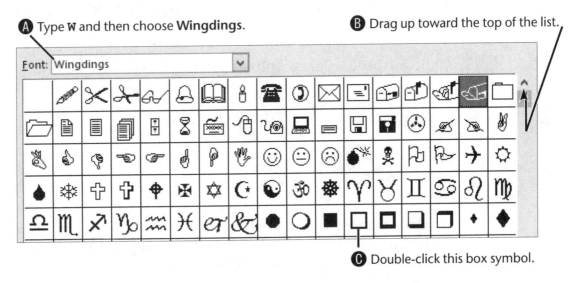

Ⓒ Double-click this box symbol.

Word displays a preview of the bullets. Let's make them a bit larger.

4. Enlarge the bullet font:

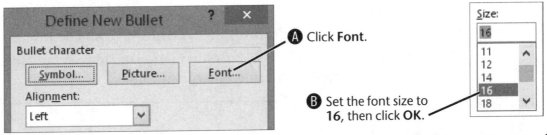

Ⓐ Click **Font**.

Ⓑ Set the font size to **16**, then click **OK**.

5. Click **OK** again.

Word displays the line with the new bullet.

6. Type the two checkbox bullet lines:

Ⓐ Type the text that follows the checkbox, then tap ⌷Enter⌷. (The next bullet appears automatically on the new line.)

☐ **I am willing to pay dues of $3/month**

☐ **I am willing to help with setup or cleanup after showings**

Ⓑ Type the text, then tap ⌷Enter⌷.

7. Choose **Home→Paragraph→Bullets** from the Ribbon.

The bullet disappears from the last line. The bullet command works like a toggle, switching the feature on and off each time you click the command.

8. **Save** 🖫 the document.

Show/Hide Codes

There are hidden codes that you can switch on and off. This can help you see exactly how lines are formatted in Word.

9. Choose **Home→Paragraph→Show/Hide** from the Ribbon.

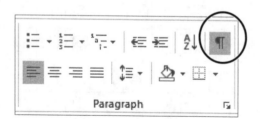

Word displays the hidden codes that control some of the document formatting. Notice the tab symbol in the form lines. There's also a paragraph mark at the end of each line. This shows where you've tapped ⌷Enter⌷.

Name:⊙→ _____ →⃝ _____ ¶

10. Choose **Home→Paragraph→Show/Hide** ¶ from the Ribbon again.

Word switches the code display off. Most users prefer to keep the codes hidden. But sometimes they can help you see where things are.

Using Cut, Copy, and Paste

One reason to multitask is to copy and paste the results from one program into another. This way you can use programs optimized for each part of a complex task. For example, you can use a spreadsheet program to create a budget with calculations and paste this into a word-processing document for a monthly report.

Cut Compared to Copy

The Cut command works just like the copy command, with one difference. Both commands place a copy of your selection into the Clipboard. Both can be pasted repeatedly. However, the Cut command deletes your selection after it's been placed into the Clipboard.

Selecting Text

Selections tell Word which parts of a document you wish to change or apply a command to. There are several ways to select text. For example, you can drag with the mouse to make a selection. A double-click can select an entire word. One of the handiest ways to select entire lines of text is to drag from the left side of the document, as you will do in the next exercise.

Cursor Keys

Cursor keys move the text cursor one character or line at a time. They are sometimes an easier way to quickly put the cursor exactly where you need it or to select just a few characters at a time.

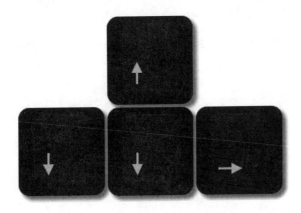

Copying and Moving Text

Command	Description
Cut	Delete my selection and place it on the Clipboard for pasting.
Copy	Leave my selection where it is and place a copy of it on the Clipboard for pasting.
Paste	Insert a copy of my most recently cut or copied item at the spot where the cursor (insertion point) is blinking.

 HANDS-ON 3.6 Use Cut, Copy, and Paste

In this exercise, you will use Cut, Copy, and Paste to reorganize and add to the form.

1. Select and cut the checkbox bullet lines:

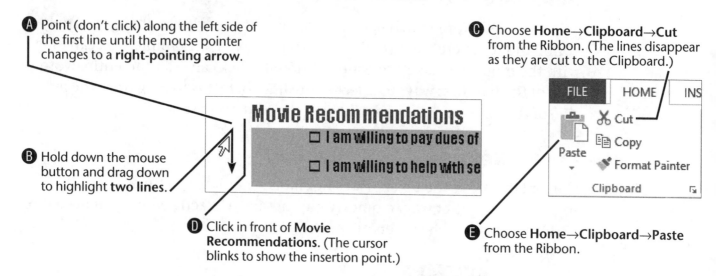

A Point (don't click) along the left side of the first line until the mouse pointer changes to a **right-pointing arrow**.

B Hold down the mouse button and drag down to highlight **two lines.**

C Choose **Home→Clipboard→Cut** from the Ribbon. (The lines disappear as they are cut to the Clipboard.)

D Click in front of **Movie Recommendations**. (The cursor blinks to show the insertion point.)

E Choose **Home→Clipboard→Paste** from the Ribbon.

Word inserts the cut lines in front of the cursor. This places them before the *Movie Recommendations* heading.

2. Select, then copy and paste two lines:

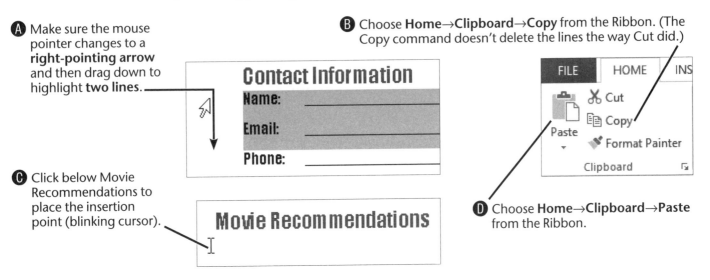

A Make sure the mouse pointer changes to a **right-pointing arrow** and then drag down to highlight **two lines**.

B Choose **Home→Clipboard→Copy** from the Ribbon. (The Copy command doesn't delete the lines the way Cut did.)

C Click below Movie Recommendations to place the insertion point (blinking cursor).

D Choose **Home→Clipboard→Paste** from the Ribbon.

Word pastes the lines at the insertion point.

3. Select and revise text:

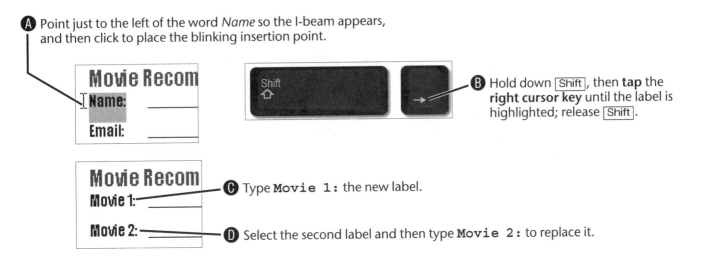

A Point just to the left of the word *Name* so the I-beam appears, and then click to place the blinking insertion point.

B Hold down Shift, then **tap** the **right cursor key** until the label is highlighted; release Shift.

C Type **Movie 1:** the new label.

D Select the second label and then type **Movie 2:** to replace it.

Select and Format Text

The lines for contact information and movie recommendations are a bit cramped. You will add some paragraph space before to spread the lines out without using Enter.

4. Drag to select the entire **Name**, **Email**, and **Phone** lines.

5. Choose **Home→Paragraph→Line Spacing→Add Space** from the Ribbon.

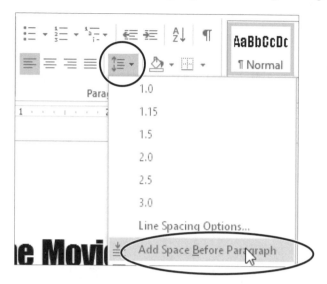

6. Select the **Movie 1** and **Movie 2** lines.

7. Tap the ⬚F4⬚ function key on the keyboard.

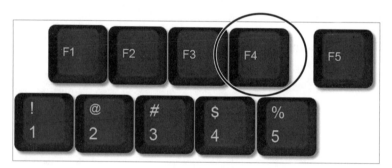

Word repeats the command without your having to select it again. Next, you'll select the entire form, then copy and paste it to repeat it at the bottom of the page.

Create a Second Copy of the Form

8. Select all the lines in the form, from the title to the line below **Movie 2**.

9. Choose **Home→Clipboard→Copy** from the Ribbon.

10. Click below the **Movie 2** line to set the insertion point.

11. Choose **Home→Clipboard→Paste** from the Ribbon.

Word pastes a second copy of the form.

12. **Save** ⊟ the document.

13. Click FILE , then choose **Close**.

    This closes the document while leaving the Word program running.

Printing Documents

Word's Print command gives you a preview before you print. You can tell Word to print the entire document, the currently viewed page, or a range of pages. If the document is to be used online, you can also save it in a form that someone who doesn't have Word installed can still open.

The Default Printer

A default setting is one a program assumes you'll want unless you change it. If a printer is set up on the computer or tablet, it's usually the default printer. If more than one printer is available, you can select which one to use. You can also "print" to a file you can send via email.

Saving as a PDF

Rather than print a document, you can choose to save it in PDF. PDF (Portable Document Format) is a world-wide standard for exchanging documents online. Saving in PDF allows others who don't have Word installed to reliably open and view your documents.

Word gives the option to save any document in PDF format.

About Printers

Computer printers can create sharp, colorful pages from documents you type or from web pages you view online. Most home users have either an ink jet or an all-in-one printer. Both are described in this section.

Ink Jet Printers   Ink jet printers spray microscopic drops of ink on the page. Most use separate black and color ink cartridges, and mix the colors as necessary to print your documents and photos. Compared to the laser printers found in most office environments, ink jet printers are slower, and the cost of printing each page is usually a few cents more. But ink jet printers are also capable of printing digital photographs in photo-realistic color.

!**TIP!** When it comes to printing photographs, the paper you use with an ink jet printer makes a huge difference in the quality of the picture.

All-in-One Printers   All-in-one ink jet printers can serve as a copier, a document or photo scanner, and a fax machine. Most all-in-ones have a USB port and a slot into which you can plug your digital camera's storage card.

Image courtesy of Epson America, Inc.

The Epson Expression Premium XP-600 Small-in-One™ Printer makes copies, scans, prints from photo storage cards, and wirelessly connects to tablets and smartphones.

Wireless Printing   Many printers now feature the ability to print wirelessly over your home network or from a mobile device, such as a tablet or smartphone. This allows you to send a file to print without a physical connection to the printer. For example, you can print from a computer on the other side of the house. Or, you can open a file on a tablet and print it without the use of another computer.

!**TIP!** Wireless printing capability goes by various vendor-specific names, including Apple AirPrintTM Epson ConnectTM, Google Cloud PrintTM, and HP ePrintTM.

Opening Recent Documents

Most Windows programs display a Recent Documents list. This makes it easy to locate and open files you've worked with lately, without the need to search.

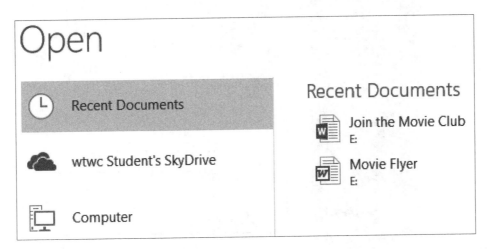

Word displays recently-opened documents.

 HANDS-ON 3.7 **Print the Document**

In this exercise, you will print a copy of the document. You will also save it in PDF format.

1. Click **FILE**.

   Word displays the Open command by default.

2. Choose **Join the Movie Club** from Recent Documents.

3. Click **FILE**.

4. Set the print options:

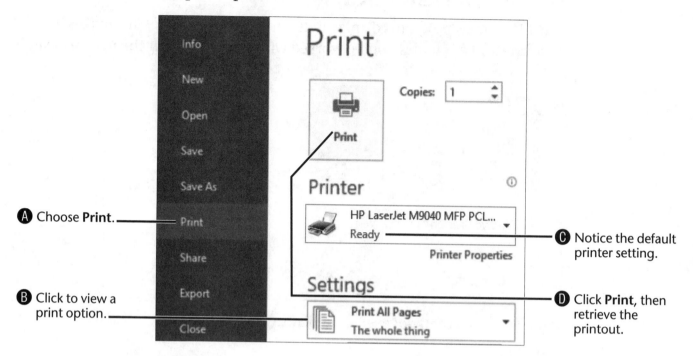

Ⓐ Choose **Print**.

Ⓑ Click to view a print option.

Ⓒ Notice the default printer setting.

Ⓓ Click **Print**, then retrieve the printout.

Save the Form in PDF

Now you will save the document to a new file that anyone can open on most any computer.

5. Click [FILE], then choose **Save As**.

⚠ **NOTE!** Skip to step 7 if you use Word 2010.

6. (Word 2013) Choose the save location:

Ⓐ Choose **Computer**.

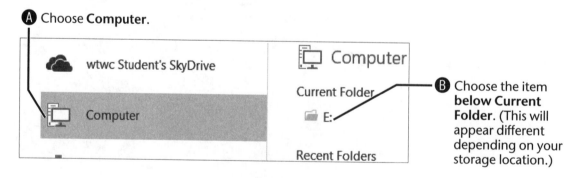

Ⓑ Choose the item **below Current Folder**. (This will appear different depending on your storage location.)

7. Change the type to PDF:

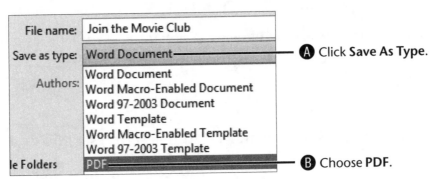

A Click **Save As Type**.

B Choose **PDF**.

8. Click **Save** or tap the Enter key.

Word 2013 saves the form in the new format, then displays it.

Word 2010 saves the file without displaying it.

9. Use **Windows** ⊞+Tab to return to the Desktop.

10. **Close** ⊠ Word.

NOTE! Skip the rest of this exercise if you aren't using a USB flash drive.

Safely Remove Your Flash Drive

Properly ejecting your flash drive is a good habit.

11. Safely eject your flash drive if you use one as your storage location.

Concepts Review

To check your knowledge of the key concepts introduced in this lesson, complete the Concepts Review quiz here or on the student resource center.

True/False Questions

Page Number

1. A template can contain a blank document with format settings. **True False** _____

2. A tab setting tells Word where to advance the cursor when you tap ⬚Tab⬚. **True False** _____

3. A theme is predesigned formatting for text. **True False** _____

4. To insert a symbol, you must memorize the key it is associated with. **True False** _____

5. The Copy command deletes the selection after it's placed on the Clipboard. **True False** _____

6. Saving a file in PDF allows a user who doesn't have Word to open it. **True False** _____

Multiple Choice Questions

7. A style is _____.

   Page Number: _____

   a. a coordinated set of predesigned formats
   b. predesigned formatting for text
   c. a way to add an underscore to a tab setting
   d. All of the above

8. A theme is _____.

   Page Number: _____

   a. a coordinated set of predesigned formats
   b. predesigned formatting for text
   c. a way to add an underscore to a tab setting
   d. None of the above

9. The Cut command _____.

   Page Number: _____

   a. copies your selection to the Clipboard and leaves it in the document
   b. copies your selection to the Clipboard and deletes it from the document
   c. allows you to repeatedly paste the selection
   d. Both b and c

10. A template _____.

    Page Number: _____

    a. is a way to apply formatting to text with a single click
    b. is another type of theme setting
    c. contains a design for some type of writing
    d. None of the above

Skill Builders

SKILL BUILDER 3.1 **Use a Calendar Template (Word 2013)**

In this exercise, you will create a calendar using a template.

Before You Begin: Skip to the next exercise if you use Word 2010.

1. If necessary, start the computer and sign on to **Windows**.

2. Start **Word**.

   Word asks which type of document you wish to create. Rather than choosing a blank document, you will search for a calendar template.

3. Open a calendar template:

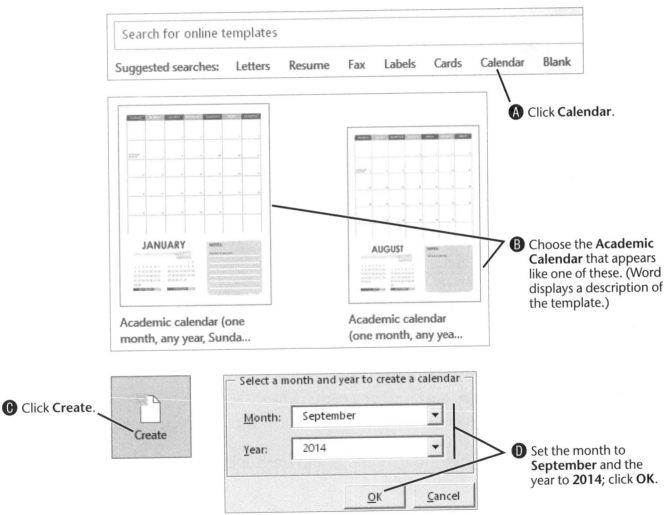

Ⓐ Click **Calendar**.

Ⓑ Choose the **Academic Calendar** that appears like one of these. (Word displays a description of the template.)

Ⓒ Click **Create**.

Ⓓ Set the month to **September** and the year to **2014**; click **OK**.

A note displays about changing the dates on the calendar.

4. Click **OK** again.

The calendar opens in Word. Notice that the title bar shows that the document is untitled. This means it hasn't been saved yet; the document only exists in RAM. Next you'll save the document to give it a name and storage location.

Save the New Document

5. Insert your **USB flash drive** if you use one to store your coursework.

6. Save the **calendar**.

Since this is the first save command for this document, Word asks where you want to store it.

7. Click **Computer**, then click **Browse**.

8. Choose your **storage location**. (Drag the scroll bar if your storage location isn't visible.)

9. **Type** the name: `Calendar - Movies`.

10. Click **Save**.

Word names the document and saves it to the new location. The title bar displays the name.

11. Close ☒ **Word**.

SKILL BUILDER 3.2 **Use a Calendar Template (Word 2010)**

In this exercise, you will create a calendar using a template.

Before You Begin: Skip to the next exercise if you use Word 2013.

1. If necessary, start the computer and sign on to **Windows**.

2. Start **Word**.

3. Click **FILE** then choose **New**.

4. Find and open a calendar template:

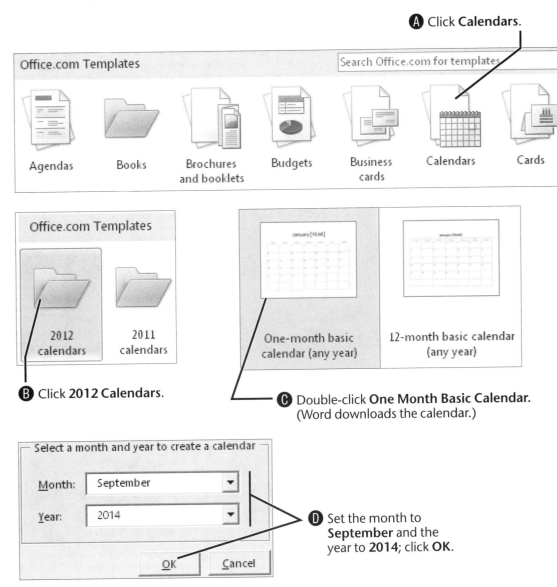

ⓐ Click **Calendars**.

ⓑ Click **2012 Calendars**.

ⓒ Double-click **One Month Basic Calendar**. (Word downloads the calendar.)

ⓓ Set the month to **September** and the year to **2014**; click **OK**.

A note displays about changing the dates on the calendar.

5. Click **OK** again.

The calendar opens in Word. Notice that the title bar shows a generic document name. This means it hasn't been saved yet; the document only exists in RAM. Next you'll save the document to give it a name and storage location.

Save the New Document

6. Insert your **USB flash drive** if you use one to store your coursework.

7. Save the calendar.

   Since this is the first save command for this document, Word asks where you want to store it.

8. Choose your storage location. (Drag the scroll bar if your storage location isn't visible.)

9. Type the name **Calendar – Movies**.

10. Click **Save**.

    Word names the document and saves it to the new location. The title bar displays the name.

11. **Close** ☒ Word.

SKILL BUILDER 3.3 ## Edit the Calendar

In this exercise, you will add dates to the calendar and observe the effects of theme and style changes.

1. Start **Word**.

2. Perform the step for your version of Word:
   - Word 2013: Click **Open Other Documents**.
   - Word 2010: Click **FILE**, then choose **Recent**.

   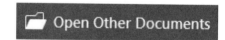

3. Open **Calendar – Movies** from the Recent Documents list.

4. Choose **View→Zoom→Page Width** from the Ribbon.

5. Point in the **first Saturday of the month** until you see the text I-beam, then click. (Depending on the calendar design, the typing area may be alongside or below the date.)

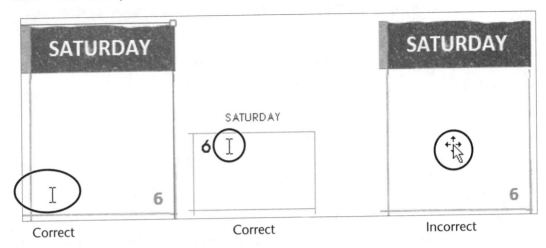

Correct   Correct   Incorrect

You'll see the cursor blinking where the insertion point is ready for typing.

6. Type the name of a favorite movie.

7. Type the names of additional favorite movies in the remaining Saturdays of the month.

8. **Save** ⊟ the calendar.

Apply Themes and Styles

9. Choose **Calendar→Themes→Themes** from the Ribbon.

10. Choose any theme from the **Theme Gallery** list.

    Depending on the calendar's original settings, the change in theme may make a dramatic difference, or very little.

11. Choose **Calendar→Themes→Themes** from the Ribbon, then apply another theme.

12. Click anywhere on the name of the month.

13. Choose **Calendar→Styles→[any style]** from the Ribbon.

    Depending on the style, the month may become small, or even disappear.

14. Click **Undo** ↺.

    Word restores the original style. Undo is a handy command when things go wrong.

15. Choose **Calendar→Styles→[any style]** from the Ribbon again.

Close Without Saving

If some commands don't produce the results you want and a document gets messed up, you can undo the commands by closing the document without saving. Then you can open the most recently saved version of the document to start over.

!**TIP!** This capability is another good reason to give the Save command often as you work on a document.

16. Click [FILE], then choose **Close**.

Word asks if you want to save changes to the document file. Let's assume there are changes you don't want to keep.

17. Choose **Don't Save**.

Word closes the document, but doesn't save your most recent work (anything you did after the Save command in step 8).

18. Click [FILE], then open **Calendar – Movies** from the Recent Documents list.

Notice that any theme or style changes weren't saved. The calendar looks just as it did after you finished adding movie names to it.

19. Close [X] Word.

SKILL BUILDER 3.4 Save the Calendar as a PDF File

In this exercise, you will save the calendar in PDF for sending via email.

1. Start **Word**.

2. Perform the step for your version of Word:

- Word 2013: Click **Open Other Documents**.

- Word 2010: **Click** [FILE], then choose **Recent**.

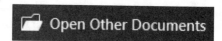

3. Open **Calendar – Movies** from the Recent Documents list.

4. Click [FILE], then choose **Save As**.

5. (Word 2013 only) Click **Computer**, then choose the **Current Folder**.

6. Set Save As Type (just below the document name) to **PDF**.

7. Click **Save**.

   Word 2013 displays the PDF file in a tablet window. Word 2010 saves the file without displaying it.

8. Use **Windows** +Tab to return to the Desktop.

9. **Close** ✕ Word. Choose **Don't Save** if you are asked to save any changes.

10. Safely eject your flash drive if you use one as your storage location.

Working with Files

When you begin working with a computer, you will have just a few files to keep track of. As your use of computers grows, so will the number of files you must manage. After several months, you may have more than one hundred files; after a year, hundreds more. Windows gives you a very effective tool for managing files: folders. With folders, you can group related files. You can even create folders inside of other folders. In this lesson, you will practice finding files, organizing them into folders, and moving them from one location to another.

LESSON OBJECTIVES

After studying this lesson, you will be able to:

- Browse files on the computer
- Open files from a folder window
- Create new folders
- Move and copy files to new locations
- Delete and undelete (restore) files
- Back up files on a USB flash drive

Case Study: Disaster Avoided

Timithy uses his flash drive every day. All his coursework is there and he carries it whenever he thinks he'll need to get something done on a computer. He organizes his work into folders; one for each course he's enrolled in. He also makes a backup of his flash drive every week, or more often if he's done some significant work on a course.

One night, Timithy couldn't find his flash drive. He looked in his backpack, on his desk, in his car. He thought back to the last time he used it. He'd saved an article on it at the library. The next morning, he rushed to the library, but no dice. No one had seen it.

Fortunately, Timithy had made a full backup of his flash drive just two days before. He'd lost some work, but only what he'd done since his last backup. He bought a new flash drive, and loaded his most recent backup on it. He also decided to learn more about cloud storage as another way to protect his work.

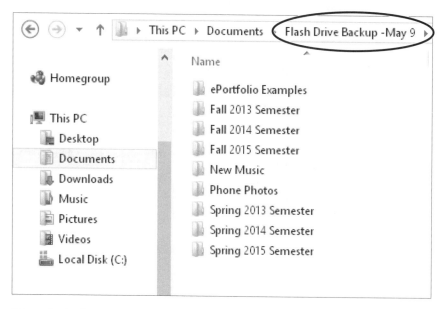

Timithy's flash drive backup took only a couple minutes to make, and saved him dozens of hours of potentially lost work, not to mention irreplaceable photos.

Using the Control Panel

There are many ways to change the way Windows looks and operates. Many of the controls for changing the properties of Windows can be found in the Control Panel.

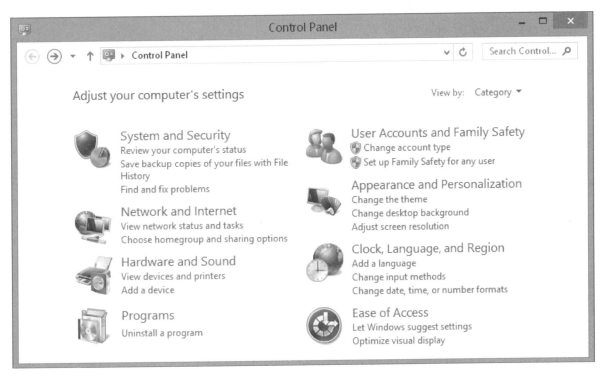

The Windows Control Panel groups various controls into several categories.

Common Control Panel Tasks

The following table describes some of the most important Windows features that you can control through the Control Panel.

Control Panel Item	Description
Add/Remove Programs	This setting allows you to uninstall programs you aren't going to use, which creates more hard drive space
Date/Time	You can set the date and time on your PC.
Display	You can control how the screen appears, such as background colors and pictures.
Mouse	This setting allows you to change the way the mouse operates.
Sounds	This controls the various sounds Windows associates with system events.
Printers	You can add a new printer or set the normal printer.

Opening the Control Panel

The Control Panel appears on the All Apps screen. You can also find it with the Search charm. Normally, the control panel displays the Category view, similar to the preceding figure. If you are studying in a computer lab, you might not have access to the Control Panel. In that case, try viewing the Control Panel on your home computer.

 HANDS-ON 4.1 **Start the Control Panel**

In this exercise, you will examine the many controls available to you in the Control Panel.

> **!NOTE!** Some computer labs do not permit student access to the Control Panel. If you cannot open the Control Panel, skip this exercise. You might try it at home if your computer or tablet runs Windows 8.1.

1. If necessary, **sign on** to Windows and display the **Start** screen.

2. Use **Windows** ⊞+Ⓢ to display the **Search charm**.

3. Search for and open the Control Panel:

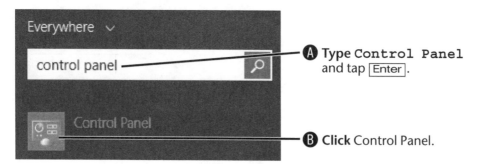

Ⓐ Type Control Panel and tap Enter.

Ⓑ **Click** Control Panel.

The Control Panel displays the Category/Home view. This groups various controls for easy access depending on the task you wish to accomplish. When you open a category to make new settings with the Control Panel, Windows displays its various controls.

Setting Mouse Properties

The mouse has numerous settings you can adjust. Probably the most important setting for a beginner is the double-click speed. You have the option of changing how quickly you must double-click for Windows to recognize it as a double click rather than two slow single clicks. If you're experiencing difficulty double-clicking, slowing down the double-click speed may help.

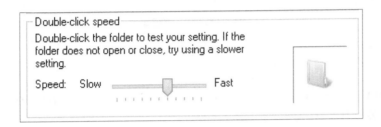

You can change the double-click speed from the Control Panel.

Double-Clicking

So far, you have used a single click to select items on the screen. You have also used the dragging motion (holding down the left mouse button as you move the mouse) to select text in Word and used the right-click motion to pin a program to the Taskbar. You can perform a double-click by tapping and releasing the mouse twice in quick succession. A double-click is essentially a shortcut.

Example

You want to open a file. You display the My Documents window, locate the file, and then use a double click to open it. You could also select the same file with a single click and then choose File→Open from the menu bar or simply tap the [Enter] key.

TIP! Some learners initially have trouble double-clicking. If you find a double click difficult, don't worry. Just use a single click to select an item and then tap [Enter] to open it. Or give a command from the command bar.

HANDS-ON 4.2 **Change the Double-click Speed**

In this exercise, you will adjust the double-click speed of the mouse. Your Mouse Properties screens may look a bit different, depending on the brand of mouse you have.

1. Open Mouse Properties:

A Choose **Hardware and Sound**. (Windows displays Control Panel items in this category; in the left panel are additional, related commands.)

B Choose **Mouse**.

A new window appears to display the mouse properties (settings). Now you will set the double-click speed slower.

2. Adjust the double-click speed:

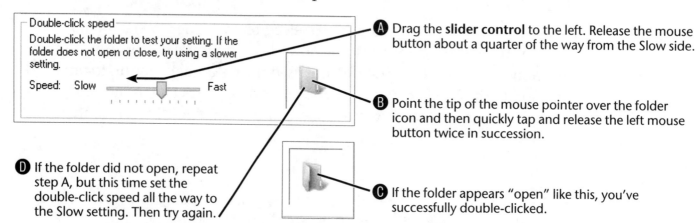

A Drag the **slider control** to the left. Release the mouse button about a quarter of the way from the Slow side.

B Point the tip of the mouse pointer over the folder icon and then quickly tap and release the left mouse button twice in succession.

C If the folder appears "open" like this, you've successfully double-clicked.

D If the folder did not open, repeat step A, but this time set the double-click speed all the way to the Slow setting. Then try again.

3. Practice double-clicking on the practice folder and adjusting the speed setting until the folder opens and closes reliably.

As your double-clicking improves, you can adjust the double-click speed higher.

4. Click **OK** when you are finished.

This closes the Mouse Properties window and the Control Panel is visible.

5. **Close** ▄x▄ the Control Panel.

Browsing Files

All of your digital documents and media are stored in files and folders on your physical computer or in Internet-based (cloud) storage. This lesson concentrates on local, physical locations of your files; Lesson 7, Using Cloud File Storage covers cloud storage. Browsing locations on your computer or tablet is a key skill. You can accumulate hundreds and later thousands of files over time. As a student, you create many new files each semester. By the end of this lesson, you'll be able to organize files so you can find something months after creating it. You'll use the File Explorer for most of these tasks.

File Explorer

File Explorer (not to be confused with Internet Explorer) is a program for browsing and managing files and folders. Like WordPad, Paint, and Word, it uses a Ribbon to organize program commands with tabs and command groups.

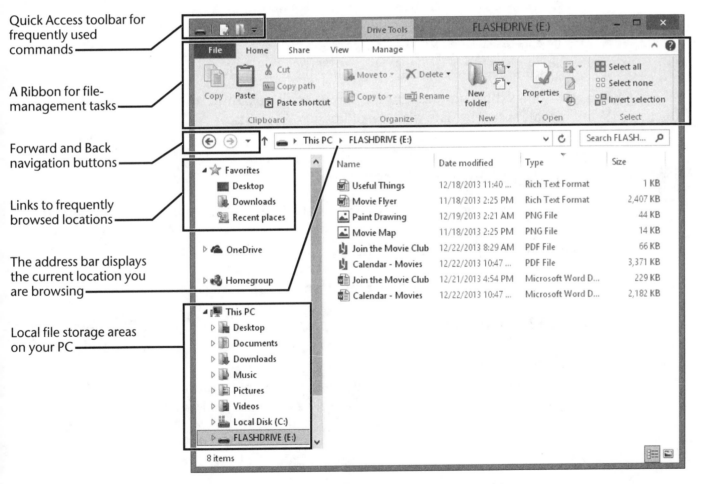

Windows 8.1 File Explorer

Changing the View

File Explorer can display files and folders in several ways. You can view files as a simple list, or choose a view that displays large icons that show previews of pictures.

Sorting Files

You can sort the view of files in File Explorer. For example, you can sort files by name, date modified, and type. The Details view is the best way to quickly sort files. The headings in this view display how files are sorted.

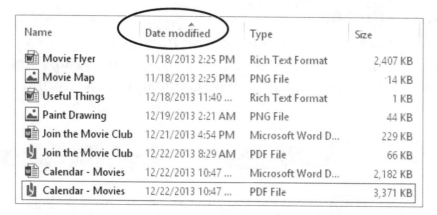

Name	Date modified	Type	Size
Movie Flyer	11/18/2013 2:25 PM	Rich Text Format	2,407 KB
Movie Map	11/18/2013 2:25 PM	PNG File	14 KB
Useful Things	12/18/2013 11:40 ...	Rich Text Format	1 KB
Paint Drawing	12/19/2013 2:21 AM	PNG File	44 KB
Join the Movie Club	12/21/2013 4:54 PM	Microsoft Word D...	229 KB
Join the Movie Club	12/22/2013 8:29 AM	PDF File	66 KB
Calendar - Movies	12/22/2013 10:47 ...	Microsoft Word D...	2,182 KB
Calendar - Movies	12/22/2013 10:47 ...	PDF File	3,371 KB

Headings show how a column is sorted. In this example, the files are sorted by date with the oldest files listed first.

 HANDS-ON 4.3 **Start File Explorer**

In this exercise, you will start File Explorer and browse significant parts of the computer.

1. If necessary, display the **Desktop**.

2. If you use a USB flash drive, plug it in.

3. Start **File Explorer**.

4. Click **This PC**.

File Explorer displays the basic locations on the computer; including standard folders and any storage drives, including your flash drive if you plugged it in earlier.

Change the View

5. Display your file storage location.

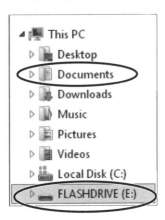

Change the View

6. Choose **View→Layout→Large Icons**.

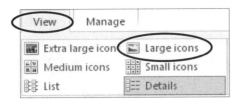

The display of your files changes. You see thumbnails of images.

7. Choose **View→Layout→Details**.

A list of files with program and file size details appears.

Change the Order

8. Sort the files:

C Click the **Name** heading.

B Click the **Date Modified** heading again to sort in descending order.

A Click **Date Modified** to sort the list by date, ascending.

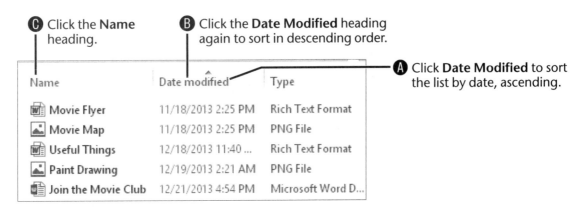

Name	Date modified	Type
Movie Flyer	11/18/2013 2:25 PM	Rich Text Format
Movie Map	11/18/2013 2:25 PM	PNG File
Useful Things	12/18/2013 11:40 ...	Rich Text Format
Paint Drawing	12/19/2013 2:21 AM	PNG File
Join the Movie Club	12/21/2013 4:54 PM	Microsoft Word D...

The File Storage Hierarchy

Windows 8.1 introduces some changes to the hierarchy used in previous versions, such as Windows 7. The four levels in the hierarchy are listed in the following table.

Windows 8.1 File Storage Hierarchy

Level	Definition	Examples
Cloud	This is Internet-based storage.	• OneDrive • Dropbox • Google Drive
This PC	This location displays folders and storage drives located on your physical computer or tablet.	• Documents • Music • Pictures • Videos • USB Flash Drive
Folder	This is an electronic location in which you store groups of related files and folders. Folders are often grouped into libraries.	• A folder to store all files for the Word program • A folder to store files you typed for a project
File	This is a collection of computer data that has some common purpose.	• A letter you've typed • A picture you've drawn

An Analogy A traditional file-cabinet system is a good analogy for the file system on a computer. Drives, folders, and files on a computer system have intuitive file-cabinet equivalents.

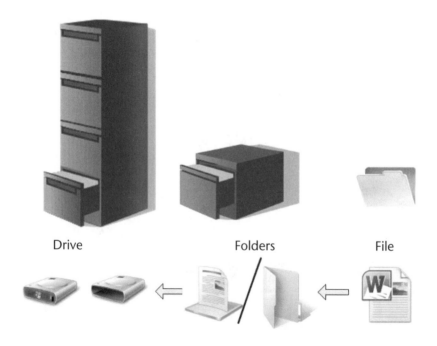

Drive   Folders   File

Folders Compared to Files

Files and folders are closely related, but quite different. Folders (like the drawers in a file cabinet) are simply electronic containers for your files. As the number of files you create grows, you create folders to organize them.

A folder you created in Documents or on your flash drive.

Movie Club

Calendar - Movies

Calendar - Movies

Join the Movie Club

Join the Movie Club

Movie Flyer

Movie Map

Document and image files grouped inside the folder.

Opening Files

One reason to use File Explorer is to locate and open a file you've created previously. The most convenient ways to open a document are from the Recent Documents list within the application you used to create the file or from File Explorer. Each method is just as effective as the other.

Default Programs

A default is a setting Windows assumes you want unless you indicate otherwise. Most files you store have a default program that opens it unless you deliberately choose a different program. A double click always opens a file with the default program. But you can choose a different program from the File Explorer.

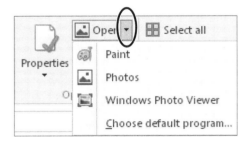

File Explorer displays programs that can open a picture file.

Drive Letter ABCs

A Windows computer assigns a letter to each storage device attached to it. If you attach a new storage device to the computer, Windows automatically assigns the next available drive letter to it. Drive letters are just another way to distinguish one storage location from another. Windows also labels each storage location with a name. You can usually change the name of a device. For example, you can change the name of your USB flash drive to something easier to identify, such as your first or last name.

Folder/Drive Displays   Windows has standard folder locations and drive letters. Following is a typical display of storage devices.

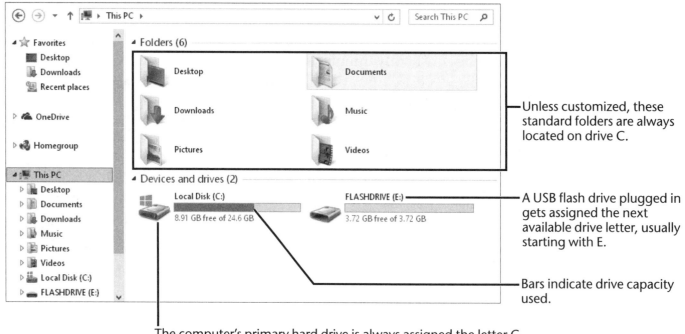

Unless customized, these standard folders are always located on drive C.

A USB flash drive plugged in gets assigned the next available drive letter, usually starting with E.

Bars indicate drive capacity used.

The computer's primary hard drive is always assigned the letter C. The Windows logo indicates that the computer starts from this drive.

HANDS-ON 4.4 **Open a File**

In this exercise, you will practice opening a file using File Explorer.

1. Double-click **Movie Map**. Or, click once on the file and tap Enter .

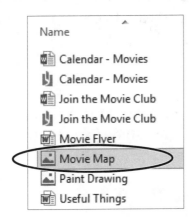

Windows starts the Photos tablet app to display the file.

2. Use **Windows** 🔳+ Tab to return to the Desktop.

3. Choose the program to open a file:

Ⓐ Make sure **Movie Map** is selected.

Ⓑ Choose **Home→Open→Open menu** ▼. (A list of common programs to open this type of file appears.)

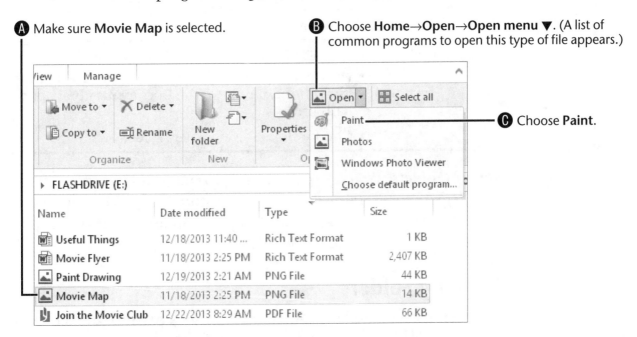

Ⓒ Choose **Paint**.

Paint starts and displays the map.

4. **Close** ⬛ x Paint.

Using Folders

In addition to using the basic Documents library window, you can create new folders of your own to store your files. For example, you may want to create a folder in which to store most of the letters you type or to store photos taken with a digital camera. Windows makes it easy to create new folders. Once you have created a folder, you can store files in it.

Creating New Folders

You can create new folders using File Explorer. Most Windows programs include a button that lets you create a new folder from within the program when you first save a file.

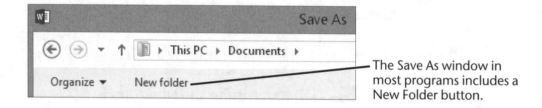

The Save As window in most programs includes a New Folder button.

QUICK REFERENCE: Creating a New Folder

Task	Procedure
Create a new folder	• Start File Explorer. • Display the location where you wish to create the new folder (for example, in the Documents library or your USB flash drive). • Choose Home→New→New Folder.

Naming Folders   You use the same rules to name folders that you use to name files. Refer to the Naming Files table in Lesson 2 (page 54). A folder name can be up to 255 characters long and can use some types of punctuation marks, such as dashes, commas, and ampersands.

Opening Folders

Use the same techniques to open a folder that you use to open files. It's easiest to open folders with a double click. As you navigate folders, the address bar shows which folder you are viewing.

The Back Button

 When you open a folder, you go "inside" it. The Back button takes you back to the previous view. One or two clicks of the Back button will usually get you back to the Documents folder or USB flash drive where you started.

HANDS-ON 4.5 **Create and Open a New Folder**

In this exercise, you will create a new folder in your file storage location, open it, and then return to the base level of your storage location.

1. Create and rename a new folder:

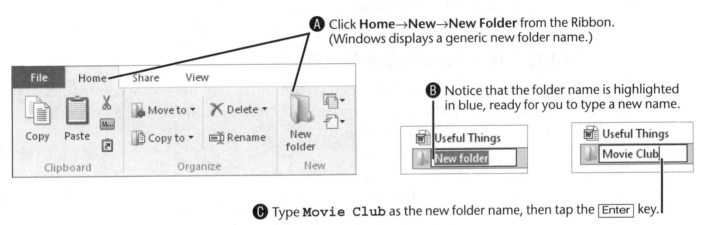

Ⓐ Click **Home→New→New Folder** from the Ribbon. (Windows displays a generic new folder name.)

Ⓑ Notice that the folder name is highlighted in blue, ready for you to type a new name.

Ⓒ Type **Movie Club** as the new folder name, then tap the Enter key.

The new name is locked in.

2. Double-click to open the folder. Or, click once on the folder, then tap Enter. Windows opens the new folder. It is empty, since you just created it.

3. Go back to the base level of your storage location:

Ⓐ Notice the folder name in the address bar. (It also appears in the title bar at the top of the window).

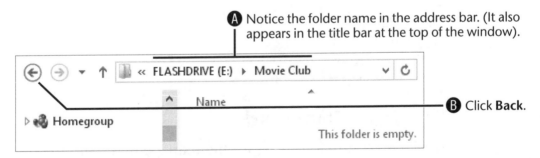

Ⓑ Click **Back**.

You are back to viewing the base level of your file storage location. Notice the name on the address bar. Now that you've learned how to create a new folder, you're ready to practice moving and copying files into it.

Moving and Copying Files

Once you save a file in a folder or drive, it does not mean the file has to *stay* in that particular location. You have the option of moving the file into another folder if it suits your needs. The easiest way to move a file to another folder is to cut it from its original location and paste it in a new location. The commands used to perform this task work similarly to the Cut and Paste commands for text.

 TIP! There are other ways to move and copy files, but Cut, Copy, and Paste is an excellent technique to get started with. It lets you use a familiar approach for a new task.

Cut, Copy, and Paste for Files

The following table summarizes how the Cut, Copy, and Paste commands work for file management. Compare this table with the Copying and Moving Text table in Lesson 3 (page 92).

Copying and Moving Files

Command	Description
Cut	Delete the selected file after it is pasted in a new location.
Copy	Leave selected file in place after it is pasted in a new location.
Paste	Place the most recently cut or copied file into the location currently in view.

FROM THE KEYBOARD

Ctrl + X to Cut
Ctrl + C to Copy
Ctrl + V to Paste

The Undo Command

The Undo command works for file-management commands too. If you get an unexpected result when you move or copy files, just use Undo to reverse it. File Explorer has an Undo button available (although it starts out hidden by default). Or, you can use the keyboard shortcut.

FROM THE KEYBOARD

Ctrl + Z to Undo

TIP! Use the Undo command immediately after you realize you've made a mistake or changed your mind about a command.

Modifying the Quick Access Toolbar

File Explorer has a Quick Access toolbar you can add a few buttons to. One of them happens to be the Undo button.

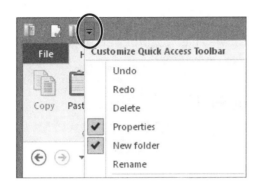

The Customize menu on File Explorer's Quick Access toolbar.

 HANDS-ON 4.6 **Move a File to a Different Folder**

In this exercise, you will use the Cut and Paste commands to move a document file to the new Movie Club folder. Then you will use the Undo feature to undo the command.

Before You Begin: Your file storage location should be displayed in File Explorer.

1. Cut a file for moving:

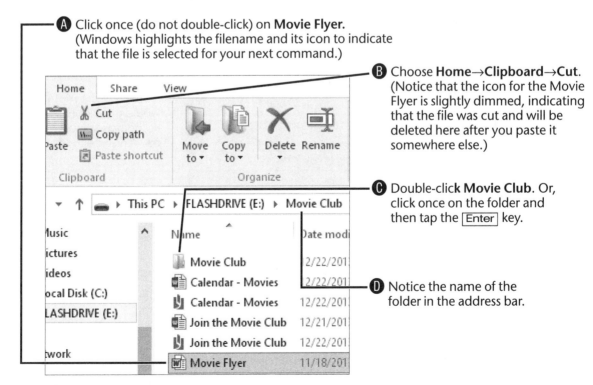

Ⓐ Click once (do not double-click) on **Movie Flyer.** (Windows highlights the filename and its icon to indicate that the file is selected for your next command.)

Ⓑ Choose **Home→Clipboard→Cut.** (Notice that the icon for the Movie Flyer is slightly dimmed, indicating that the file was cut and will be deleted here after you paste it somewhere else.)

Ⓒ Double-click **Movie Club.** Or, click once on the folder and then tap the Enter key.

Ⓓ Notice the name of the folder in the address bar.

Whenever you wonder exactly what you are viewing in the main (right) panel in File Explorer, take a quick look at the address bar. Now that you are viewing the destination, you can paste the file in the next step.

2. Choose **Home→Clipboard→Paste** from the Ribbon.

The file appears in the folder. Now let's see what happened to the file where it was originally stored.

3. Click **Back** ⬅.

You are back to viewing the base of your storage location. Notice the location in the address bar. Notice also that the Movie Flyer document is no longer in this folder. You successfully moved it into the Movie Club folder.

Undo the Cut and Paste Command

Let's say that you've changed your mind and do not wish to move the file after all. You can simply undo the previous command. First, you need to make sure the command is visible.

4. Display Undo on the Quick Access toolbar:

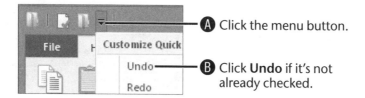

Ⓐ Click the menu button.

Ⓑ Click **Undo** if it's not already checked.

The command appears on the Quick Access toolbar. This doesn't actually give the command, however.

5. Undo the previous command:

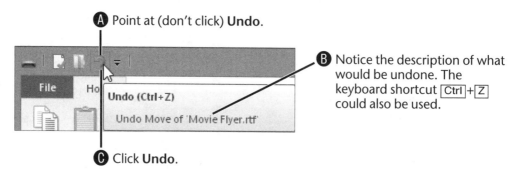

Ⓐ Point at (don't click) **Undo**.

Ⓑ Notice the description of what would be undone. The keyboard shortcut Ctrl + Z could also be used.

Ⓒ Click **Undo**.

The Movie Flyer file reappears in your storage location.

6. Double-click the **Movie Club** folder, or click once on the folder and tap Enter.

The folder is empty again after the Undo command you performed in step 5.

7. Click **Back** ⬅.

You are back to viewing the base level of your storage location.

Moving and Copying Multiple Files

You may wish to move or copy more than one file with the same command. Normally, Windows only selects one file at a time whenever you give a single click. However, you can use the Ctrl and Shift keys to add files to your selection.

The location of the Ctrl key on most keyboards.

Selecting Files with Ctrl and Shift

Method	How It Works
Ctrl+click	Adds a new item to your selection with each click, or deselects any already selected item.
Shift+click	Selects all the items between two clicks.

Using Select All

You can also tell File Explorer to select all items in the folder or drive you are currently viewing. This is especially useful when you want to create backup copies of your flash drives or of some other location with numerous files and folders.

FROM THE KEYBOARD

Ctrl+A to Select All

Copying Files with the Copy Command

The Copy and Paste commands work just like the Cut and Paste commands, with one exception. As you would expect, the Copy command keeps the original file where it was after you give the Paste command.

HANDS-ON 4.7 **Copy Multiple files to a Folder**

In this exercise, you will use Copy and Paste to copy several files to the Movie Club folder.

Before You Begin: Your file storage location should be displayed in File Explorer.

1. Select multiple files using the mouse and keyboard:

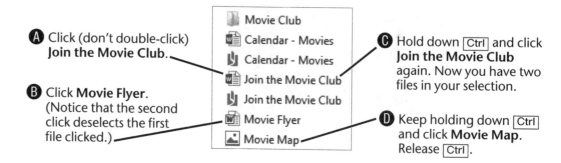

Ⓐ Click (don't double-click) **Join the Movie Club**.

Ⓑ Click **Movie Flyer**. (Notice that the second click deselects the first file clicked.)

Ⓒ Hold down `Ctrl` and click **Join the Movie Club** again. Now you have two files in your selection.

Ⓓ Keep holding down `Ctrl` and click **Movie Map**. Release `Ctrl`.

2. Choose **Home→Clipboard→Copy** from the Ribbon.

   Windows copies all three files to the Clipboard for pasting. Notice that this time the document icons are not "dimmed" as when you used the Cut command.

3. Double-click the **Movie Club** folder to open it.

   The folder is still empty after the Undo command you used at the end of the previous exercise.

4. Choose **Home→Clipboard→Paste** from the Ribbon.

   The three files appear in the folder as Windows pastes them. Since we used the Copy command, the files should also still be their previous location. Let's go back and see.

5. Click **Back** ⊖.

   All the files are still at the base level of your storage location. Leave the File Explorer window open.

Backing Up Flash Drives

It is critical to back up your flash drive regularly. USB flash drives are extremely compact and convenient. They are also easily lost! The last thing you want is to lose an entire semester's work on your flash drive during the final weeks of the term. The best way to avoid a loss is to make regular backups of your flash drive onto your computer's hard drive, or onto some form of cloud storage. Then, at most you might lose a day or two of work—but not weeks or months.

⚠**TIP!** Make a backup of your coursework files at least once a week, or even more often.

Storing Backups

Flash Drive Backup A
File folder

Flash Drive Backup B
File folder

Creating a special folder in your Documents folder for flash drive backups is a great idea. That way the backup is easy to find. You could even rename the backup folder with the date you made the backup. This can help you keep track of how recently you backed up your files. Or you can create an "A" and a "B" backup, alternating between the two. This provides extra protection against the loss of a file through corruption or accidental overwriting.

An example of two sets of flash drive backups.

QUICK REFERENCE: Backing Up Flash Drive Files

Task	Procedure
Create a new folder for backups	• Start File Explorer and display the Documents folder. • Choose Home→New→New Folder from the Ribbon. • Name the folder *Flash Drive Backups* and tap Enter.
Back up files from the flash drive to a hard drive	• Insert your flash drive into a USB port. • Start File Explorer and display the USB flash drive. • Use Ctrl+A to select all files and folders on the flash drive. • Use Ctrl+C to copy the selection. • Display the Documents folder, then open the Flash Drive Backups folder. • Use Ctrl+V to paste the copied files/folders. (If you've previously made a backup, Windows will ask if you wish to overwrite it.) • Choose Yes to All to confirm the replacement. • (Optional) Click the Back button and add today's date to the end of the Flash Drive Backups folder name.

HANDS-ON 4.8 **Back Up Flash Drive Files**

In this exercise, you will copy all of the files from your USB flash drive to a storage drive. Note that this exercise requires a flash drive, and should be completed in order for you to proceed through this lesson sequentially.

⚠️ **NOTE!** Skip this exercise if you are not using a USB flash drive.

1. Display the contents of your flash drive.

   Windows displays the files and folders on your flash drive.

2. Copy all the files on the flash drive:

   Ⓐ Choose **Home→Select→Select All.**

   Ⓑ Choose **Home→Clipboard→Copy.**

   Windows notes all the items to be copied when you give the Paste command.

3. Click **Documents**.

   Windows displays your Documents folder. Now you will make a new folder to store your backup files.

   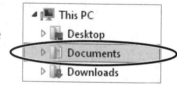

4. Choose **Home→New→New Folder** 📁 from the Ribbon.

5. Type **Flash Drive Backup** and tap ⌷Enter⌷.

6. Double-click the new **Flash Drive Backup** folder.

   Now that you are at the destination, you can paste the copied files.

7. Choose **Home→Clipboard→Paste** from the Ribbon or use ⌷Ctrl⌷+⌷V⌷ from the keyboard.

   All files and folders from your flash drive appear in the backup folder.

8. Go **Back** ⬅ to the Documents folder.

   Your Flash Drive Backup folder appears in the file/folder list. You will use these files in the next two exercises. At the end of the lesson, you will delete all of these files.

Deleting Files and Folders

You can delete unneeded files and folders to free up space on a storage drive. When you delete a folder, any folders and files inside that folder are deleted as well. However, the Delete command doesn't necessarily mean erase. Windows takes steps to help avoid the loss of files you may not have meant to delete.

What Happens to Deleted Files and Folders?

Windows does not physically erase a deleted file from the hard drive. Instead, the file is placed in the Recycle Bin. (Exception: See the warning below.) The Recycle Bin holds the deleted files until you give a command to empty it, or until it runs out of the space allotted to store deleted files.

WARNING! Files and folders deleted from USB flash drives or a network drive *are not* sent to the Recycle Bin! They are *immediately deleted* when you issue the Delete command.

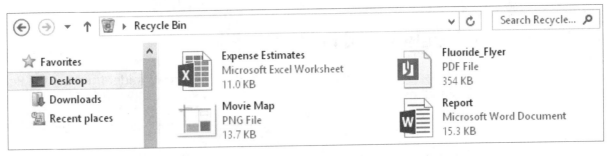

Recently deleted files and folders reside in the Recycle Bin.

TIP! If you accidentally delete files from a flash drive, *stop using the drive immediately* and find an IT professional to help you recover them. In most cases, you should be able to recover the accidentally deleted files.

Restoring Files from the Recycle Bin

Files cannot be opened if they are located in the Recycle Bin. If you decide you need a file you previously deleted, and it hasn't been permanently deleted from the Recycle Bin, you can restore the file to its original location by right-clicking the file and choosing Restore from the pop-up menu. The Recycle Bin also has a Restore All Items command to restore all files it presently contains.

Recovering Accidentally Deleted Files If you accidentally empty one or more files or folders from the Recycle Bin, you may still be able to recover them. However, you should not try to do this yourself. Instead, get assistance from an information technology (IT) professional. IT experts have special software that may be able to recover some or all of the lost files.

> **!TIP!** If you need help recovering files, don't use the drive again until the recovery attempt is made.

Emptying Files from the Recycle Bin

Files located in the Recycle Bin are "permanently" deleted from your computer when you issue an Empty Recycle Bin command, or automatically when the Recycle Bin runs out of space to keep deleted files. Depending on your computer's configuration, the Recycle Bin is set to store a certain amount of files. Once that limit is reached, the oldest files in the Recycle Bin are automatically and "permanently" deleted to make room for additional files.

 HANDS-ON 4.9 **Delete and Restore a File**

In this exercise, you will delete a file in the Documents folder then use the Recycle Bin to view and restore it.

Before You Begin: The Documents folder should be displayed in File Explorer.

1. (Flash drive users) Double-click to open the **Flash Drive Backup** folder.

2. Double-click to open the **Movie Club** folder.

3. Click once (do not double-click) on the **Movie Map** file.

4. Choose **Home→Organize→Delete** from the Ribbon.

   Windows may display a prompt asking you to confirm deletion of the file. (It's very rare for this default option to be switched off.) Some details about the file to be deleted are also displayed.

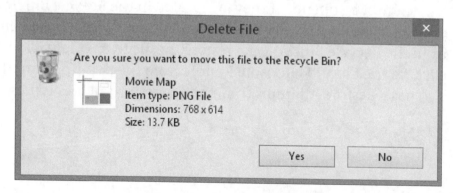

5. Choose **Yes** to confirm deletion of the file; skip to the next step if the confirmation prompt was switched off.

The file disappears as Windows moves the document from My Documents into the Recycle Bin. Now, you will open the Recycle Bin to see where the file has gone.

Open the Recycle Bin

6. **Minimize** ▬ File Explorer.

7. Double-click the **Recycle Bin** icon on the Desktop.

A window displaying the contents of the Recycle Bin appears. Depending on files others have deleted, you may see just the Movie Map document or numerous documents in the Recycle Bin. There may be so many documents that it will be difficult to find your file, but we will.

8. Follow the appropriate step:

- Click once on the **Movie Map** file if it is visible.

- Tap M on the keyboard (the first letter of the filename) until the **Movie Map** file appears highlighted. (Windows will move to each file with a name beginning with the letter you press.)

The Movie Map file is highlighted, ready for your next command.

9. Restore the file:

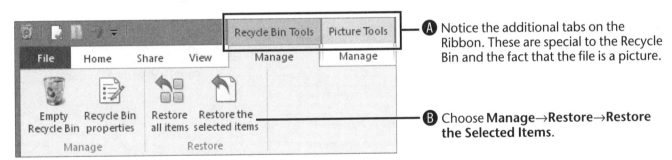

Ⓐ Notice the additional tabs on the Ribbon. These are special to the Recycle Bin and the fact that the file is a picture.

Ⓑ Choose **Manage→Restore→Restore the Selected Items**.

The file disappears from the Recycle Bin. Windows has restored it to the Movie Club folder (from which you deleted it in step 3).

10. **Close** ☒ the Recycle Bin.

The Desktop should be clear again. Now you will use the taskbar to restore the Documents library to the screen and confirm that the Movie Map file has been undeleted.

11. Click **File Explorer** on the Taskbar or use Alt + Tab to restore it.

The previously minimized Documents library window reappears.

12. Look for the **Movie Map** file in the folder. It should be visible again.

Using the Save As Command

There will be times when you want to use an existing file as the starting point for a new one. The File→Save As command lets you give a file a new name and/or save it to a new location. Then the original file is left untouched and you can modify the newly saved copy.

 HANDS-ON 4.10 **Create a New File with Save As**

In this exercise, you will open a document, then use the Save As command to create a copy of it. You'll also delete your flash drive backup.

Before You Begin: Your flash drive backup folder should be displayed in File Explorer.

1. **Double-click** to open the **Join the Movie Club** Word document.

   Word starts and opens the document.

2. Click ▐ FILE ▐ , then choose **Save As**.

3. Choose a new location and rename the file:

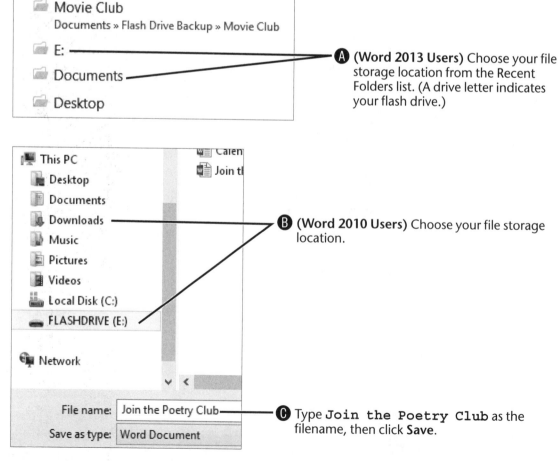

> **A** **(Word 2013 Users)** Choose your file storage location from the Recent Folders list. (A drive letter indicates your flash drive.)

> **B** **(Word 2010 Users)** Choose your file storage location.

> **C** Type `Join the Poetry Club` as the filename, then click **Save**.

Word saves the file at the new location and changes the name. Notice the new name in the title bar.

Edit the New Document

4. Select a word:

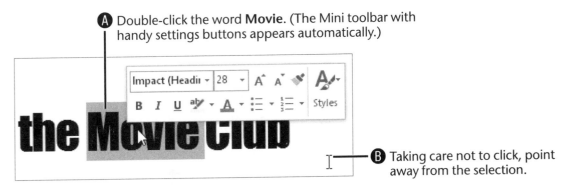

Ⓐ Double-click the word **Movie**. (The Mini toolbar with handy settings buttons appears automatically.)

Ⓑ Taking care not to click, point away from the selection.

The Mini toolbar fades away, but your selection remains highlighted.

5. Type **Poetry** in place of *Movie*.

Word replaces the selection with your typing.

6. Use the double-click method to select and replace *movie* with **poet** in these three places.

Copy and Paste Changes to the Form

The top of the form is revised. Now you'll copy and paste the changes to the bottom half.

7. Choose **View→Zoom→One Page** ▤ from the Ribbon.

Word displays the entire page on the screen. Now you won't have to scroll.

8. Select the top half of the form:

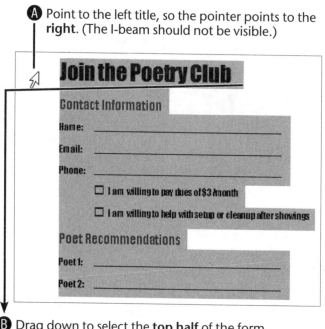

Ⓐ Point to the left title, so the pointer points to the **right**. (The I-beam should not be visible.)

Ⓑ Drag down to select the **top half** of the form.

9. Choose **Home→Clipboard→Copy** from the Ribbon.

10. Select the **bottom half** of the form and then choose **Home→Clipboard→ Paste** from the Ribbon.

The paste command replaces your selection. Now both halves of the form are the same.

11. Save 🖫 the document; **close** ☒ Word.

Delete the USB Backup Folder

!NOTE! Skip the steps below if you did not create a backup of a flash drive.

12. Select and delete a folder:

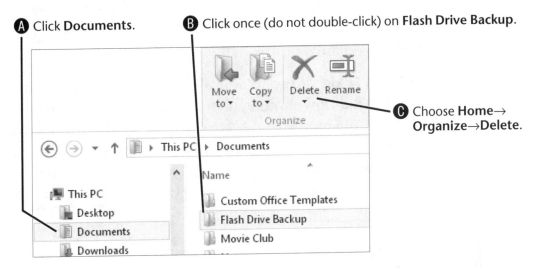

A Click **Documents**.   **B** Click once (do not double-click) on **Flash Drive Backup**.

C Choose **Home→ Organize→Delete**.

Move to ▾   Copy to ▾   Delete ▾   Rename

Organize

This PC ▸ Documents

Name

This PC
Desktop
Documents
Downloads

Custom Office Templates
Flash Drive Backup
Movie Club

13. Choose **Yes** if Windows asks you to confirm the deletion.

The folder disappears into the Recycle Bin.

14. **Close** ⬛x File Explorer.

Empty the Recycle Bin

Someone could restore the just-deleted folder from the Recycle Bin. So you must empty it.

15. Double-click the **Recycle Bin**.

16. Choose **Manage→Manage→Empty Recycle Bin** from the Ribbon.

Windows asks if you are sure you want to permanently delete the Recycle Bin contents.

17. Choose **Yes** to confirm the command.

18. **Close** ⬛x the Recycle Bin.

19. Safely remove your USB flash drive.

Organizing Digital Photos

Most computers come with a program that helps you transfer photos from your digital camera or smartphone. However, unless you transfer photos frequently, they probably won't be organized in a way that makes photos from specific events easy to identify. Your skills with file management will work with photo organization as well.

Organizing Folders Chronologically   To organize the photos, you'll want to use folders. But how should you name the folders? Naming the folders by year, followed by the month and event is a good method. The months work best as two-digit numbers. So, the photos you took in February 2012 would go into a folder named *2012-02-[Event Name]*, for example 2012-02-Concert Photos. When you scan a list of folders, every event will be in chronological order.

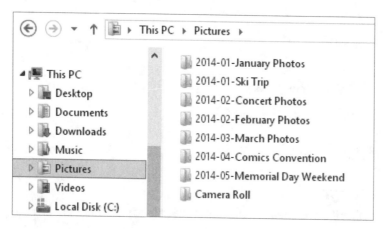

Using year-month prefixes, folders for photos arrange in a neat chronological order.

!TIP! Ten years from now, the program used to view or tag these photos may not exist, but a rational folder organization will.

Cutting and Pasting   Once you create a folder, you can cut and paste photos into it. Cutting a file will move it upon pasting; just like text in Word. You can use the cut and paste commands to move groups of photos for a specific event into a folder of their own.

Concepts Review

To check your knowledge of the key concepts introduced in this lesson, complete the Concepts Review quiz here or on the student resource center.

True/False Questions

				Page Number
1.	File cabinets and file drawers are a good analogy of file organization in Windows.	**True**	**False**	_____
2.	The Documents folder is located on the computer's disk drive.	**True**	**False**	_____
3.	You can control the double-click speed of the mouse.	**True**	**False**	_____
4.	You cannot store folders inside of other folders; only files can be stored in folders.	**True**	**False**	_____
5.	You can use the Cut and Paste commands to move files from one location to another.	**True**	**False**	_____
6.	You must move or copy files one at a time.	**True**	**False**	_____

Multiple Choice Questions

7. What happens when you delete a file on a computer's disk drive?

   Page Number: _____

   a. The file is immediately erased.
   b. The file is marked for future deletion.
   c. The file is placed in the Recycle Bin.
   d. The file is permanently deleted.

8. When can you create a new folder?

   Page Number: _____

   a. When you move a file.
   b. When you copy a file.
   c. While you browse files in the My Documents window.
   d. All of the above

9. What does the Back button in the File Explorer do?

   Page Number: _____

   a. Takes you back to the most recently used program
   b. Takes you back to the previous folder you were browsing
   c. Undoes your most recent command
   d. None of above

10. File→Save As lets you _____.

    Page Number: _____

    a. create a new copy of a file
    b. change the name of a file
    c. save a file in a new location
    d. All of the above
    e. Only a and b

Skill Builders

SKILL BUILDER 4.1 **Browse to Open a File**

In this exercise, you will open a previously created document and save it with a new name.

1. Display the Desktop, then open **File Explorer** and maximize the window.

2. Display your **file storage location** (Documents folder or flash drive).

3. Double-click to open the **Movie Club** folder.

Windows displays the contents of the folder. The address bar displays the current folder location.

4. Double-click to open the **Join the Movie Club** document.

There is a pause as Windows starts Word.

5. Choose **File→Save As**.

6. **(Word 2013)** Click **Movie Club** under the current folder.

7. Rename the document **New Member Forms**

8. **Close ☒** Word. Choose **No** if Word asks if you wish to save any changes to the document.

You are back to viewing the Movie Club folder in File Explorer.

9. Click **Back ⬅** to return to viewing the base level of your storage location.

Leave File Explorer open. You will create a new folder here in the next exercise.

SKILL BUILDER 4.2 **Create and Rename a Folder**

In this exercise, you will create a new folder in your storage location, then copy files and a folder to it. You will also delete a folder, then copy it back to its old location.

1. If necessary, start **File Explorer** and display your **file storage location** (flash drive or Documents folder).

2. Choose **Home→New→New Folder** from the Ribbon.

   Windows displays a new folder. The folder name is highlighted so you can replace it with a new name.

3. Name the folder **Practice** and then tap ⌷Enter⌷.

4. Click once on a clear area of the screen.

Rename the Folder

5. Click (don't double-click) the **Practice** folder name (not the icon).

6. Click the **Practice** folder again.

   The folder name is highlighted, ready for you to rename it.

7. Type **Backups**, then tap ⌷Enter⌷.

   Windows displays the new name. It's easy to rename a folder if necessary.

Copy Files to the Folder

   Now you will create a backup copy of every file and folder in your storage location.

8. Choose **Home→Select→Select All** from the Ribbon.

   Every file and folder is highlighted. However, you don't need to copy the Backups folder. So in the next step you will deselect that folder. The ⌷Ctrl⌷ key lets you add and remove individual files from the selection. Since Backups is already selected, ⌷Ctrl⌷+click will deselect it.

9. Deselect a folder:

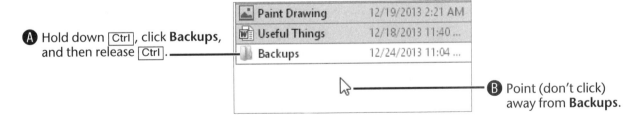

A Hold down ⌷Ctrl⌷, click **Backups**, and then release ⌷Ctrl⌷.

B Point (don't click) away from **Backups**.

   Backups is no longer highlighted. It will be left off from your next command.

10. Choose **Home→Clipboard→Copy** from the Ribbon.

11. Double-click to open **Backups**.

    The folder is empty since you have not yet saved, moved, or copied any files to it.

12. Choose **Home→Clipboard→Paste** from the Ribbon.

There is a pause as Windows shows the progress of the copy command. The files and folder you copied earlier are all pasted to the new location.

Delete a Folder

13. Click **Back** ⊕ to return to viewing the base level of your storage location.

14. Click once to select the **Movie Club** folder and then tap the ⌈Delete⌉ key on the keyboard. Or, choose **Organize→Delete** from the command bar.

Windows asks to confirm deletion of this folder. Since you know you have a copy of it in Backups, it is safe to delete the folder.

15. Choose **Yes** to confirm the deletion.

The folder disappears. If it was on a USB flash drive, the folder is deleted. If it was in the Documents folder (which is on a disk drive), it's been moved to the Recycle Bin.

Copy the Folder

Now you will copy the Movie Club folder from your Backups folder back into its old location.

16. Double-click to open **Backups**.

17. Click (don't double-click) the **Movie Club** folder.

18. Choose **Home→Clipboard→Copy** from the Ribbon.

19. Click **Back** ⊕.

The Address bar shows you back at the base of your storage location. Since this is the destination, you can next give the Paste command.

20. Choose **Home→Clipboard→Paste** from the Ribbon.

Windows displays the progress of the paste command. Notice that it's at the bottom of the list, not in alphabetical order.

21. Refresh the view and order of items:

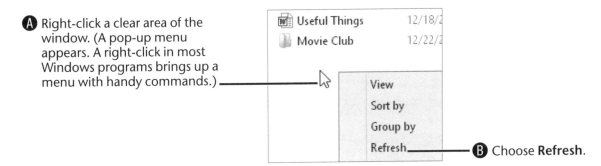

Ⓐ Right-click a clear area of the window. (A pop-up menu appears. A right-click in most Windows programs brings up a menu with handy commands.) ——————————

| 📄 Useful Things | 12/18/2 |
| 📁 Movie Club | 12/22/2 |

View
Sort by
Group by
Refresh ——————— Ⓑ Choose **Refresh**.

Windows refreshes the list and the two folders appear at the top. Windows normally displays all folders in alphabetical order at the top, followed by files in alphabetical order.

22. Close ❌ File Explorer.

SKILL BUILDER 4.3 ## Back Up a USB Flash Drive

In this exercise, you will copy everything from your USB flash drive to the Documents folder.

To perform this exercise, you need a USB flash drive.

1. Start **File Explorer** and display your **file storage location**.

2. Choose **Home→Select→Select All** from the Ribbon.

3. Choose **Home→Clipboard→Copy** from the Ribbon.

4. Display the **Documents** folder.

5. Choose **Home→New→New Folder** from the Ribbon.

6. Type **USB Backup** as the folder name.

7. Double-click to open the **USB Backup** folder.

8. Choose **Home→Clipboard→Paste** from the Ribbon.

Windows pastes the entire contents of the flash drive to the folder. That didn't take very long, did it? If you make a habit of backing up your flash drive at least once a week, or after completing work on an important project, you can rest easier in case the flash drive ever gets lost or corrupted.

Delete the Backup

Because this backup might contain personal files you don't want to leave on a public computer, you will delete the backup folder.

9. Click **Back** ⬅.

10. Click once (don't double-click) to select the **USB Backup** folder.

11. Choose **Home**→**Organize**→**Delete** from the Ribbon.

12. Choose **Yes** if Windows asks you to confirm the deletion.

    This backup folder was on the computer's storage drive. So it's now in the Recycle Bin. The last step is to empty the Recycle Bin.

13. **Close** ☒ File Explorer.

14. Double-click the **Recycle Bin**.

    The folder should be in the Recycle Bin, unless there are so many other items there that it's deep in a long list.

15. Choose **Manage**→**Manage**→**Empty Recycle Bin** from the Ribbon.

16. Choose **Yes** to confirm the command.

    Its entire contents is emptied out of the Recycle Bin.

17. **Close** ☒ the Recycle Bin.

The Internet

In this unit, you will go online! In Lesson 5, you will be introduced to the Internet and the Internet Explorer web browser. You will navigate with the address bar, hyperlinks, and navigation buttons. In Lesson 6, you will search for websites using the instant search box and keywords. You will also use Internet Explorer's tabbed browsing features. Other topics in this lesson include bookmarks and favorites, the History panel, and printing web pages. In Lesson 7, you will fly into the cloud as you explore new ways of interacting and collaborating with others. An important topic of this lesson is watched folders. And finally, in Lesson 8, you will learn various ways of sharing your files with others, including via email and cloud storage.

The Internet

Lesson 5: Browsing Web Pages 147

Lesson 6: Searching for Websites 175

Lesson 7: Using Cloud File Storage................................... 213

Lesson 8: Sharing Files 249

Browsing Web Pages

The World Wide Web ("the web") is the richest information resource in human history. There are tens of millions of websites in the world, and you can navigate to any of them with just a few keystrokes and clicks. The web organizes information onto pages connected by links, which you click to navigate to other web pages. You view web pages with an application program called a web browser. One of the most popular web browsers is Microsoft's Internet Explorer, which comes installed with all versions of Windows. In this lesson, you will learn the basics of browsing web pages with Internet Explorer.

LESSON OBJECTIVES

After studying this lesson, you will be able to:

- Define the Internet
- Navigate to web pages by typing in the browser's address bar
- Describe how a computer connects to the Internet
- Navigate in a website via hyperlinks
- Navigate using the browser's controls
- Browse web pages in full-screen view

Case Study: Using an Online Encyclopedia

Brooke has browsed the web since she first learned to use a computer. She's pretty amazed by the incredible variety she finds on the web. She starts to wonder if the web isn't a watershed of human progress on a par with writing, the sailing ship, even the wheel. To learn more about the origins of this technology, Brooke goes to a website a friend recommended: Wikipedia. It's an online encyclopedia that people all over the world create entries for and revise to every day. The friend gives Brooke Wikipedia's web address (URL). Brooke types the address into the address bar of her web browser, and soon she's found an article.

Browsing the article, Brooke discovers that spots in the articles called hyperlinks let her swiftly jump to related topics and enlarge pictures. Connections to past and recent events and discoveries abound in most every paragraph.

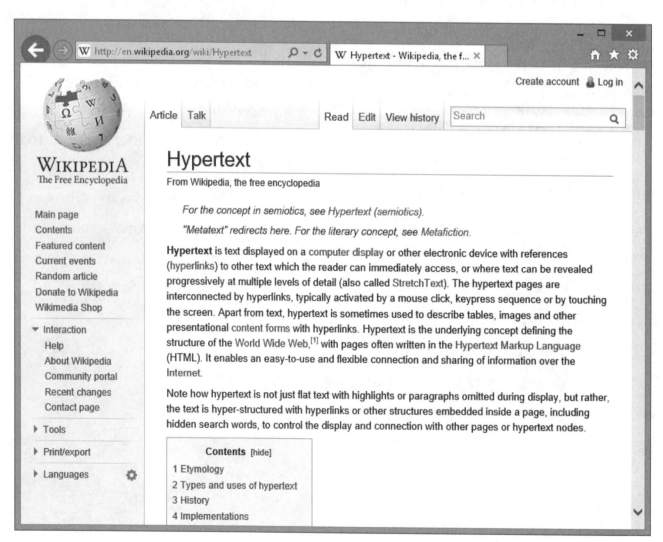

Wikipedia.org contains tens of thousands of articles in a vast online encyclopedia.

Defining the Internet

The Internet is the world's largest computer network. It is an interconnected system of computers residing on every continent. These computers "talk" to each other with a common set of rules (called protocols). Every computer on the Internet has the capability to send information to any other computer that is also connected to the Internet.

The Internet supports many services for global communications. The two most commonly used services on the Internet are the web and electronic mail (email). However, the Internet also supports many other types of services.

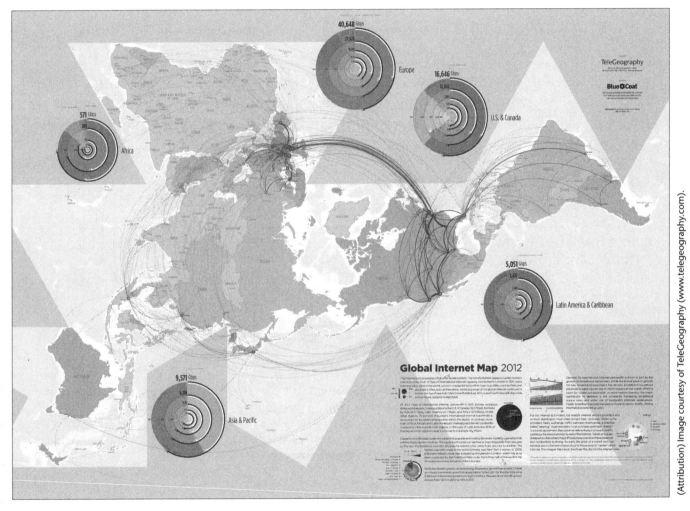

(Attribution) Image courtesy of TeleGeography (www.telegeography.com).

A connectivity map shows the major Internet network lines throughout the world.

Using Internet Explorer

Internet Explorer is an application program—similar to a word processor or spreadsheet—designed for viewing and navigating web pages on the Internet. There are several ways to launch Internet Explorer. When you start the browser, it will begin searching for a page on either the Internet or your hard drive.

Two Versions

There are actually two different flavors of Internet Explorer installed in Windows 8.1.

- **Traditional Desktop version** – This version runs on the Traditional Desktop and works just like previous versions of Internet Explorer.

- **Tablet version** – This version has a different interface that's optimized for use with touchscreens. It has the address bar at the bottom and a visual representation of the various "tabs." Microsoft calls the tablet version the "immersive browser."

QUICK REFERENCE: Starting Internet Explorer

Task	Procedure
Start the Tablet version (Immersive Browser)	• On the Start screen, click the Internet Explorer tile. • Or right-click a tab on the Desktop version, then choose Open in Immersive Browser.
Start the Desktop version	• Click the Internet Explorer button on the Taskbar.

!NOTE! This book concentrates on the use of the Desktop version of Internet Explorer 11, which comes installed with all new Windows 8.1 computers and is also available on computers running Windows 7.

Other Browsers

Although Internet Explorer is one of the most popular web browser programs, there are many others you can install and use in its place. These include Firefox, Chrome, and Safari. Most of these browsers have similar features to Internet Explorer. You can download and install them directly from the web.

The Homepage

When you launch Internet Explorer, the first page you see displayed is the homepage. Internet Explorer allows you to set any page on the web as your homepage. The homepage you are viewing now may be the Microsoft Network (MSN) website, or it may be set to a page for your educational institution.

NOTE! Later in this lesson you will learn how to set your own homepage.

 HANDS-ON 5.1 **Start Internet Explorer**

In this exercise, you will start the Internet Explorer browser program.

1. Display the **Desktop**, then click **Internet Explorer** on the taskbar.

The browser window appears and displays the homepage.

2. Tap **Windows** 🏴 to display the Start screen.

3. Click **Internet Explorer**.

The tablet version of Internet Explorer starts. This app fills the screen. Notice the address bar at the bottom of the screen. There are also some control buttons there.

4. Right-click a clear (non-link) area of the screen.

The Tabs area appears. This may display tabs you haven't opened during this session, but may have been opened at another time.

5. Use **Windows** ⊞+⌈Tab⌉ to return to the Desktop.

6. Maximize □ Internet Explorer if it doesn't already fill the screen.

The rest of this lesson concentrates on the Desktop version of Internet Explorer 11.

Internet Explorer Window Features

Like many other application programs, Internet Explorer has menus and a toolbar that allow you to give commands, such as to navigate back and forth between web pages, print, or return to the homepage. The following figure displays some of the most significant features of the Internet Explorer window. Depending on how Internet Explorer is set up on your computer, additional features may be visible as well. You will use many of these features in this lesson.

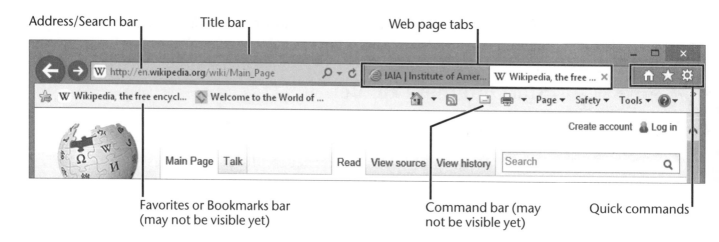

Navigating with the Address/Search Bar

Internet Explorer features an integrated address and search bar. When you type a valid web address Internet Explorer displays that web page. When you type something else in the address/search bar, Internet Explorer performs a search with the currently set search engine (see Lesson 6, Searching for Websites).

Typing Web Addresses

In order to navigate the web, you need to tell your browser which sites you wish to view. Every page on the web has a unique identifying address, called a URL. When you enter a URL in the address/search bar, the browser loads the web page found at that address.

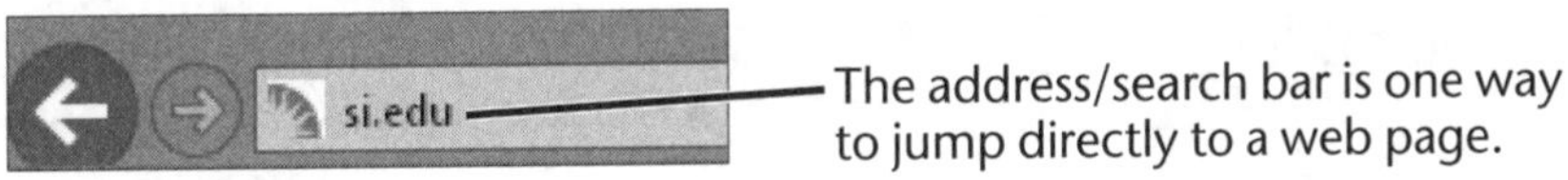

The address/search bar is one way to jump directly to a web page.

NOTE! From now on the address/search bar will simply be called the "address bar."

URLs

A URL (pronounced "you are el") is an address for a web page. Similar to residential addresses, URLs contain several parts to locate a specific page. Every URL contains a domain name, for example. A URL may also contain file and folder names that point to a specific web page. If page names and folder names are part of a URL, each is separated by a forward slash (/). The following illustration identifies each part of a URL.

http://labyrinthelab.com/wtwc5/index.php

Protocol   Domain name   Folder names   Page name

NOTE! When you type a URL in the address bar, you can leave out the http:// protocol portion because the browser adds this automatically.

The Refresh Button

The Refresh button reloads any web page currently displayed. Use the Refresh button when it appears that a web page did not load completely or it is out of date.

Internet Domains

About Domains   A domain is a computer network connected to the Internet. A domain may consist of a single computer or hundreds of computers networked together. Every computer connected to the Internet is part of a domain. Most domains use a domain name to make them easy to identify. The most basic identifier for a domain is its top-level domain.

Top-level Domains   The characters that follow the period at the end of a domain name indicate the top-level domain a website belongs to. There are many types of top-level domains. When domain names were first created, several top-level domains were designated. Additional top-level domains have been added to the list over the years. The following table lists several different top-level domains and the types of organizations they usually represent.

Top-level Domain	Description	Examples	Organization Name
.com	A commercial website	microsoft.com sears.com	Microsoft, Inc. Sears, Roebuck & Co.
.edu	An educational institution	berkeley.edu sfcc.edu	U.C. Berkeley Santa Fe Community College
.org	A nonprofit organization	npr.org amnesty.org	National Public Radio Amnesty International
.gov	A government agency	irs.gov state.gov	Internal Revenue Service US Secretary of State
.jp	An organization based in Japan	japantimes.co.jp yahoo.co.jp	Japan Times Publications Yahoo! Japan

Example   Brooke views some web pages about national parks in the American Southwest. She notices that the domain names that end in ".gov" are official National Park Service websites. Web pages that end in ".com" are nearly always commercial websites independent of the national parks.

HANDS-ON 5.2 **Navigate with the Address Bar**

In this exercise, you will navigate to the National Park Service web page, the student resource center, and a linked page from the student resource center.

1. Click once in the address bar to highlight the current address (the highlighted URL will differ from the one shown here).

   The current address turns blue to show it is highlighted. Now it will be replaced by whatever you type. (There is no need to use Backspace or Delete.)

2. Type **nps.gov** and tap Enter.

   The National Park Service web page appears. The .gov domain name at the end of the URL lets you know that this is a governmental website (the official National Park Service website) and not a commercial site.

3. Click once to highlight the current address, type **google.com** in the address bar, and tap Enter.

   The Google search engine website appears.

Navigate to a Web Page

Now you will navigate to a specific web page. Be sure to type the URL below exactly as it is written. Incorrectly typing even a single letter can cause you to miss the page.

4. Click once in the address bar to highlight the current address, type **labpub.com/wtwc5/broadband.htm** exactly as shown, and tap Enter.

   A web page about broadband Internet connections appears. This page is one of several that support this book. Now you will go to the student resource center for this book by deleting part of the URL.

5. Change the width of the address bar:

   Ⓐ Point at the right border of the address bar until you see a **double-pointed arrow**.

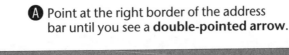

   Ⓑ Hold down the mouse button and drag right or left to adjust the width until the entire URL is visible.

6. Follow these steps to modify the current URL:

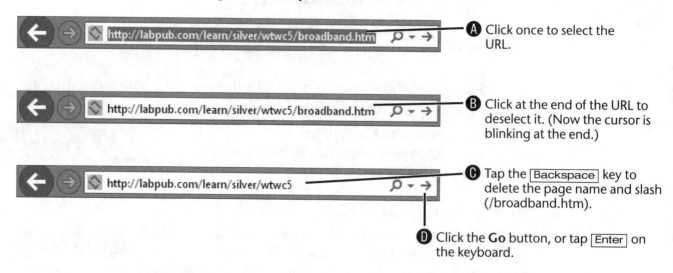

A Click once to select the URL.

B Click at the end of the URL to deselect it. (Now the cursor is blinking at the end.)

C Tap the Backspace key to delete the page name and slash (/broadband.htm).

D Click the **Go** button, or tap Enter on the keyboard.

A new web page appears. When you don't indicate a specific page in a URL, Internet Explorer displays the default page found in the address. In this case, it's a replica of the student resource page for this book.

7. Click the link to the real student resource center page.

The new page appears similar, but it's actually at a different URL.

The Smart Address Bar

Internet Explorer's address bar incorporates AutoComplete technology to help you enter URLs of previously visited websites more quickly. As you type a URL, the address bar checks it against your previous browsing history, and favorites (bookmarks), looking for possible matches. It displays the potential matches as you type.

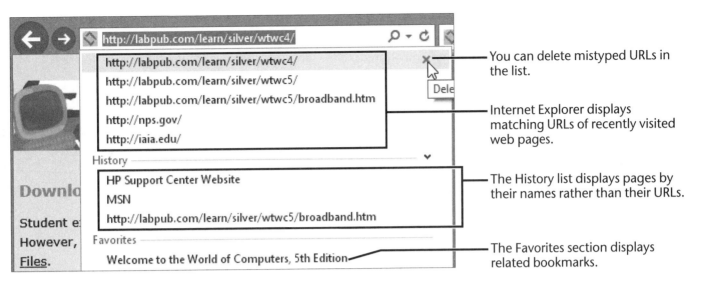

You can delete mistyped URLs in the list.

Internet Explorer displays matching URLs of recently visited web pages.

The History list displays pages by their names rather than their URLs.

The Favorites section displays related bookmarks.

Recently Viewed Pages

Internet Explorer also displays all recently visited web pages. This feature allows you to view the list, then immediately select a page from the list to navigate back to the page.

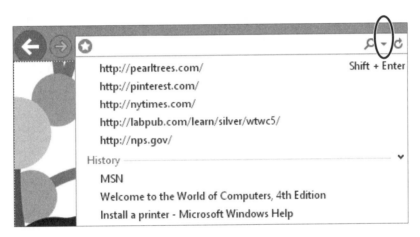

The AutoComplete menu ▼ button displays recently visited web pages.

HANDS-ON 5.3 Navigate Recently Entered URLs

In this exercise, you will navigate to the student resource center via AutoComplete.

1. Return to the book web page:

Ⓐ Click **Home**.

Ⓑ Click the **URL** in the address bar and type **labyrinthelab** (Internet Explorer's AutoComplete adds the .com automatically. However, you will need to then supply the folder name **/wtwc5** to reach this book's student resource center).

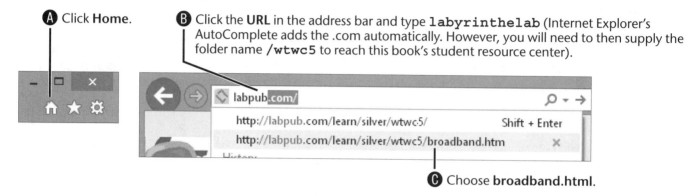

Ⓒ Choose **broadband.html**.

Internet Explorer displays the selected page you viewed earlier.

2. Use the Recently Entered Sites list:

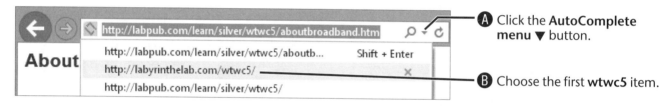

Ⓐ Click the **AutoComplete menu ▼** button.

Ⓑ Choose the first **wtwc5** item.

Internet Explorer displays the student resource center again.

Navigating with Links

After URLs, a link (short for hyperlink) is the most basic tool for web navigation. A link is essentially an object on a web page that can point to some other location on the same page, a different page, or even a different website. Web pages with links are examples of hypertext. Ted Nelson coined this term in 1963 while a sociology student at Harvard. He envisioned a book with hypertext connections to all human knowledge. Links usually navigate you to a web page or a specific location on a web page. Some links may perform other functions, such as generating an email message that is addressed automatically to a particular recipient.

Varieties of Links

A link can take on several forms. It may be some text on a web page or an image or part of an image. There is one feature that is consistent for *all* forms of links. Whenever you place the mouse pointer over a link, the mouse pointer changes to a hand. On many, but not all, websites links are often indicated by underscored text. However, not all links are underscored and many are buttons or images.

Anything on a web page that causes the pointer to change to a hand is a link. A picture and some underscored text on these web pages each serve as links.

TIP! When in doubt, point at a potential link. If the pointer changes to a hand 🖑, you know you're pointing at a link.

About WebSims

In the following exercise, you will perform the steps on a special type of web page. A WebSim is a simulation of a real website. Because most websites change over time, these instructions might not work on the "live" version of the site. A copy of the actual website is stored on the website for this book and will always work exactly according to the exercise instructions.

NOTE! All WebSim pages are clearly identified with the word *Simulation* in a corner of the WebSim screen. Most of the links on WebSim pages are disabled. Only links used in the exercise are active.

Click the Forward button if a step does not work. This will get you to the next step in most cases.

Many (but not all) WebSims have a control similar to this one.

HANDS-ON 5.4 **Navigate with Links**

In this exercise, you will search a topic in Wikipedia. Then you will use links to navigate to related topics.

Before You Begin: The student resource center should be open in Internet Explorer.

1. Click **Lesson 5: Browsing the Web**.

A list of lesson links appears, including links to WebSims.

2. Click **Hands-On 5.4: Navigate with Links**.

There will be a pause as the WebSim loads. When the WebSim starts, the Wikipedia homepage appears. It displays the various languages in which you can view its articles.

3. Search for a term:

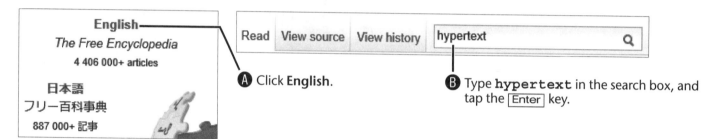

A Click **English**.

B Type **hypertext** in the search box, and tap the Enter key.

The Wikipedia article devoted to this topic appears. Notice the words that appear in blue in the first paragraph and the Contents box below it. Each of these words is a link.

4. Navigate links:

A Point (don't click) over the **History** link.

B Notice that the mouse pointer has changed to a hand, indicating this is a link. There is also a pop-up note of where this link will take you.

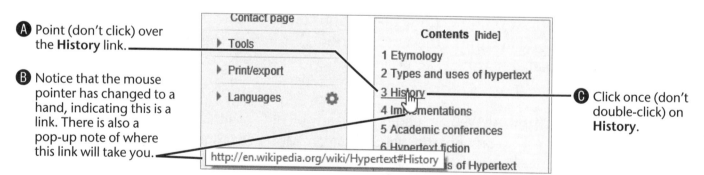

C Click once (don't double-click) on **History**.

The History section of the article immediately appears. This part of the article also features numerous links, each marked in blue.

5. Click **Vannevar Bush** in the second paragraph of the History topic. (The line that begins "In 1945, ...")

   This link jumps you to a brief biography of the American academic whose essay "As We May Think" pioneered many ideas that we now use daily on the web.

History [edit]

Main article: History of hypertext

In 1941, Jorge Luis Borges created The inspiration for the concept of hypertext.[

In 1945 Vannevar Bush wrote an article device he called a Memex. This was a n document standard.

6. Click **Continue to Next WebSim**.

   The title of the next WebSim appears since it begins where this one leaves off. Read the next topic until you reach the next Hands-On exercise.

Browsing Controls

Web pages may or may not have navigation controls (such as *next* and *previous* links) built into them. Fortunately, your web browser has basic navigation controls that are always available. These basic navigation controls allow you to navigate reliably in any type of website. They also have some features that ordinary links lack.

Basic Navigation Buttons

The most basic navigation controls on Internet Explorer are the Forward and Back buttons. Normally, the Back/Forward buttons jump you one page at a time. However, you can also make multipage jumps, rather than having to click back page by page.

Back/Forward buttons — http://en.wikipedia.org/wiki/Hypertext#History

Making Multipage Jumps

The Back button allows you to jump several pages at once. This can be much faster than clicking the Back/Forward buttons repeatedly. For example, you can jump from deep within a website back to its homepage with a single jump.

A right-click on the Back button displays a list of recently visited pages.

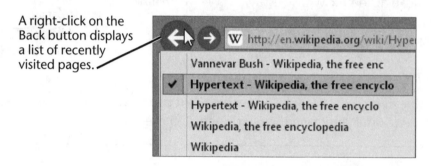

 HANDS-ON 5.5 **Navigate Back and Forward**

 In this exercise, you will navigate back and forth through web pages you've already visited.

Before You Begin: The Navigate Back and Forward exercise should be displayed. If it's not, click the link for this exercise on the student resource center.

Notice that the Forward button is presently grayed out. This is because you cannot move forward until you have moved back at least one page.

1. Click **Back** .

   Internet Explorer returns to the display of the previous web page. Now the Forward button is colored and active.

2. Click **Forward** .

   Internet Explorer returns to the web page you'd moved back from. Notice that the Forward button is grayed-out again, since there's once again no page you've moved back from. Next you'll jump back multiple pages.

3. Navigate back multiple pages:

   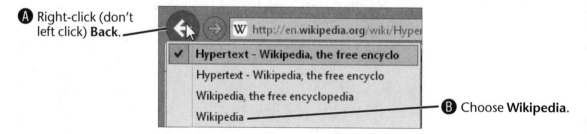

   Internet Explorer jumps you back to the Wikipedia homepage. However, this is the simulation version of the page, so in the next step you will close the simulation window.

4. Click **Back to Course** at the top-right corner of the page.

WebSims links on the student resource center page are visible again.

Back To Course

The Home Button

The Home ⌂ button jumps you back to your homepage (the page the browser displayed when you first started Internet Explorer). Internet Explorer allows you to set more than one homepage. All of these homepages open simultaneously when you first start Internet Explorer or whenever you click the Home button.

Setting a Custom Homepage

You do not have to use the homepage originally programmed for Internet Explorer. For example, a computer vendor may program its own website as the homepage on a new computer. You can change the homepage whenever you wish and set a web page as an additional homepage.

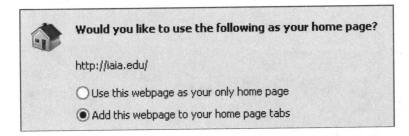

The Add or Change Home Page dialog box lets you choose to create multiple homepages or to use just one.

Multiple Homepages Example   Brooke checks her Facebook page, webmail account, and Twitter when she first starts web browsing. She sets these three websites as her homepages.

Brooke's Home displays three pages when she starts Internet Explorer or clicks Home.

QUICK REFERENCE: Setting Homepages in Internet Explorer

Task	Procedure
Add a new homepage	• Display the web page you wish to use as a homepage. • Right-click (don't left-click) Homepage 🏠. • Choose Add or Change Home Page.
Change your homepage to a set of tabs	• Open the set of pages you wish to use as your new homepages, each in its own tab on the same Internet Explorer window. • Right-click (don't left-click) Homepage 🏠. • Choose Add or Change Home Page from the pop-up menu. • Choose Use the Current Tab Set As Your New Home Page, and then choose Yes.

 HANDS-ON 5.6 Set a Custom Homepage

In this exercise, you will add a new page to your homepage set. Then you will reset the homepage.

1. Make sure that the student resource center page is displayed in Internet Explorer.

2. Change the homepage:

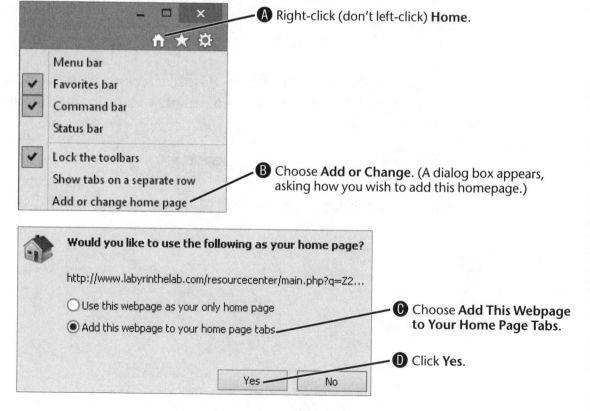

Ⓐ Right-click (don't left-click) **Home**.

Ⓑ Choose **Add or Change**. (A dialog box appears, asking how you wish to add this homepage.)

Would you like to use the following as your home page?

http://www.labyrinthelab.com/resourcecenter/main.php?q=Z2...

○ Use this webpage as your only home page
◉ Add this webpage to your home page tabs

Ⓒ Choose **Add This Webpage to Your Home Page Tabs**.

Ⓓ Click **Yes**.

Internet Explorer adds the page to the Home button.

View Multiple Homepages

3. **Close**  Internet Explorer. Choose **Close All Tabs** if Internet Explorer asks for confirmation.

4. Click **Internet Explorer** on the Taskbar to restart the program.

   Notice that two tabs (not just one) opened when you started Internet Explorer.

!**NOTE!** If someone else has already defined any additional homepages, there might be more than two tabs visible in Internet Explorer.

Reset Your Homepage

5. Set the homepage back to a single page:

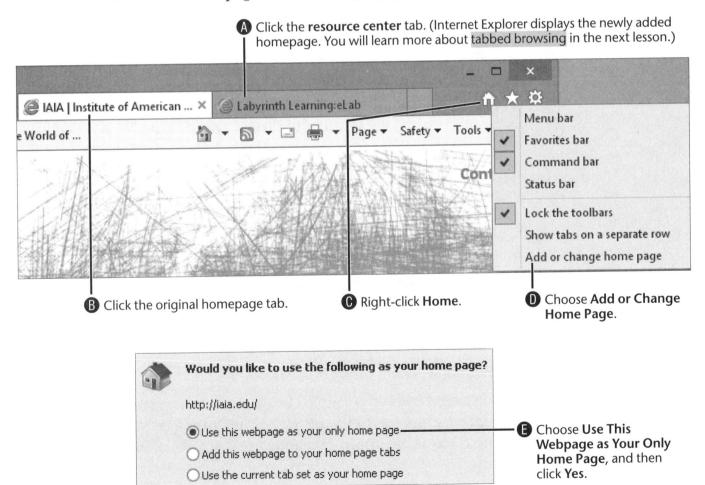

A Click the **resource center** tab. (Internet Explorer displays the newly added homepage. You will learn more about tabbed browsing in the next lesson.)

B Click the original homepage tab.

C Right-click **Home**.

D Choose **Add or Change Home Page**.

E Choose **Use This Webpage as Your Only Home Page**, and then click **Yes**.

Internet Explorer resets the homepage to just a single page. However, the other home page tab will still be visible in the Internet Explorer window until you navigate away from it.

6. Click the **student resource center page** tab again.

7. Left-click (don't right-click) **Home** 🏠.

Internet Explorer displays the homepage again.

8. Click **Back** ◀.

The student resource center page should be visible again.

Viewing Web Pages

Once you find the web page you wish to read, Internet Explorer and your mouse have controls to bring parts of it into view and make it easier to read.

The Mouse Scroll Wheel

Most modern mice have a scroll wheel between the left and right mouse buttons. Rolling the wheel with your index finger intuitively scrolls the web page up and down. In addition to the scroll wheel, many mice have additional controls to control web pages similar to the following figure.

Photo courtesy of Logitech

Program window switcher button

Scroll wheel (also provides left/right scroll control)

Forward/Back buttons

A mouse has useful controls for web browsing. Try the scroll wheel and it will be hard to imagine how you did without it.

Full-screen View

Even with Internet Explorer's compact browser controls, you may wish to see more of a web page and less of the controls. The full-screen view reduces the browser controls to a bare minimum, allowing you to concentrate on the web page content.

Zooming the View

You can also adjust the scale of text and images on most web pages to make them easier to view. For example, you can magnify the size of text on an article that has small print. The zoom changes the size of images on the page as well. You can zoom the view in and out using the keyboard.

QUICK REFERENCE: Adjusting the View of a Web Page

Task	Procedure
Scroll a web page using the mouse	• Click once over the part of the web page you wish to scroll. • Roll the scroll wheel up and down with your forefinger.
Shift into/out of Full Screen view	• Tap the F11 function key on the keyboard. • Tap F11 again to toggle out of full-screen mode.
Scale web page text larger and smaller	• Hold down Ctrl on the keyboard. • Use Ctrl+ + to zoom in or Ctrl+ - to zoom out.
Navigate a web page using the keyboard	• Tap Home to jump to top of page. • Tap End to jump to bottom of page. • Tap the PgUp and PgDn to jump one screen up or down.

 HANDS-ON 5.7 Adjust the View of a Web Page

In this exercise, you will switch between full-screen and normal view. You will also see how the browser window uses the most recent view mode. You will use the scroll wheel to move up and down in the page and also zoom in and out on the text.

Before You Begin: The student resource center should be displayed in Internet Explorer.

1. Click **Hands-On 5.7: Adjust the View of a Web Page**.

   This link opens the About Broadband web page.

2. Roll the **scroll wheel** in the center of the mouse to scroll up and down through the page.

   Skip to the next step if your mouse doesn't have a scroll wheel.

Navigate with the Keyboard

> ⚠️ **NOTE!** Computer keyboards can vary, so the figure below may not represent your keyboard exactly.

3. Navigate with the keyboard:

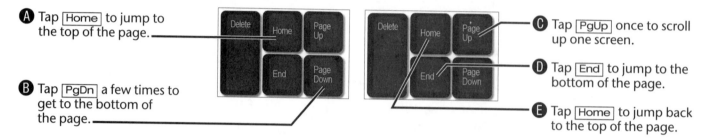

Ⓐ Tap Home to jump to the top of the page.

Ⓑ Tap PgDn a few times to get to the bottom of the page.

Ⓒ Tap PgUp once to scroll up one screen.

Ⓓ Tap End to jump to the bottom of the page.

Ⓔ Tap Home to jump back to the top of the page.

Zoom the View

4. Zoom in using the keyboard:

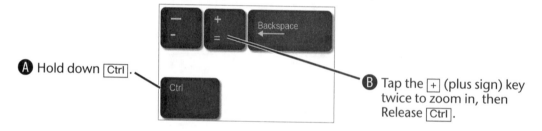

Ⓐ Hold down Ctrl.

Ⓑ Tap the + (plus sign) key twice to zoom in, then Release Ctrl.

The view zooms closer each time you tap Ctrl + +.

5. Use Ctrl + - (minus sign) to zoom out again.

Practice Full-screen Mode

6. Tap the F11 function key. If necessary, move the mouse pointer away from the top of the web page.

Internet Explorer shifts to full-screen mode. The address bar and other controls disappear, leaving maximum space to display the web page.

7. Tap F11 again to toggle back to normal view.

8. Tap F11 again to toggle back to full-screen view.

Close and Open Internet Explorer in Full-screen Mode

If you were in full-screen mode when you closed Internet Explorer, the program opens full-screen the next time you start it. This often confuses users. So this part of the exercise shows you what to do if the address and title bars don't appear at first.

9. Point (don't click) over the picture and wait until the address bar disappears.

10. Point above the title near the top of the page so that the pointer turns into an arrow.

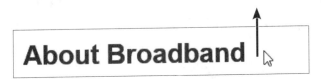

The address bar and other controls reappear in black rather than their normal colors. You can always get them to reappear by pointing at the top of the page. Now you will close Internet Explorer.

11. Close Internet Explorer in full-screen mode:

Ⓐ Without moving below the top of the web page, slide the mouse to the right toward the Close button. Point again at the top of the screen if the buttons disappear before you get to them.

Ⓑ Click **Close**.

Internet Explorer asks if you wish to close all of the tabs. This is because Internet Explorer opened with two tabs in the previous exercise.

12. Choose **Yes** to close all the tabs in the Internet Explorer window.

13. Click **Internet Explorer** on the taskbar to restart the program.

Notice that the program starts in full-screen view, since that was the view when you closed it.

14. Tap F11 to toggle back to normal view.

15. **Close** ❎ Internet Explorer again.

When you restart Internet Explorer the next time, it will open in normal (not full-screen) mode.

16. Choose **Yes** to close all the tabs.

Concepts Review

To check your knowledge of the key concepts introduced in this lesson, complete the Concepts Review quiz here or on the student resource center.

True/False Questions

Page Number

1. A URL is the address of a website. **True   False** _____
2. The Forward button navigates you to the next web page on a site. **True   False** _____
3. You can navigate back only one page at a time. **True   False** _____
4. You can change the homepage. **True   False** _____
5. When you type a URL, you must always include http://. **True   False** _____
6. You can set more than one homepage in Internet Explorer. **True   False** _____

Multiple Choice Questions

7. A link can be a _____.

   Page Number: _____

   a. word or text phrase on a web page
   b. a button on a web page
   c. an image on a web page
   d. All of the above

8. A URL is very similar to _____.

   Page Number: _____

   a. a highway sign
   b. a computer terminal
   c. a mailing address
   d. None of the above

9. Internet Explorer's smart address bar feature _____.

   Page Number: _____

   a. lists the names of recently visited web pages similar to what you are typing
   b. allows you to choose URLs from a list
   c. appears below the address bar
   d. All of the above

10. The Forward button _____.

    Page Number: _____

    a. is always active
    b. takes you forward to a new next page on a website
    c. only works after you use the Back button
    d. jumps you to the next homepage

Skill Builders

Browse National Parks

In this exercise, you will visit the National Park Service website and view information about some parks.

1. Start **Internet Explorer**.

2. Type the URL **labyrinthelab.com/wtwc5** in the address bar and then tap **Enter**.

   The student resource center appears.

3. Click **Lesson 5: Searching the Web**.

4. Click **Skill Builder 5.1: Browsing National Parks**.

   ⚠ NOTE! The first part of this exercise will be a WebSim. The second part will use the "live" NPS.gov website.

   The National Park Service website appears. Notice the long green navigation bar below the main image. This provides navigation links to various main sections of the website. Virtually all websites have some sort of navigation bar or scheme that's readily apparent on the homepage.

5. Click **Find a Park**.

   This page offers different ways to locate a park. Let's search by park name.

6. Navigate to a park by name:

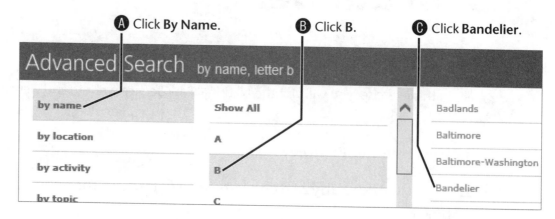

Ⓐ Click **By Name**. Ⓑ Click **B**. Ⓒ Click **Bandelier**.

The Bandelier site's web page appears.

7. Click the **scroll bar** to simulate scrolling down the page.

Notice the navigation links along the left side of the page.

8. Navigate to a virtual tour:

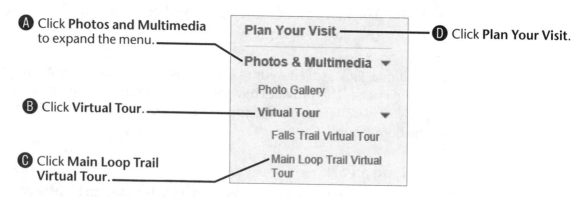

Ⓐ Click **Photos and Multimedia** to expand the menu.

Ⓑ Click **Virtual Tour**.

Ⓒ Click **Main Loop Trail Virtual Tour**.

Ⓓ Click **Plan Your Visit**.

The Photos and Multimedia items collapse, and the Plan Your Visit section expands. Many websites have dynamic navigation menus such as this to help you locate the web pages and information you wish to view.

Browse the Live National Park Service Website

9. Click the **National Park Service logo**.

A new browser window opens to display the homepage of the National Park Service website. Many websites feature a link like this that always returns you to the homepage.

!NOTE! You are now viewing the live National Park Service website. (Notice the URL in the address bar.) For the rest of this exercise, the site may look and act differently from the WebSim in the previous steps.

10. Navigate the site using these guidelines:

- Choose a park near where you live.

- Visit some of the pages that show maps and features of the park.

- Use the scroll wheel, PgDn, and Home to move up and down on each page.

- Right-click the Back button to jump back to the main NPS website page.

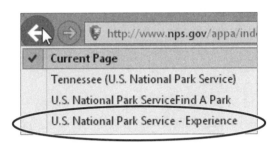

- Browse pages for at least two other parks in your area.

11. **Close** x Internet Explorer when you are finished.
The WebSim window reappears.

12. **Close** x the WebSim window.

Browse Web Pages

In this exercise, you will navigate to web pages with the address bar.

Live Links: These are live web links. It is possible for a link to have changed locations or to have shut down since this book was printed. A link may also be down temporarily due to technical problems. If you try a link and it does not work, go on to another link.

1. If necessary, start **Internet Explorer**.

2. Navigate to the homepage of a website on the following list by typing its URL in the address bar. If you see an error message, check for a typo in the address bar and try again.

   !NOTE! Notice that some of the URLs below use a "www" at the front. Usually, you can omit the www. However, if the site you expect does not appear, try adding www. to the front of the URL.

Website	URL
Smithsonian Institution	`www.si.edu`
Library of Congress	`lcweb.loc.gov`
Project Gutenberg	`gutenberg.org`
National Aeronautics and Space Administration	`www.nasa.gov`
Louvre Museum (France)	`louvre.fr/en`
United Nations	`un.org`

3. If you find a website that interests you, explore the site for a few minutes.

4. Navigate to at least one other website that interests you and explore.

Searching for Websites

The growth of the web has been explosive. In June 1993, there were approximately 130 websites on the Internet. Nobody knows exactly how many websites and web pages are available on the Internet today, but by mid-2008, there were more than a trillion unique URLs (web addresses) available on the web. While highly useful information is available on the web, its very volume makes finding what you need difficult. Good search techniques will help you quickly locate the most useful web pages. In this lesson, you will use the most significant aid to finding information on the web: the Internet search engine and Internet Explorer's Instant Search feature.

LESSON OBJECTIVES

After studying this lesson, you will be able to:

- Describe what an Internet search engine does
- Perform a basic instant search
- Use Internet Explorer's tabbed browsing feature
- Use favorites to mark and navigate to websites
- Navigate using the History panel
- Print a web page

Case Study: Planning a Rail Trip

Spring break is approaching, and Joaquin wants to travel. He calls a cousin, and they decide to visit the Grand Canyon together. Neither of them has visited the Grand Canyon before, so there's no literature close at hand. Joaquin goes on the web to find out what's available at the Grand Canyon, where to stay, and what to see. He knows that the best way to find information on the web is to use a search engine. With the choice of a few keywords, Joaquin discovers some good general information and learns about a railroad with daily trains traveling into and out of the Canyon.

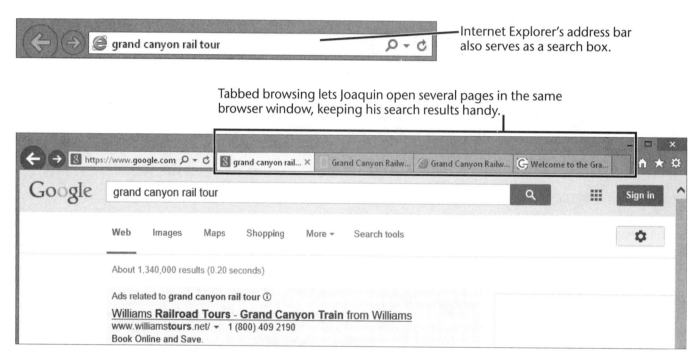

Internet Explorer's address bar also serves as a search box.

Tabbed browsing lets Joaquin open several pages in the same browser window, keeping his search results handy.

Searching from the Address Bar

Internet Explorer features an integrated address/search bar. Previously, users had to navigate to a search engine's web page in order to use it for a search. Now you can type one or more words into the Address bar and immediately see search results from the search provider of your choice.

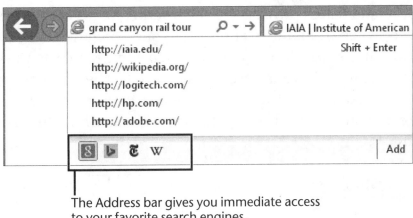

The Address bar gives you immediate access to your favorite search engines.

> **!NOTE!** The address/search bar will be referred to as the address bar for the remainder of this lesson.

About Search Engines

A search engine is a website designed to locate and navigate to web pages. Search engines typically display a list of search result links. There are many types of search engines, specializing in specific approaches to finding information.

> **!NOTE!** Most of the exercises in this lesson use the Google.com search engine because it is an excellent general search engine that is easy to use. The techniques you use to work with Google.com will also work well with other search engines.

Choosing a Search Engine

No single search engine is ideal for every type of search. Some search engines may consistently produce search results highly relevant to the actual information you are seeking. Other search engines may perform a search so complete you don't have time to make your way through all of the hits and yet may be perfectly suited to searching for a very obscure piece of information. Over time you will likely begin to favor one search engine in particular, though there may be occasions when you seek additional search engines because the one you usually use does not provide the results you need.

Adding Search Providers

You can add search providers to the Internet Explorer's Address bar, making it easy to switch from one to another as your search needs dictate. For example, you might use Google as a general search engine and then switch to a different search engine to run a more complete search. The Internet Explorer Gallery has many categories of search providers to choose from. For example, there are search providers for shopping, news, music, and other specialized search needs.

The Internet Explorer Gallery displays search providers you can add to the Address bar.

!NOTE! You can only add search providers listed in the Internet Explorer Gallery to the Address bar. But you can still navigate to other provider's websites to perform searches.

Setting a Default Search Provider

You can tell Internet Explorer to use a particular search provider by default. This means any keyword search in the Address bar will use this provider unless you choose a different provider. You can alter your default search provider at any time.

QUICK REFERENCE: Searching with the Address Bar

Task	Procedure
Perform an instant search	• Type one or more search keywords into the Address bar and then tap [Enter].
Change the default search provider	• Click Tools . • Click Manage Add Ons. • Click Search Providers on the left panel. • Right-click the desired search provider and choose Set as Default.
Add a new search provider	• Click the address bar Search menu [🔍 ▾]. • Click Add.

HANDS-ON 6.1 Add a Search Provider

In this exercise, you will add a new search provider to the Instant Search box.

On the Web

1. Start **Internet Explorer**. If necessary, **Maximize** 🗖 the window.

2. Navigate to the student resource center by typing `labyrinthelab.com/wtwc5` into the address bar of your web browser.

3. Click **Lesson 6: Searching the Web**.

4. Click **Hands On 6.1: Add a Search Provider**.

   As it starts, Internet Explorer is already running in the WebSim.

5. Start adding a new search provider:

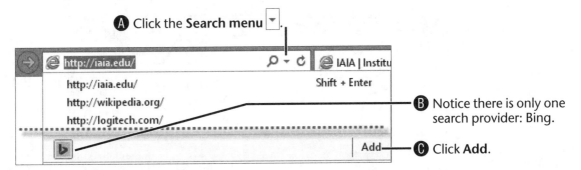

Internet Explorer displays a new tab with the first of several pages listing popular search providers. To the left is a navigation panel displaying various categories of providers.

6. Point (don't click) over **Google**.

A rating for the search provider appears. As with many ratings you see on the Web, this one should be taken with a grain of salt. However, it may help you spot particularly ineffective search providers.

7. Click **Google**.

The search provider's Internet Explorer Gallery page appears.

8. Finish adding Google:

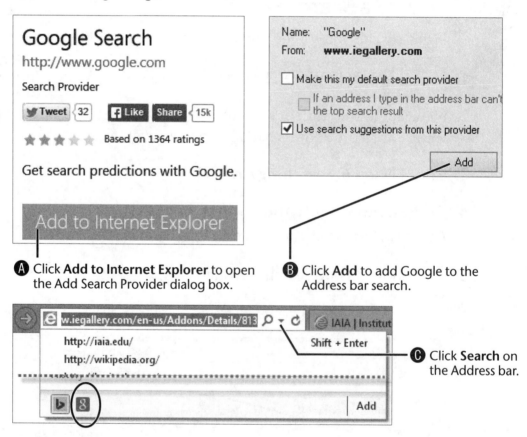

Ⓐ Click **Add to Internet Explorer** to open the Add Search Provider dialog box.

Ⓑ Click **Add** to add Google to the Address bar search.

Ⓒ Click **Search** on the Address bar.

Notice that Google has been added to the search provider list. You can now switch to this provider at any time.

9. Click anywhere on the **web page** to dismiss the Search list.

Set the Default Search Provider

Now you will set the search provider that Internet Explorer always uses when you first start the program. (You could also have set this when you added Google, but it's good to know how to make this choice later.)

10. View manage add-ons:

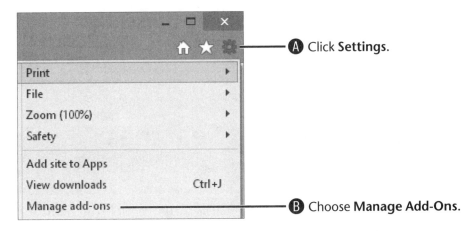

Ⓐ Click **Settings**.

Ⓑ Choose **Manage Add-Ons**.

The Manage Add-Ons window appears.

11. Set the default search provider:

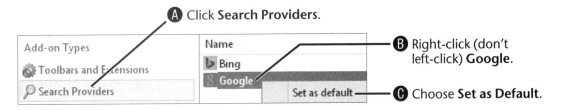

Ⓐ Click **Search Providers**.

Ⓑ Right-click (don't left-click) **Google**.

Ⓒ Choose **Set as Default**.

Google is indicated as the new default search provider.

12. **Close** [x] the window.

13. Verify the new setting:

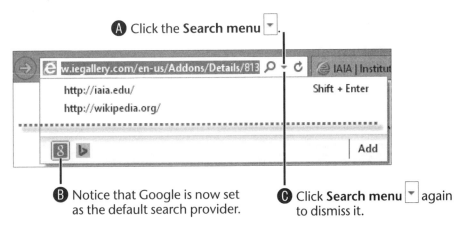

Ⓐ Click the **Search menu** [▾].

Ⓑ Notice that Google is now set as the default search provider.

Ⓒ Click **Search menu** [▾] again to dismiss it.

14. Close  the Internet Explorer Gallery tab.

15. Click **Continue to Next WebSim**.

The next Websim loads into Internet Explorer, ready for the next exercise. Continue reading the next topic.

Performing Basic Keyword Searches

A basic keyword search asks the search engine to find web pages with a specific word or several specific words. Basic searches are quick and easy to execute and will often yield the information you are seeking. Search results are typically reported as a list of search results with a short summary of each page. Sometimes a search may yield no results at all, while other times you may get millions of results—more than you could possibly browse.

Selecting Search Words

The more words you include in a keyword search, the more likely it is that the search results will be relevant to your needs. However, you don't want to start out with so many search words that you overlook websites that did not include some of the search words but would still be of interest. When you perform a keyword search with more than one word, most search engines will show you the pages that contain all the words first, then pages that contain only a few of the words.

> **!TIP!** Every search engine has its own rules and conventions (syntax) for searching. However, the two rules described in the following table work with most search engines.

Rule	Examples
Use capital letters only when typing proper nouns. If you type more than one proper name in a search, separate each name with a comma.	Mahatma Gandhi, Grand Canyon
If you wish to search for an exact phrase, enclose the phrase in quotation marks.	"global warming trends" "hybrid automobile"

Search Suggestions

Internet Explorer's search suggestions feature displays likely searches as you type in the Address bar. This feature works by sending your keystrokes to the active search provider. There are privacy issues related to search suggestions. However, Internet Explorer 11 turns on this feature by default when you add a new search provider. You can turn this feature off if you don't want to use it.

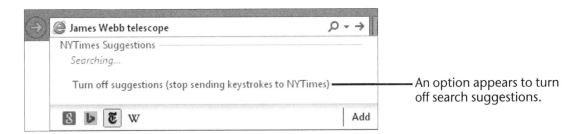

An option appears to turn off search suggestions.

How Internet Search Engines Work

All Internet search engines maintain some type of database of web pages and their content. When you perform a search, the search engine uses its database to list all web pages that meet your search criteria. Search engines differ in the techniques they use to locate websites and add them to their databases.

Metasearch Engines   The web also has search engines that search other search engines. Essentially, a metasearch engine sends your search to several search engines and other resources with a single command. This approach takes advantage of the strengths of several search engines simultaneously. However, you may end up with more search results than you bargained for.

This metasearch engine searches three popular search engines simultaneously.

Search Result Order   Different search engines usually list the same sites in a different order. There are a few factors that can affect the order of sites in the search-results list.

- **Content of the page**—The text on the web page can make a difference in the order a site is listed. The search engine reviews the homepage to determine the level of relevance of the site to your search terms.

- **Search relevance rating**—Each search engine has its own system for rating the relevance of a website to the terms you used in your search. How this relevance rating is processed will change the order of sites in the search-results list.

- **Content of the metatag for a page**—Many web pages have some hidden code (metatag) that contains search keywords. Some search engines use this information to determine the order of the web page in a search-results list.

- **Sponsored links/money**—Yes, it's true. Many websites pay a search engine to give them a higher position in the search-results list. The logic is that the first sites in the search-results list are much more likely to be browsed. Conversely, if a web page is deep in the list, it is much less likely that a searcher will make it that far down the list to view the page.

Ads related to **grand canyon** ⓘ

Grand Canyon Tours - Choose from Bus, Air, or Boat
www.**canyon**tours.com/ ▾
Tours Departing from Vegas Daily!

    Bus Tours   Skywalk Combo Tour

    Helicopter Tours   South Rim Deluxe Bus Tour

Visit The **Grand Canyon** - NationalParks.org
www.nationalparks.org/ ▾
Take A Trip The **Grand Canyon** And Do Trip Research With Our Online Guide
National Park Foundation has 1,678 followers on Google+
Explore Our Parks - Support National Parks - Connect With National Parks

Grand Canyon National Park (U.S. National Park Service)
www.nps.gov/grca/ ▾
7 days ago - Official National Park Service site. News and events, information on camping and lodging, facilities and fees, maps and volunteer openings.
Plan Your Visit - Fees & Reservations - Directions - Operating Hours & Seasons

Two sponsored (paid) links push their websites to the top of Google's search results. The paid links appear before the much more popular National Park Service website (the first unpaid result). Not all search engines mark sponsored links.

HANDS-ON 6.2 ## Search with the Address Bar

In this exercise, you will search on a specific keyword via the address bar.

Before You Begin: The Search with the Address Bar WebSim should be open. If it's not, click the link for this exercise on the student resource center.

The WebSim begins with an Internet Explorer browser window open.

1. Type **gran** in the address bar.

   Google displays search suggestions based on what you've just typed. Notice that it's already suggesting Grand Canyon. It does this because the words *Grand Canyon* are very popular search keywords.

2. Choose **Grand Canyon** from the Google Suggestion list.

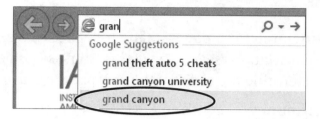

The first page of Google's search results appears. Notice that this initial search found more than 76,000,000 (!) results.

3. Navigate various search results:

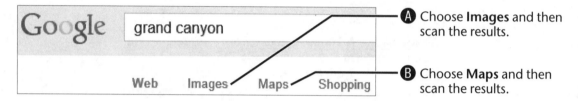

Ⓐ Choose **Images** and then scan the results.

Ⓑ Choose **Maps** and then scan the results.

Google displays a map of the Grand Canyon. Notice that the list of search categories near the top of the page has disappeared.

4. Click **Back** ⊙.

You return to the Images page, and the search categories list reappears.

5. Choose **Web** from the search result categories.

You are back to the original search results. Next, we'll look at the details of interpreting search results.

6. Click **Continue to Next WebSim**.

Interpreting Search Results

Most search engines display basic information about each result turned up by a search. This helps you select the results most likely to have the content you want. This is one area where search engines can differ quite a bit. The following figure displays features of a search-results list from Google.

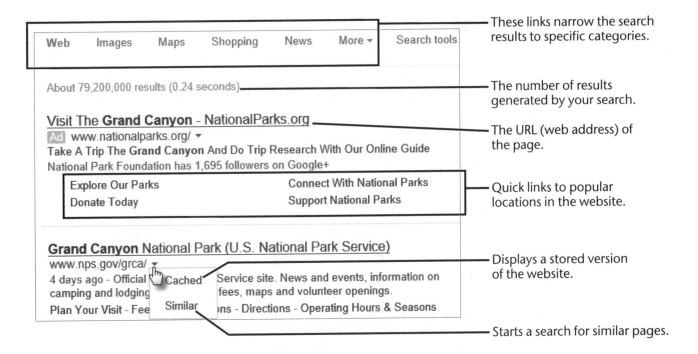

These links narrow the search results to specific categories.

The number of results generated by your search.

The URL (web address) of the page.

Quick links to popular locations in the website.

Displays a stored version of the website.

Starts a search for similar pages.

Searching for Specific Types of Results

Good search engines also allow you to search for specific types of results. For example, you can search specifically for images or maps of a particular locale. You tried this at the end of the previous exercise.

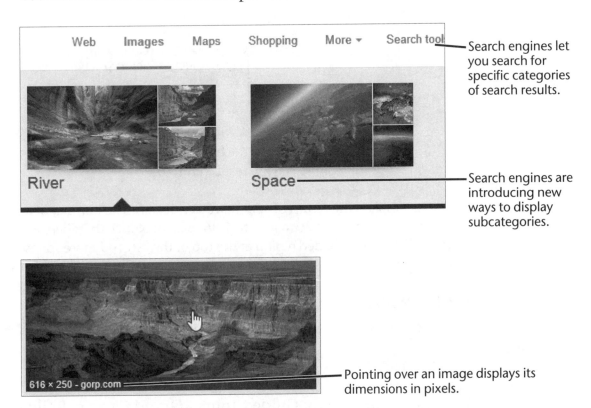

Search engines let you search for specific categories of search results.

Search engines are introducing new ways to display subcategories.

Pointing over an image displays its dimensions in pixels.

Narrowing a Search

When a search yields millions or even just thousands of results, it could be quite time-consuming to browse through even a fraction of the pages to find the information you need. Fortunately, you can easily narrow a search by adding search keywords. This means that you can conduct a broad search first and then add more keywords to the search to reduce the number of results. This is called narrowing your search, because a narrower cross-section of websites will match your additional keywords.

Example   Since Joaquin and his cousin have decided to take a rail trip into the Grand Canyon, Joaquin decides to narrow his search to pages that contain references to railroad and railway trips.

 HANDS-ON 6.3   Narrow a Search

 In this exercise, you will add keywords to narrow a search for visits to the Grand Canyon by railway.

Before You Begin: If necessary, start the WebSim for this exercise.

In the next step, you could narrow your search in the Search box or in the Google web page showing the search results. Be sure to use the Google web page as shown.

1. Narrow your search:

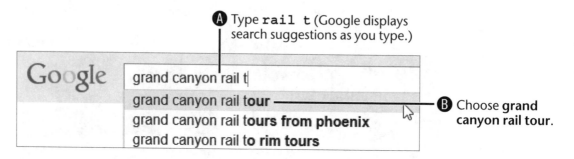

Google displays the results of your narrowed search. The number of results has gone down from more than 76 million to 1.35 million. Notice that there are three sponsored (paid) links in the shaded region at the top of the list, and more sponsored links to the right. These paid links are a major income generator for Google and other search engines.

2. Click **Williams Railway Tours – Grand Canyon Train**.

   Let's say this page doesn't show quite what you need. So you return to the search results.

3. Click **Back** 🔙.

4. Click **Grand Canyon Guided Tours – Grand Canyon Railway** (near the bottom of the page).

5. Click **Back** .

Going back and forth between search results is one way to go about finding the information you need. But going back and forth between different sites is tedious. There is another method to open web pages that makes this type of search much more effective: tabbed browsing. You'll work with this feature in the next topic.

6. Click **Back to Course**.

The links to the WebSims on the Student Resource Center page reappear.

Back To Course

Using Tabbed Browsing

Tabbed browsing is the capability to open multiple web pages within the same browser window. Instead of going back and forth between web pages or having to open multiple browser windows, you can open a new tab for each page you wish to view. You can also open a new tab and start a new search or navigate to a new web page via the Address bar.

Your search results   The currently viewed tab

Opening Links in a New Tab

You can open links in new tabs by using a right-click rather than a left click. A right click opens a pop-up menu with the option to open the link in a new tab or in a new browser window.

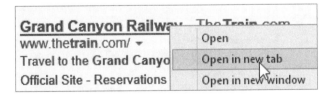

Right-clicking a link displays Open in New Tab in a pop-up menu.

⚠**TIP!** When you want to view several results from a search, use the right mouse button to open each search result in its own tab.

HANDS-ON 6.4 **Open Links in Tabs**

In this exercise, you will open links in new tabs and then switch from one tab to another.

1. Click **Hands-On 6.4: Open Links in Tabs** on the student resource center page. A simulation of Google search results appears in a new tab.

2. Create a new window for a tab:

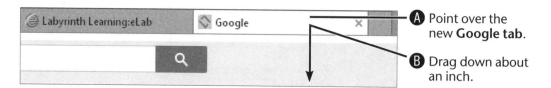

Ⓐ Point over the new **Google tab**.

Ⓑ Drag down about an inch.

The tab now has its own window. This is an easy way to separate any tab from a window with several open tabs.

3. **Maximize** ☐ the window.

4. Open a link in a new tab:

Ⓐ Right-click **Williams Railway Tours – Grand Canyon Train.**

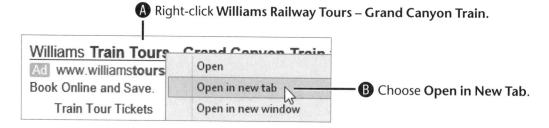

Ⓑ Choose **Open in New Tab.**

Internet Explorer opens a new tab for this web page. However, you are still viewing the search results in the original (leftmost) tab.

5. Open two more tabs:

Ⓐ Right-click **Grand Canyon Railway – The Train.com** and then choose **Open in New Tab.** (Another new tab appears.)

Ⓑ Scroll down the page and then right-click and open **Motorcoach & Railway Tours** in a new tab.

You could actually open a dozen or more new tabs, but these three new ones will do.

Navigating Tabs

You can switch from one tab to the next using the mouse or convenient keyboard commands. It's also easy to close a tab once you are finished viewing it. Internet Explorer can even help you open recently closed tabs for another look.

QUICK REFERENCE: Using Tabbed Browsing

Task	Procedure
Open a link in a new tab	• Right-click the link. • Choose Open in New Tab.
Close a tab	• Point over the tab you wish to close. • Click the tab's Close ☒ button. Or, display the tab and press Ctrl+W.
Close all tabs but one	• Right-click the tab you wish to keep. • Choose Close Other Tabs.
Close all tabs	• Close ☒ Internet Explorer. • Choose Yes to confirm closing the tabs.
Switch to a new tab using the keyboard	• Use Ctrl+Tab to switch to the next tab. • Use Ctrl+Shift+Tab to switch to the previous tab.
Open a new tab	• Click New Tab ▢ or use Ctrl+T from the keyboard.
Open a recently closed tab	• Right-click any tab. • Choose Recently Closed Tabs.

HANDS-ON 6.5 Navigate Tabs

In this exercise, you will use various techniques to navigate between tabs.

Before You Begin: The search results page should be open, and there should be four tabs visible. If necessary, repeat the previous exercise.

1. Click **Williams Tours**.

The web page for this tab appears immediately. One advantage of opening web pages in new tabs is that the pages can load in the background while you choose additional pages, which can be helpful if you access the Internet via a slow connection.

NOTE! In the next step, hold down one key and then tap the other key. *Do not* try to hold down both keys at the same time.

2. Jump to the next tab using the keyboard:

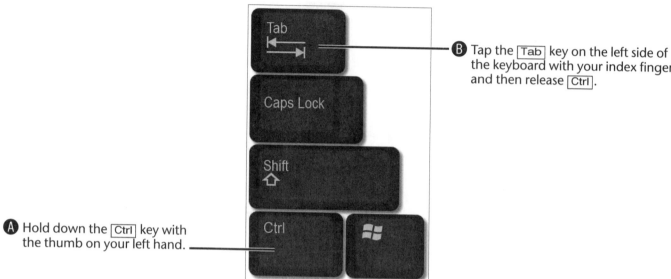

Ⓑ Tap the Tab key on the left side of the keyboard with your index finger, and then release Ctrl.

Ⓐ Hold down the Ctrl key with the thumb on your left hand.

Internet Explorer jumps you to the next available tab. This keyboard method can be a very handy way to navigate tabs without having to reach for the mouse.

3. Use Ctrl + Tab again to jump to the next tab.

Now you are at the end of the tabs for this Internet Explorer window. The next time you jump to a new tab, you will start over with the first tab.

4. Use Ctrl + Tab one more time to jump to the next tab.

The Google search tab appears. Now you could perform a new search, or choose additional links to open in new tabs.

NOTE! Do not try to hold down all three keys at once in the next step.

5. Use the keyboard to jump back one tab.

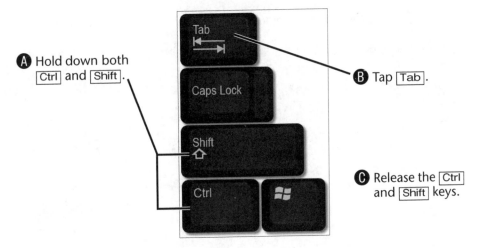

Ⓐ Hold down both ⌨Ctrl⌨ and ⌨Shift⌨.

Ⓑ Tap ⌨Tab⌨.

Ⓒ Release the ⌨Ctrl⌨ and ⌨Shift⌨ keys.

Internet Explorer jumps you back to the previous tab.

Close Tabs

Next you will use two methods to close tabs.

6. Close  the The Train tab.

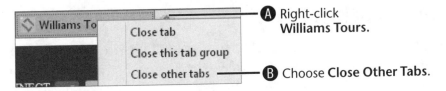

7. Close multiple tabs:

Ⓐ Right-click **Williams Tours**.

Ⓑ Choose **Close Other Tabs**.

All of the other tabs immediately disappear.

8. Reopen recently closed tabs:

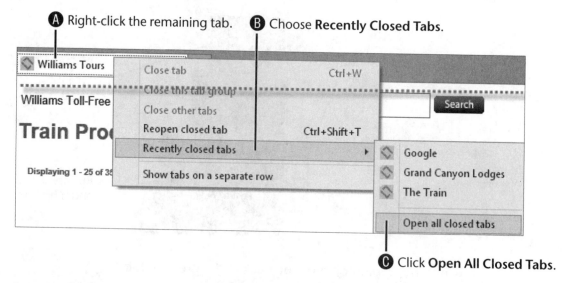

Ⓐ Right-click the remaining tab. Ⓑ Choose **Recently Closed Tabs**.

Ⓒ Click **Open All Closed Tabs**.

Internet Explorer opens the closed tabs, ready for you to use in the next exercise.

Bookmarking Favorite Websites

A favorite (also called a bookmark) is a way to mark a web page so you can open it later without needing to type the URL. Favorites make it easy to locate the web pages you browse most often. For example, you can use a favorite to view the local weather report or to check your favorite online news source.

The Favorites Bar

Internet Explorer has a toolbar to display favorites bookmarks. Use the Favorites bar to get one-click access to the websites you visit regularly. The Favorites bar may not be visible when you start using Internet Explorer.

!NOTE! Depending on how your computer lab is set up, favorites may not yet be visible on your screen.

Creating Favorites

Any time you are viewing a web page you think you will visit often, you can create a new favorite for it using either the mouse or keyboard. If you have several web pages open in tabs, you can create a folder of favorites that you can open with a single click.

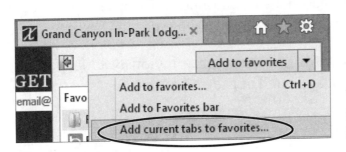

You can add all currently displayed tabs to a folder in your Favorites list with a single command.

Hidden Controls

To maintain a clean and uncluttered look, Internet Explorer hides some familiar toolbars and menu when the program is first installed (such as on a new Windows computer). However, you can call them up easily.

A right-click on the Title bar (above the tabs) displays a pop-up menu.

 HANDS-ON 6.6 Add Favorites

In this exercise, you will add a favorite for a single web page and for a group of currently displayed tabs, and then navigate within Favorites.

Before You Begin: If you are not continuing from Hands-On 6.5, then complete Hands-On 6.4 before beginning this exercise. (No need to repeat Hands-On 6.5).

1. Add a favorite for a web page:

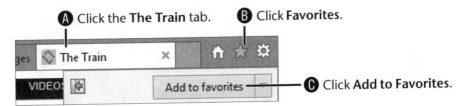

Ⓐ Click the **The Train** tab. Ⓑ Click **Favorites**.

Ⓒ Click **Add to Favorites**.

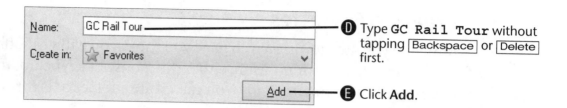

D Type `GC Rail Tour` without tapping Backspace or Delete first.

E Click **Add**.

If someone else has added the same favorite, you may see a prompt from Internet Explorer asking if you wish to overwrite the old favorite with this new one.

2. Choose **Yes** to confirm overwriting a previously added favorite with the same name if a prompt appeared at the end of step 1.

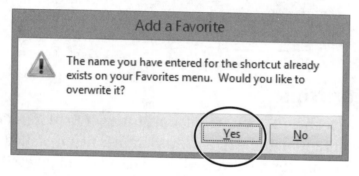

Internet Explorer adds the web page to your Favorites list. Now you will add all of the currently displayed tabs to your Favorites.

Add an Entire Tabbed Group to Favorites

Rather than adding Favorites one at a time, you can create them for an entire Internet Explorer window.

3. Add a Tab Group to Favorites:

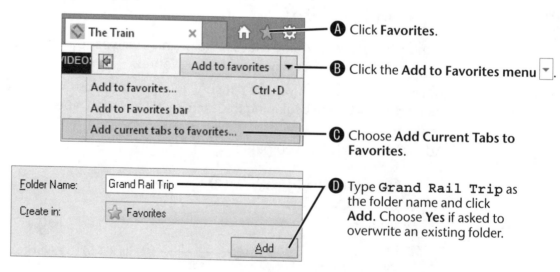

A Click **Favorites**.

B Click the **Add to Favorites menu** ▾.

C Choose **Add Current Tabs to Favorites**.

D Type `Grand Rail Trip` as the folder name and click **Add**. Choose **Yes** if asked to overwrite an existing folder.

Internet Explorer creates a new folder containing favorites for all currently open tabs in that window.

Display Hidden Controls

Next you will display some Internet Explorer controls that might be hidden in your current computer setup.

4. Turn on display of the Command bar:

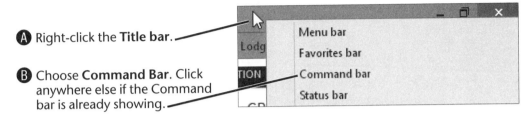

Ⓐ Right-click the **Title bar**.

Ⓑ Choose **Command Bar**. Click anywhere else if the Command bar is already showing.

Internet Explorer displays the Command bar. Depending on whether the Favorites bar is displayed, the Command bar may appear on the left or right side.

5. Right-click the **Title bar** and choose **Favorites Bar**. Click anywhere else if there is already a checkmark beside the Favorites bar command.

   Internet Explorer displays the Favorites bar, just below the Back/Forward buttons. You can place buttons on this bar for single-click access to websites you visit frequently.

6. Click **Add to Favorites**.

   Internet Explorer adds a button for the currently displayed webpage to the Favorites bar.

Navigate to a Favorite

Now you will open a new browser window and navigate with your new favorites.

7. Open a new Internet Explorer window:

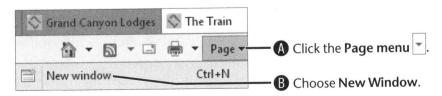

Ⓐ Click the **Page menu** ▾.

Ⓑ Choose **New Window**.

   Internet Explorer opens a new browser window. This new window displays the same web page you were viewing when you gave the New Window command.

!**NOTE!** For the rest of this book, a command like this will be written: Choose **Page→New Window** from the Command bar.

8. Click **Home** 🏠 on the Command bar.

   The homepage appears.

9. Open a favorite:

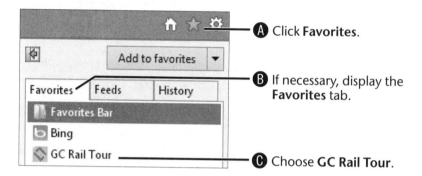

Ⓐ Click **Favorites**.

Ⓑ If necessary, display the **Favorites** tab.

Ⓒ Choose **GC Rail Tour**.

Internet Explorer immediately displays the web page.

10. Click **Back** ⬅.

Open Tab Group Favorites

Next you will open an entire folder of Favorites with a single command.

11. Click **Favorites** ⭐.

12. Open a tab group:

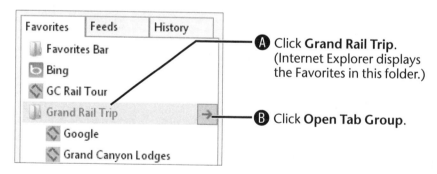

Ⓐ Click **Grand Rail Trip**. (Internet Explorer displays the Favorites in this folder.)

Ⓑ Click **Open Tab Group**.

!**NOTE!** If another student performed this exercise without deleting the tab group, more than four tabs may open.

13. Right-click the first tab, then choose **Close Other Tabs**.

14. Click the button for the website you created on the Favorites bar previously.

Internet Explorer displays the Favorite. The Favorites bar is a great place to put buttons for websites you visit most often.

15. Close x Internet Explorer.

The first window you worked with (and its open tabs) should now be visible.

The Favorites Center

The Favorites Center panel displays all of your available favorites. You can open the panel briefly to choose a favorite and it will close when the favorite opens, or you can "pin" the Favorites Center panel so it remains open until you close it.

You can "pin" the Favorites Center panel open so it does not close after you click a favorite.

You can temporarily open the Favorites Center whenever you wish.

A single-click opens a folder to display its Favorites.

Organizing Favorites into Folders

When you create a favorite, you have the option of placing it in an existing folder in your Favorites list or creating a new folder. This allows you to group favorites so you can find them more easily.

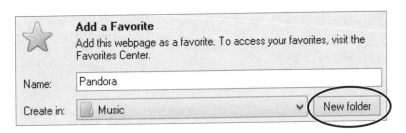

New Folder creates a new folder for a favorite, or you can choose an existing folder.

⚠️ **NOTE!** Skill Builder 6.3 gives practice with organizing favorites.

Deleting Favorites

When you no longer need a favorite, it's easy to delete it. You can also delete an entire folder of favorites by deleting the folder.

QUICK REFERENCE: Creating and Using Favorites

Task	Procedure
Create a favorite for a single web page	• Display the web page for which you wish to create a favorite. • Click the Favorites button, then click Add to Favorites; or, use Ctrl + D .
Create a favorite for a group of pages	• Open each web page for the group in its own tab. • Click the Favorites button, then click the Add to Favorites menu and choose Add Current Tabs to Favorites.
Navigate to a favorite	• Click the Favorites button. • If necessary, display the Favorites tab in the Favorites panel. • Click the favorite you wish to open.
Open a folder of favorites	• Click the Favorites button, then click the folder to open. • Click Open Tab Group →.
Delete a favorite or folder of favorites	• Click the Favorites button. • Right-click the favorite or folder you wish to delete and choose Delete.
Pin the Favorites panel open	• Click the Favorites button. • Click Pin the Favorites Center.

Using the History View

The History view in the Favorites panel displays all of the web pages you've visited. This can be handy when you want to quickly revisit a web page you've seen before. By default, the History view keeps track of web pages you've viewed up to 20 days before. You can increase or decrease this setting if you wish.

Changing the History View

There are several ways to view your browsing history. By default, the History view displays browsing history by date. You can alter this view as your needs dictate. For example, you might want to display your history in order starting with the most recently viewed pages, or you could display the entire history by website. You can even perform a search on items in your browsing history.

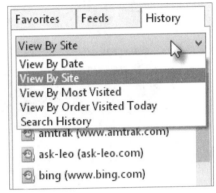

You can view your browsing history in a variety of ways.

HANDS-ON 6.7 **Use the History View**

In this exercise, you will use the History view to navigate previously viewed web pages.

Before You Begin: The Internet Explorer window displaying four tabs should be open. If this is not the case, repeat Hands-On 6.4.

1. Click **Favorites** ⭐.

   Since you most recently used the Favorites panel to navigate favorites, this is what it displays until you shift to History view.

2. View the History:

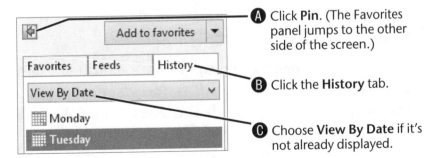

   Ⓐ Click **Pin**. (The Favorites panel jumps to the other side of the screen.)

   Ⓑ Click the **History** tab.

   Ⓒ Choose **View By Date** if it's not already displayed.

Internet Explorer may display a list of days and weeks, or it may display a list of the websites visited on the currently expanded day/week.

3. Navigate with History:

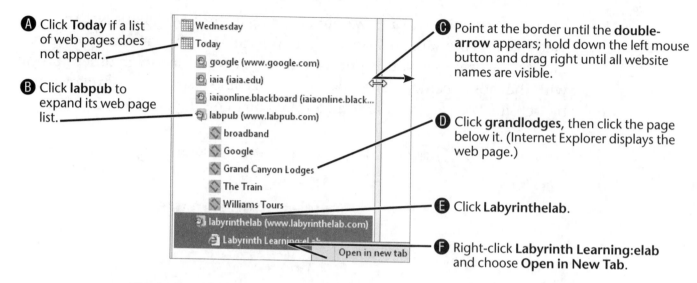

A Click **Today** if a list of web pages does not appear.

B Click **labpub** to expand its web page list.

C Point at the border until the **double-arrow** appears; hold down the left mouse button and drag right until all website names are visible.

D Click **grandlodges**, then click the page below it. (Internet Explorer displays the web page.)

E Click **Labyrinthelab**.

F Right-click **Labyrinth Learning:elab** and choose **Open in New Tab**.

The history item opens in a new tab, although you still see the current tab.

4. Close **History**.

Now you are viewing webpages in the full screen again.

5. Close [x] Internet Explorer and then choose **Close All Tabs**.

You should now be back on the student resource center page.

Printing Web Pages

You may wish to print a web page. Modern websites make it easy to print an article only, omitting the navigation and other features of the webpage. Many articles have buttons to share via email or a social network. For example, you can email an article to yourself or someone else.

Selecting What to Print

Printing a single web page may result in several printed pages. This can be wasteful of paper and ink or toner. If you select only the part of a page that you need, it's possible to print only the selection. The Print dialog box and Print Preview have settings for this.

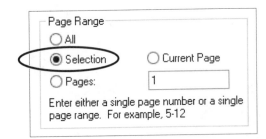

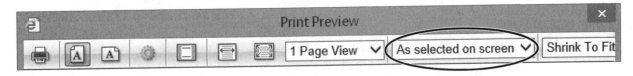

> **!TIP!** Many websites include a Print link on a page (such as for an article) that allows the page to print more efficiently. For example, the print mode may omit online advertisements around the article.

QUICK REFERENCE: Printing Web Pages

Task	Procedure
Display a print preview	• Click the Print 🖶 ▾ menu ▾. • Choose Print Preview.
Print a web page directly	• Click Print 🖶 ▾ on the Command bar.
Print only a selected portion of a web page	• Select the portion of the web page to print. • Click the Print 🖶 ▾ menu ▾ and then choose Print. • Choose an option in Page Range.

 HANDS-ON 6.8 **Print a Web Page**

In this exercise, you will preview and print a web page.

Before You Begin: The student resource center page should be open in Internet Explorer.

1. Click **Hands-On 6.8: Print a Web Page**.

   A new browser window appears to display a simulation of the James Webb Space Telescope website. The Webb telescope is the successor to Hubble. This web page compares the two.

2. Click the **Size** link.

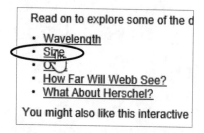

3. Select part of the page:

Ⓐ Point (don't click) by **Size** so the mouse pointer is an arrow (not a text I-beam).

Ⓑ Hold down the mouse button, then drag down and to the right.

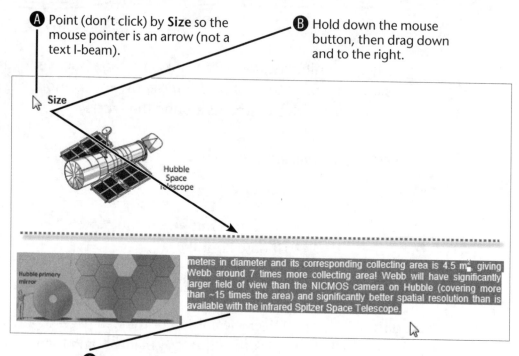

Ⓒ Release the mouse button here, so all the text is highlighted. (The screen will scroll down automatically to bring the end of this section into view.)

4. Choose **Settings→Print→Print Preview**.

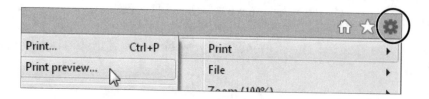

A preview of the entire page appears. But you can limit this to just the selection.

5. Click the **menu button**, then choose **As Selected On Screen**.

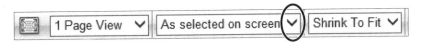

Now print preview just shows your selection. Internet Explorer changes the printout to include only what you selected previously. The additional (unnecessary) parts of the page won't print.

6. Click **Print** 🖶.

The normal Print dialog box appears. Notice that the Page Range setting is already set to Selection. There's no need to actually print this page, so you'll simply close the various windows.

7. Cancel the print command.

8. **Close** ▮x▮ the Print Preview.

9. **Close** ▮x▮ the WebSim window.

10. **Close** ▮x▮ the student resource center web page.

You'll use live web pages for the end-of-lesson Skill Builder exercises.

Concepts Review

To check your knowledge of the key concepts introduced in this lesson, complete the Concepts Review quiz here or on the student resource center.

True/False Questions

Page Number

1. You can save all of the tabbed web pages in an Internet Explorer window as a tab group favorite. **True False** _____

2. In general, the more results you get on a search, the better. **True False** _____

3. The address bar allows searches only with the default search provider you have chosen. **True False** _____

4. You can open a link in a new tab. **True False** _____

5. You can print a selected portion of a web page rather than the entire page. **True False** _____

6. You cannot add a search provider to the address bar that does not appear in the Add Search Provider page. **True False** _____

Multiple Choice Questions

7. Adding search words to reduce the total number of results is called _____.

   Page Number: _____

   a. narrowing the search
   b. widening the search
   c. compressing the search
   d. performing an advanced search

8. If a web-search provider is not listed on a Search Providers page, _____.

   Page Number: _____

   a. you can add it to the address bar search providers
   b. you cannot add it to the address bar search providers
   c. you must add it as a Topic search provider
   d. None of the above

9. Adding a favorite for a website allows you to _____.

   Page Number: _____

   a. change the homepage that appears when you start Internet Explorer
   b. designate a new address bar search provider
   c. navigate to the site without typing its URL in the address bar
   d. None of the above

10. The quickest way to close many open tabs in Internet Explorer while keeping the window open is to _____.

   Page Number: _____

   a. close each tab individually
   b. close the browser window and open a new one
   c. use the Close Other Tabs command
   d. use the Close All Tabs command

Skill Builders

SKILL BUILDER 6.1   ## Add New Instant Search Providers

In this exercise, you will add another Instant Search provider. Please take notice of the following details:

- Since this exercise is performed on *live web pages*, the screen may vary from the detailed instructions here.

- These exercises are designed specifically for the desktop version of Internet Explorer, not the tablet version.

1. If necessary, start **Internet Explorer**.

2. Click the **Search** menu 🔍▾ and then click **Add**.

   The web page with popular search providers appears.

3. Type **Wikipedia**, and then tap ⟨Enter⟩.

   ⚠️**NOTE!** Keep in mind that these are live web pages and the list and the item for Wikipedia may differ from the figure below.

4. Find **Wikipedia Visual Search**, and then click **Add to Internet Explorer**.

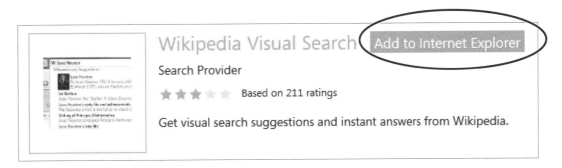

   The Wikipedia Visual Search page appears with a new button to add this search provider.

5. Click **Add to Internet Explorer**.

   An Add Search Provider window appears. Or you may see a prompt that Wikipedia is already a search provider.

6. Click **Add**. (Or click **OK** if Wikipedia is already installed.)

   Internet Explorer installs the new search provider.

7. Click the **Search menu**  and then choose **Wikipedia**.

   Now Wikipedia will temporarily be your address bar search provider until you choose another one, or until you close all Internet Explorer windows and open a new one (at which point your default search provider will appear in the Instant Search box).

8. Click the **Search menu** 🔍▾ again to dismiss the menu.

Search with Various Search Providers

9. Type one or more words in the address bar about a topic you find interesting. It could be related to a hobby, technology, history, or most any other topic.

   Wikipedia (the chosen search provider) displays an article it thinks is most closely related to your search word(s), or it may display a list of articles.

10. Click the **Search menu** 🔍▾, and then choose a different search provider or add a new one, then use it.

11. Repeat your search with the same keywords, or try different keywords.

   A different set of search results appears from the newly chosen search provider.

SKILL BUILDER 6.2 ## Compare Search Engines

In this exercise, you will attempt identical searches with two different search engines and compare the search results. There may be significant or minor differences in the results. The search engine that most reliably finds the types of web pages you are looking for is usually the one you will use first.

Search with One Search Provider

1. Think of a topic on which you would like to perform a web search, such as a travel destination, music, or a current news item.

2. Choose two or three search words closely related to your topic and write them on the line.

   _____

3. Choose a **search provider** from the address bar **Search menu** 🔍▾ (or you can add a new one).

4. Enter your search words and review the first page of search results.

5. Right-click a search result in the list that looks closely related to your topic and then choose **Open in New Tab**.

   Internet Explorer opens the web page in a new tab (but you are still viewing the search results). This makes it easy to return to your search results later.

6. Click the new tab. Spend a few minutes browsing this website.

7. Click the tab with your search results and then open another search result in a new tab.

8. Click the new web page tab, then review that website.

Search with Other Search Providers

9. View the search results tab again.

10. Click the address bar **Search menu** 🔍▾ and choose a different search provider. Then perform the same search with this new provider.

    The search results you see may closely match your previous search or may be quite different.

11. Open two new tabs with search results that look the most promising.

12. Try a third search provider and open two of its search results in new tabs.

    ⚠️**TIP!** In the next step, use the ⌨️Ctrl+Tab keyboard shortcut for switching tabs without the mouse.

13. Go from tab to tab, comparing your search results.

14. On the line below, write down which search engine you feel came up with the most useful results for your search.

   _____

15. Right-click any tab and then choose **Close Other Tabs**.

SKILL BUILDER 6.3 Practice with Favorites

In this exercise, you will organize new favorites into folders, delete a favorite, and rename a favorite.

1. If necessary, open an **Internet Explorer** window.

2. Make sure Internet Explorer is **maximized** ▫.

3. Use the address bar to search for web pages related to a personal interest.

4. Using the **Right-click + Open in New Tab** technique, open three links found by your search in new tabs.

5. View one of the web pages discovered in your search.

6. Click **Favorites** ⭐ and then choose **Add to Favorites**.

   This time, you will create a new folder in which to store the favorite.

Create a Favorite in a Custom Folder

7. Create a new favorite:

Ⓐ If desired, edit the default name.

Ⓑ Click **New Folder**, give the folder an appropriate name, and click **Create**.

Ⓒ Notice the new folder name.

8. Click **Add**.

   Internet Explorer creates the new favorite in the new folder.

9. Click **Favorites** ⭐, and choose **Add to Favorites**.

Notice that Internet Explorer displays the name of the new folder you just created as the *Create In* setting. You could choose a different folder here if you wish, but in this case you'll continue with the new folder.

10. Edit the name, then click **Add**.

Add a Tab Group to Favorites

11. Click **Favorites** ⭐ again, choose **Add to Favorites menu** ▾, and then choose **Add Current Tabs to Favorites**.

Notice that this time the *Favorites* folder appears in the Create In box.

12. Type **[Topic] Pages** as the tab group name.

13. Choose your new folder from the Create In list and then click **Add**.

Open Favorites from the New Folder

14. Right-click any web page tab, then choose **Close Other Tabs**.

15. Click **Favorites** ⭐, then click the **Favorites tab**.

16. Click the new folder you just created, then click a link.

The web page opens. The Favorites bar disappears since it was not pinned.

17. Click **Favorites** ⭐, then **Pin** 📌 the Favorites panel.

The panel jumps to the left side of the window and stays open until you close it.

18. Open a tab group:

A If necessary, click once to expand the new folder.

B Click to open the entire tab group (folder).

Internet Explorer opens all of the favorites in the folder.

Delete Your New Favorites Folder

19. Right-click the new folder, and then choose **Delete**.

Internet Explorer asks you to confirm the deletion.

20. Choose **Yes** to confirm the deletion of the folder and its contents.

You can use this same technique to delete individual favorites, too.

Using Cloud File Storage

Carrying your files with you on a device is becoming a thing of the past. Cloud storage based on the Internet allows access to documents, music, photos, and data from almost any connected device. The cloud also supports new ways to interact with classmates and coworkers. In this lesson, you will learn about online file storage, sync, sharing, and online applications. Thus far, you've used traditional storage devices on your local computer to store your work. In this lesson, you store these files in the cloud.

LESSON OBJECTIVES

After studying this lesson, you will be able to:

- Use cloud-based file storage
- Upload and download files to cloud storage
- Organize cloud storage using folders
- Describe sync and watched folders

Case Study: No Space, No Problem

Jasmine just bought a new tablet. With its touchscreen and solid-state drive (SSD), it's very fast. But it doesn't have much storage space and Jasmine has lots of files. She'd use a flash drive with it, but it doesn't have a standard USB port. Besides, the whole idea is to have a light portable device she can take anywhere; not something with a flash drive dangling off of it. Her laptop computer has plenty of drive space, but she doesn't want to connect the tablet to it every time she needs a file or photo.

Jasmine's friend, Angelica, uses a cloud storage service called Dropbox and loves it. Going into her Windows 8.1 tablet, Jasmine sees that it comes with a cloud storage service built in: OneDrive. Anything she stores in the OneDrive folder on her computer is automatically available to her tablet. But OneDrive doesn't physically copy the files to her tablet. Instead, a file is sent via the Internet when she opens it. This conserves the limited storage space on her tablet.

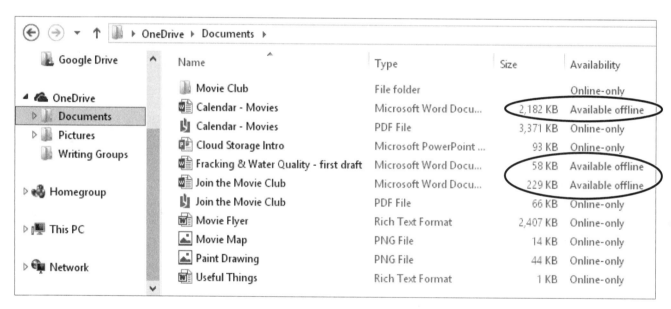

All of Jasmine's OneDrive files are available via the Internet. But she can also set files to be available even when she's offline.

Jasmine discovers that changes she makes to files in OneDrive on her tablet synchronize automatically to her laptop. In fact, the same files are also available on her smartphone, or via the web at a library computer. So she can look something up, share a file, or even work on it from any of her devices. Problem solved!

Defining the Cloud

The cloud is services and storage (typically running via the Internet) with an unknown physical location. You can use the cloud to store files, run software, or access additional computing power. This is called cloud computing. The cloud enables new levels of collaboration. Since the physical location doesn't matter, you can share files and other information with anyone anywhere.

Using Servers

A *server* is a computer that stores files in the cloud and transfers them to/from local devices. Most servers reside in huge server farm warehouse installations containing thousands of computers/storage drives.

A Google server farm somewhere in the U.S.

Services

The cloud supports numerous services. New services are added constantly. A few have become popular quite rapidly.

- **Cloud-based storage:** Online storage space from 2 gigabytes (GB) on up.

- **Cloud-based file sharing:** The ability to share files and/or folders with a link, without sending it via email or other means.

- **Cloud-based synchronization:** Files, settings, and program data that's automatically updated between multiple computers/devices.

Cloud Storage Options

This book uses Microsoft OneDrive to teach the principles of cloud storage. There are two basic reasons for this:

- OneDrive Pro is part of every Office 365 subscription (a popular way to install the Microsoft Office Suite programs, such as Word 2013.)

- OneDrive is provided for free if you use a Microsoft account to log on to Windows 8.1.

However, OneDrive is but one of numerous cloud storage services. Each service has strengths and weaknesses. Other services you could consider include:

- Dropbox
- Google Drive
- Copy.com
- Amazon Cloud Drive

Technology Moves Forward

This lesson and its exercises were based on the latest version of OneDrive at the start of 2014. However, cloud-based applications continue to grow in sophistication and capability. The appearance of OneDrive may differ from these exercises when you try it yourself. For example, some commands may change location. But the principles covered in this lesson will not change.

Using Web Access to Cloud Storage

Cloud storage gives you access to your files wherever you have an Internet connection (web access). When you're not at your computer, or using some other device such as a tablet or smartphone, you can access your files via a web browser.

For example, imagine you are doing research at a library and need to look over some notes and diagrams. You start a web browser and type the URL for your cloud storage service. You log in to your account, then open the folder for your research project. You display a mind map you created about your research.

Navigating Cloud Storage

Cloud storage services let you view and open various folders. There will usually be links along the top of the page to help you move back to the base level of your cloud storage.

Link to the base level of online storage.

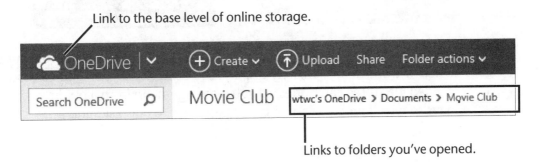

Links to folders you've opened.

!NOTE! The OneDrive tablet app on the Start screen functions differently from the web browser interface. It's designed primarily to browse your OneDrive files, not manage them. Because the web interface has more commands and versatility, this lesson concentrates on the browser version rather than the Windows 8.1 app.

  HANDS-ON 7.1 **Browse Cloud Storage via the Web**

In this exercise, you will view files in a OneDrive folder. As the exercise begins, you are logged in as a guest at a library computer.

!NOTE! All of the cloud storage exercises in this lesson use WebSims.

1. Display the **Desktop**, then start **Internet Explorer** and navigate to the student resource center by typing `labyrinthelab.com/wtwc5` into the address bar.

2. Click **Lesson 7: Using Cloud File Storage**.

3. Click **Hands-On 7.1: Browse Cloud Storage**.

   As the WebSim begins, Internet Explorer is already running and a fresh tab is in view.

   !NOTE! This lesson assumes that you sign in to Windows with a Microsoft account. This won't likely be the case in a computer lab setting, but it will be on your personal computer or tablet.

4. Sign in to OneDrive:

A Type `onedrive.live.com` into the browser's address bar.

B Click **Sign In**.

Windows uses the email address and password for your Microsoft account to sign in to OneDrive, which immediately displays the contents of your cloud storage. It starts out divided into three categories. (If you were signing in from a public computer, you would have to type your email address and password to finish signing in.)

Navigate Online Folders

5. Click once on **Documents**. (There's no need to double-click to navigate on this web page.)

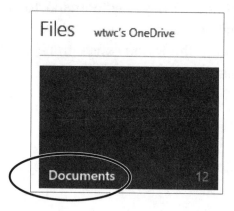

This space is empty, since you haven't placed any files into it yet. You'll load your files into this cloud storage space in the next exercise.

6. Click **wtwc's OneDrive** to return to the base level of your cloud storage.

7. Click **Continue to Next WebSim**.

The next WebSim loads. Read on to the next exercise.

Online Storage Privacy

Free online storage often comes at a price. Many services claim nonexclusive ownership and access to any files stored on their servers. This co-ownership may continue even if you delete the files or close your account.

Rights to Your Content   The rights a service has to your files are usually described in their terms of service agreement. There may be additional details in the services' privacy rights statement. These terms define their access to your files and how long that access may last. These terms may change from time to time. Some services may define their rights to last *forever*; that is, anything you upload to their service is theirs to use as they see fit, even if you terminate your account. The terms often give cloud storage services the right to develop new products based on your files, without limitation.

!TIP! Terms of service can vary widely, so it pays to review them with care. Check out the buzz with a web search related to privacy rights on any service you choose.

Online Ads   Many services survey your files to target online ads that help fund the free storage. (This is frequently done with free email services, too.) The content of your files may give clues to personal interests and concerns that accumulate in an online profile. The service then offers use of the profile details to advertisers. Revenue is earned every time a targeted ad is displayed, and even more if it is clicked.

Downloading and Uploading

As you work with cloud-based storage, you will frequently need to transfer files and folders from one storage location to another. Some commands will only work with files stored on a drive in your computer or tablet. While watched folders make file transfer commands for you automatically, sometimes you'll need to transfer files manually with download and upload commands.

- **Downloading:** Transfers a file from a remote server to your local computer.

- **Uploading:** Sends a file from your local computer to a remote server.

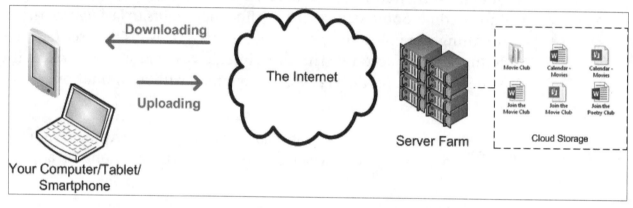

Download and upload commands transfer files between local and remote storage.

> ⚠️ **NOTE!** A more convenient alternative to uploads and downloads is synchronized storage via a watched folder. You'll learn this method later in this lesson. For now, you'll perform this task manually.

 HANDS-ON 7.2 **Upload Files**

 In this WebSim, you will upload files to the Documents folder of OneDrive from a USB flash drive.

Before You Begin: If necessary, start the WebSim for this exercise.

1. Navigate to the upload destination folder:

A Click **Documents** to return to the folder where you'll upload files. (You always start uploads at the destination folder.)

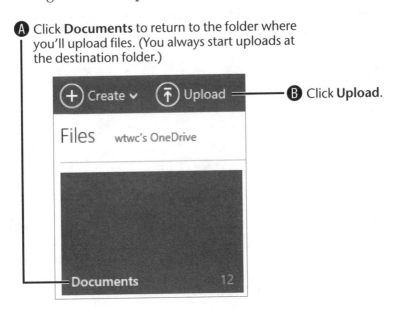

B Click **Upload**.

C Click the **scrollbar** to simulate scrolling down.

D Choose the **USB flash drive**.

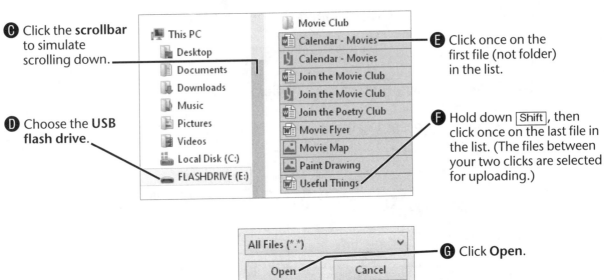

E Click once on the first file (not folder) in the list.

F Hold down Shift, then click once on the last file in the list. (The files between your two clicks are selected for uploading.)

G Click **Open**.

OneDrive displays the progress of copying your files from the computer to cloud storage. Depending on the size of the files and the speed of your Internet connection, this could take a minute or so.

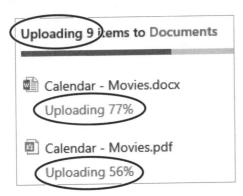

Create and Copy a Folder

OneDrive doesn't let you upload a folder directly. Instead, you will create the folder, open it, then copy from the flash drive into the new folder.

2. Create a folder:

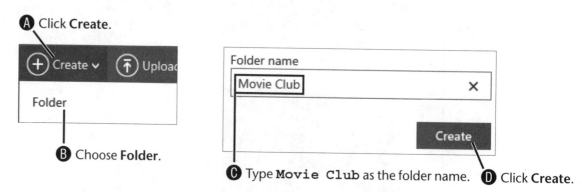

Ⓐ Click **Create**.

Ⓑ Choose **Folder**.

Ⓒ Type **Movie Club** as the folder name.   Ⓓ Click **Create**.

OneDrive displays a large tile for the new folder.

3. Click **Movie Club** to open the new folder.

4. Click the **Upload** button.   ⬆ Upload

5. Scroll down, then click your **flash drive**.

6. Select and upload files:

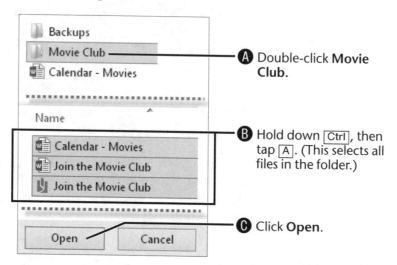

Ⓐ Double-click **Movie Club**.

Ⓑ Hold down ⌈Ctrl⌉, then tap ⌈A⌉. (This selects all files in the folder.)

Ⓒ Click **Open**.

OneDrive displays the progress of the upload. There aren't as many files, so this upload should take less time.

7. Navigate online folders:

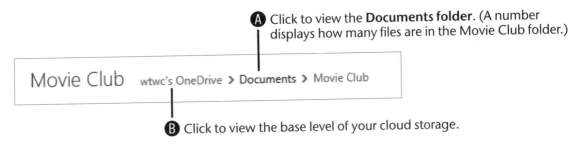

Ⓐ Click to view the **Documents folder**. (A number displays how many files are in the Movie Club folder.)

Movie Club   wtwc's OneDrive > Documents > Movie Club

Ⓑ Click to view the base level of your cloud storage.

8. Click **Continue to the next WebSim**.

Downloading Files

Downloading is copying a file from cloud (remote) storage to your local computer or tablet. You've likely downloaded many times to view photos, get music, or other forms of file sharing. Most programs are installed by first downloading the software.

Downloading is the way you can get a file from your cloud storage to work on. After the work is done, you can upload the file again. But it is inconvenient to constantly download, then upload changes. This method is mainly useful when you work with files on a computer that's not your own.

> **!NOTE!** In the next topic, you'll learn how OneDrive (and other cloud storage services) can automatically upload from and download to your computer and other devices. It's called synchronized storage, or simply synching.

Changing the View

You can view files in OneDrive as tiles or as a list. The tiles view displays thumbnails of pictures, but takes quite a bit of space. The List view is more compact, but doesn't display previews.

HANDS-ON 7.3 Change the View and Download a File

In this exercise, you will download a file from OneDrive to a USB flash drive. This is what you would do if you were using a library computer and needed to work on one of your files.

Before You Begin: If necessary, start the WebSim for this exercise.

1. Click **Documents**.

2. Change the view:

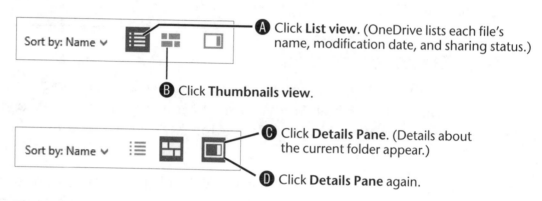

Ⓐ Click **List view**. (OneDrive lists each file's name, modification date, and sharing status.)

Ⓑ Click **Thumbnails view**.

Ⓒ Click **Details Pane**. (Details about the current folder appear.)

Ⓓ Click **Details Pane** again.

The pane toggles off.

3. Download a file:

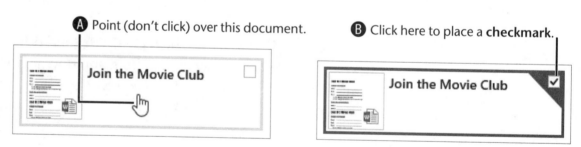

Ⓐ Point (don't click) over this document.

Ⓑ Click here to place a **checkmark**.

Join the Movie Club

Join the Movie Club

This selects the file for your next command.

4. Click **Download**.

OneDrive asks what you want to do with the file.

5. Save the file:

Ⓐ Click **Save menu** button (not just Save).

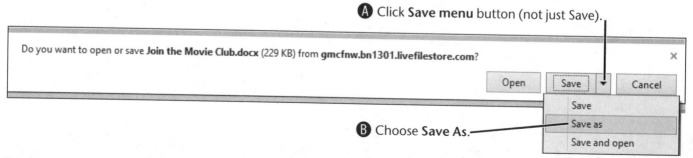

Do you want to open or save **Join the Movie Club.docx** (229 KB) from **gmcfnw.bn1301.livefilestore.com**?

| Open | Save | ▼ | Cancel |

Save
Save as
Save and open

Ⓑ Choose **Save As**.

A Save As dialog box asks where you wish to save the file. Let's save it to Documents.

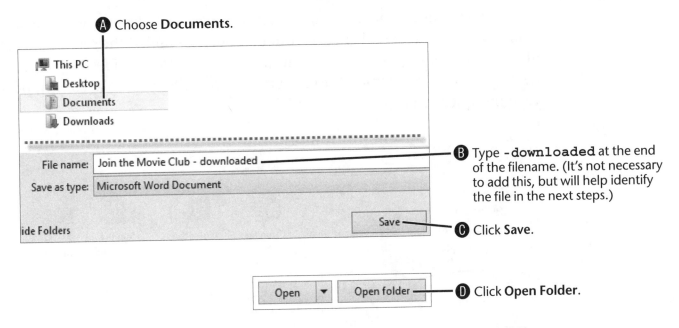

🅐 Choose **Documents**.

This PC
Desktop
Documents
Downloads

File name: Join the Movie Club - downloaded

Save as type: Microsoft Word Document

ide Folders

Save

🅑 Type **-downloaded** at the end of the filename. (It's not necessary to add this, but will help identify the file in the next steps.)

🅒 Click **Save**.

Open ▾ | Open folder — 🅓 Click **Open Folder**.

A File Explorer window appears to display the newly downloaded file.

6. Double-click to open **Join the Movie Club – downloaded**.

The document opens in Word. Since it was downloaded from the Internet, Word displays a warning bar at the top of the window. Notice also that the normal Ribbon isn't visible. Word won't let you work on the file until you confirm that you know it's safe.

7. Click **Enable Editing**.

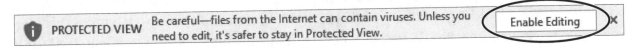

PROTECTED VIEW Be careful—files from the Internet can contain viruses. Unless you need to edit, it's safer to stay in Protected View. | Enable Editing | ✕

The full Word Ribbon appears.

8. **Close** ✖ Word.

If you had edited this file, you would upload it to OneDrive in order to save your latest changes.

9. Click **Continue to Next WebSim**.

Using Synchronized Storage

Synchronized storage makes sure the latest versions of files are available on all your devices. When you log in to your computer or tablet, the service checks files stored online against the ones in the watched folder. If files online are newer, the service downloads them. Older online files are replaced with new versions uploaded from your computer.

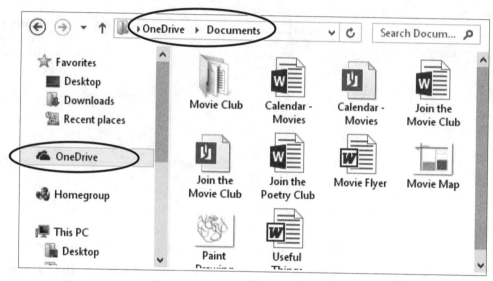

Files as they appear in OneDrive on your computer.

Watched Folders

A watched folder is a location on your local computer that responds to file/folder activity. Cloud storage services usually set up a watched folder on your computer. When you create or store a file or folder in a watched folder, a copy uploads to online storage automatically. OneDrive is an example of a watched folder. Anything changed in this folder gets uploaded to your cloud storage automatically.

Other cloud storage services often create their own watched folders. For example, anything you add or modify in the Dropbox folder is automatically synced to your Dropbox.com cloud storage. Google Drive uses a similar approach.

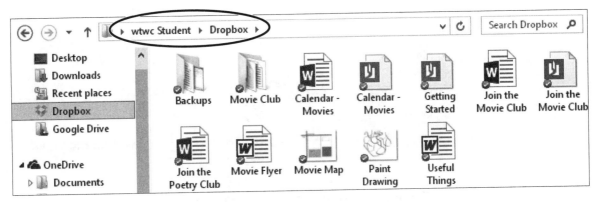

Dropbox creates a convenient link to its watched cloud storage folder.

 HANDS-ON 7.4 **View a Watched Folder and Sync**

In this exercise, you will view OneDrive through the File Explorer. You will delete files and observe how everything you do in the watched folder syncs to cloud storage automatically. This exercise assumes that you've signed on to Windows using a Microsoft ID. This activates OneDrive.

Before You Begin: If necessary, start the WebSim for this exercise.

1. Start **File Explorer** .

2. View a OneDrive folder:

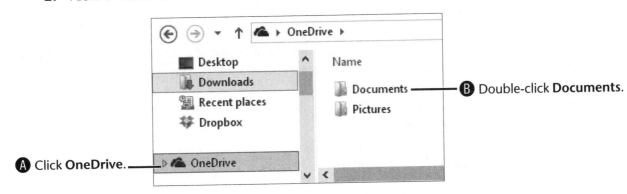

Ⓐ Click **OneDrive**.

Ⓑ Double-click **Documents**.

The contents of this folder match what you've viewed via the web earlier in this lesson. That's because everything taking place in your cloud storage has been happening here too. Let's delete a couple of files and see what happens.

3. Select files for deletion:

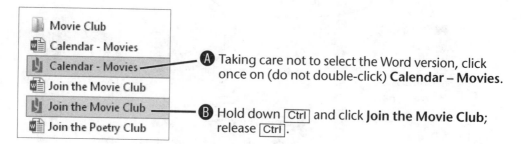

A Taking care not to select the Word version, click once on (do not double-click) **Calendar – Movies**.

B Hold down `Ctrl` and click **Join the Movie Club**; release `Ctrl`.

Both files are selected for your next command.

4. Choose **Home→Organize→Delete** from the Ribbon. Choose **Yes** if asked to confirm the deletion.

The files go into the Recycle Bin. This is because everything in OneDrive is also on the storage drive inside the computer.

5. Use `Alt`+`Tab` to flip to the **OneDrive web page**.

The deleted files may take up to thirty seconds to disappear on the web. Clicking Refresh in the next step will refresh the display and show the change.

6. Wait a few seconds, then click **Refresh**.

Notice that the two files you deleted are now gone from cloud storage. OneDrive synced these files to the command you gave in the OneDrive watched folder. Now you will undelete the files.

Undelete the Files

7. Use `Alt`+`Tab` to return to the **File Explorer**.

8. Click **Undo** or use `Ctrl`+`Z` from the keyboard.

The two deleted files reappear. That's because their deletion was your most recent command. You could also have opened the Recycle Bin and restored them from there.

9. Use `Alt`+`Tab` to flip back to the **OneDrive web page**.

Within thirty seconds, the undeleted files reappear here too.

10. Click **Continue to Next WebSim**.

Saving to Watched Folders

You can save and open directly to/from a watched folder from within applications. This saves you the inconvenience of uploading and downloading files. All you need to know is the watched folder location.

OneDrive and Office 2013

Office 2013 applications have a OneDrive location built into their Save As command. This makes it especially convenient to save new documents to OneDrive, or to open them from cloud storage.

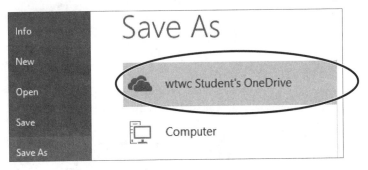

Dropbox Example

Dropbox doesn't have a save location listed in Word 2013, but it's just as easy to save directly into its cloud storage (or into other cloud storage services).

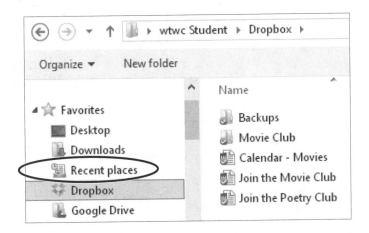

HANDS-ON 7.5 Save to a Watched Folder

In this exercise, you will save a Word document to OneDrive.

Before You Begin: If necessary, start the WebSim for this exercise.

As the WebSim begins, you have a document already open in Word 2013. Assume it was originally created on a USB flash drive, but now you want to save it to OneDrive.

1. Click ▮FILE▮ then choose **Save As**.

2. Choose a location with Word 2013:

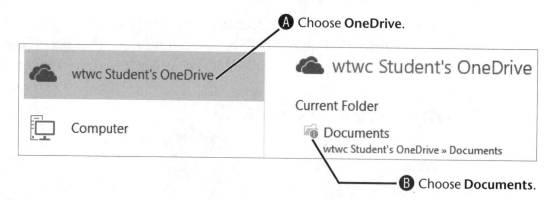

Ⓐ Choose **OneDrive**.

Ⓑ Choose **Documents**.

A Save As dialog box opens to complete the command. Notice that the Documents folder in OneDrive is already chosen.

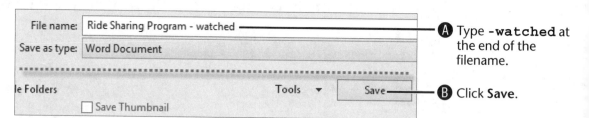

3. Change the filename:

Ⓐ Type **-watched** at the end of the filename.

Ⓑ Click **Save**.

Word saves the document to the watched folder.

4. Close ☒ Word.

5. Start **File Explorer** 📁.

6. Choose **OneDrive**, then double-click **Documents**.

The newly saved document appears. The OneDrive Save As location always saves the file to this location inside your computer.

7. Use [Alt]+[Tab] to view the **OneDrive web page** then click **Refresh** 🔄.

The document is here too, synced automatically from the watched folder.

8. Click **Continue to Next WebSim**.

Deleting Files from Cloud Storage

You can delete unneeded files and folders from cloud storage. When you do, this change syncs to all locations. For example, if you delete a document from the OneDrive web page, the file also disappears from the OneDrive folder on your computer or tablet.

Deleted Online Files and the Recycle Bin

Deleted files and folders in cloud storage go into the recycle bin of each computer or tablet you use with OneDrive. As you may recall from Lesson 4, Working with Files, Windows does not physically erase a deleted file from the storage drive. So you could still restore a file or folder deleted from OneDrive on any device and it will be synced back on all other devices on your account. OneDrive also has its own cloud-based Recycle Bin.

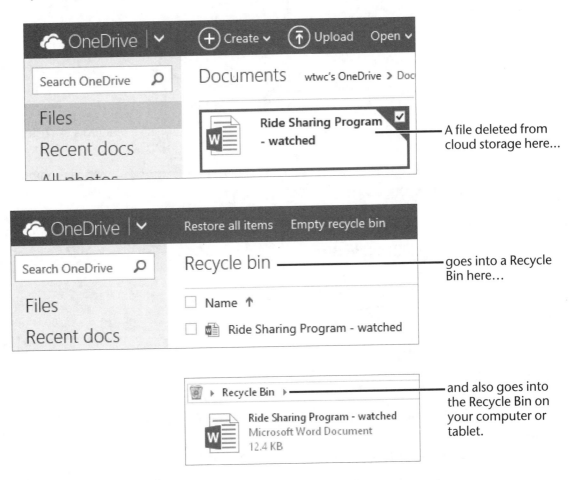

A file deleted from cloud storage here...

goes into a Recycle Bin here...

and also goes into the Recycle Bin on your computer or tablet.

In this exercise, you will delete a file from the web view of OneDrive, and then observe the file in the Recycle Bin online and on the computer.

Before You Begin: If necessary, start the WebSim for this exercise.

As the WebSim begins, you are viewing OneDrive in File Explorer.

1. Delete a file:

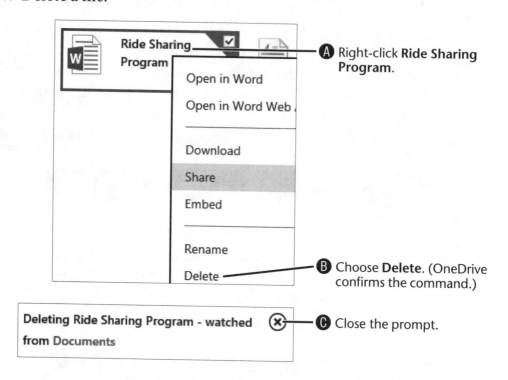

Ride Sharing
Program

- Open in Word
- Open in Word Web
- Download
- Share
- Embed
- Rename
- Delete

A Right-click **Ride Sharing Program**.

B Choose **Delete**. (OneDrive confirms the command.)

Deleting Ride Sharing Program - watched
from Documents

C Close the prompt.

2. Click **Recycle Bin**.

6.98 GB available

Recycle bin

Get more storage

Get SkyDrive apps

The file you just deleted is visible. Now let's check the Recycle Bin on the computer.

3. Click **View Computer Recycle Bin**.

A view of the Recycle Bin on the computer appears. Notice that the file you just deleted appears here, too. Wherever you give the Delete command, the result is synced everywhere.

4. Click **Continue to Next WebSim**.

Viewing Files Offline

OneDrive sets files in watched folders to be visible only when you have an Internet connection. Although the file list is always visible, if you try opening a file when you're not online, such as when your tablet or laptop is in Airplane Mode (no wireless), an error message appears. The advantage of this setting is that these files won't take up limited space in the storage of a tablet or smartphone.

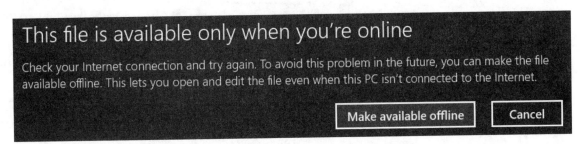

This file is available only when you're online

Check your Internet connection and try again. To avoid this problem in the future, you can make the file available offline. This lets you open and edit the file even when this PC isn't connected to the Internet.

[Make available offline] [Cancel]

Double-clicking a file while offline can result in this message.

Setting Files for Offline Viewing

You can set specific files and folders for offline viewing. These files get stored inside each device. Although they take up space, they are also available everywhere. If you make changes to a file while offline, these sync to cloud storage once you get online again.

QUICK REFERENCE: OneDrive: Setting Files for Offline Viewing

Task	Procedure
Set a file for offline viewing	• Navigate to the file in its OneDrive folder on the computer. • Right-click, then choose Make Available Offline.
Switch off offline viewing	• Navigate to the file in its OneDrive folder on the computer. • Right-click, then choose Make Available Online Only.

HANDS-ON 7.7 **View a File Offline**

In this exercise, you will set a file for offline viewing, then switch off the Internet connection and open it on a tablet.

Before You Begin: If necessary, start the WebSim for this exercise.

As the WebSim begins, you are viewing OneDrive in File Explorer.

1. Make a file available offline:

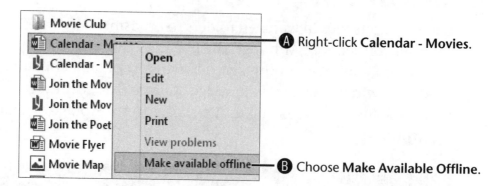

OneDrive notes the change. Notice the change in the Availability column. Next let's see what happens when there's no Internet connection available.

Name	Date modified	Type	Size	Availability
Movie Club	1/1/2014 3:06 PM	File folder		Online-only
Calendar - Movies	12/22/2013 10:47 ...	Microsoft Word...	2,182 KB	Available offline
Calendar - Movies	12/22/2013 10:47 ...	PDF File	3,371 KB	Online-only

2. Click **Enter Airplane Mode.**

You're at 32,000 feet on a flight to somewhere nice. Now you are viewing your OneDrive in File Explorer on a tablet.

3. Double-click **Calendar - Movies.**

Because it's set for offline viewing, the document opens normally.

4. **Close** ☒ Word.

Now let's try opening a file set for online-only (the default setting for OneDrive files).

5. Double-click **Join the Movie Club.**

An availability message appears. This file isn't available now, but you can set it to be available the next time you're offline.

6. Click **Make Available Online.**

The file will be downloaded to the tablet's storage the next time you're online. From then on it will be available offline too. For now, hope you have a window seat. :)

7. Click **Continue to Next WebSim.**

Creating a File in the Cloud

You can create and edit several types of files in OneDrive cloud storage without downloading them. This saves you the chore of downloading a file for editing, then uploading the edited file back into cloud storage. There are some downsides to web apps, but also times when they are the right tool for the job.

OneDrive Web Apps

OneDrive's online apps are reduced versions of Office 2013 programs you normally have to install on your computer's storage drive. They run entirely off the Internet and never need installation. They are available from any computer you can sign in on OneDrive.

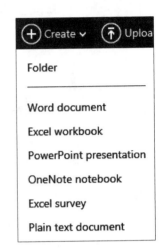

Web App Capabilities

A comparison of the Word Online app with its full Word 2013 version highlights their different capabilities. Word Online isn't nearly as capable as the full version. Some differences between Word Online and the full version of Word 2013 include:

OneDrive has web apps for six popular types of files.

- Word Online doesn't handle complex formatting very well.

- Word Online has far fewer commands and options.

- Word Online has no access to templates for creating new documents.

These differences aside, however, Word Online is very convenient when you need to edit or create a basic document. And you can always add to the Word Online draft of a document in the full Word 2013 program later. Similar remarks would apply to comparisons of the Excel and PowerPoint Online apps.

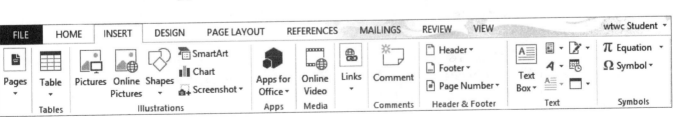

The Word 2013 Insert tab contains numerous commands.

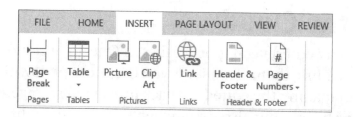

The Word Online Insert tab contains far fewer and less sophisticated commands.

NOTE! Web-based apps continue to become more sophisticated. In coming years, there will be less and less difference between drive-based programs and web-based apps.

Missing Save Button

Word Online doesn't have a Save button or command. That's because it saves your work directly to cloud storage with every keystroke. You simply close the web page tab to stop editing. This is a nice feature. Even if your Internet connection or computer/tablet fail, whatever you drafted in Word Online is safe online.

HANDS-ON 7.8   Create a File in Word Online

In this exercise, you will create a flyer from scratch in Word Online.

Before You Begin: If necessary, start the WebSim for this exercise.

As the WebSim begins, you are viewing OneDrive in File Explorer.

1. Create a new document online:

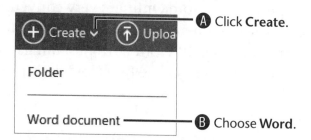

Ⓐ Click **Create**.

Ⓑ Choose **Word**.

OneDrive opens Word Online for a new document. Notice that it's got a Ribbon very similar to the one in Word 2013. Let's start the flyer with an image. Word Online has thousands of clip art images available.

2. Choose **Insert→Pictures→Clip Art** from the Ribbon.

3. Find and insert a photo:

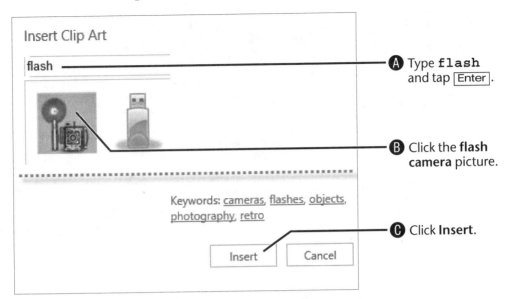

Insert Clip Art

flash ———————————————————————— **Ⓐ** Type **flash** and tap Enter.

Ⓑ Click the **flash camera** picture.

Keywords: cameras, flashes, objects, photography, retro

Ⓒ Click **Insert**.

Insert Cancel

There is a pause as Word Online inserts the picture.

Type and Format the Flyer Text

4. Click to the right of the picture, then tap Enter.

5. Choose **Home→Styles→Style Menu** from the Ribbon.

Word Online expands the style list to display all available styles.

6. Choose the **Title** style.

You'll see the effect of this formatting as you start typing.

7. Finish typing the flyer:

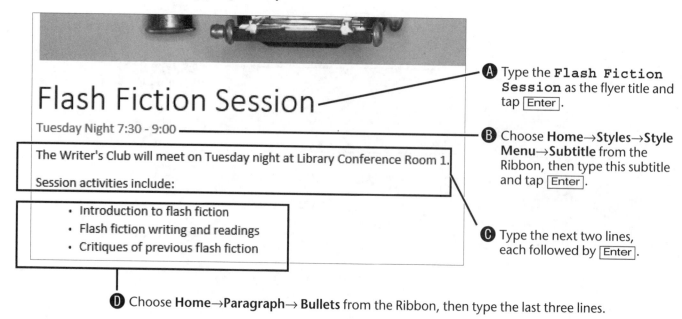

Flash Fiction Session

Tuesday Night 7:30 - 9:00

The Writer's Club will meet on Tuesday night at Library Conference Room 1.

Session activities include:

- Introduction to flash fiction
- Flash fiction writing and readings
- Critiques of previous flash fiction

Ⓐ Type the **Flash Fiction Session** as the flyer title and tap ⎡Enter⎤.

Ⓑ Choose **Home→Styles→Style Menu→Subtitle** from the Ribbon, then type this subtitle and tap ⎡Enter⎤.

Ⓒ Type the next two lines, each followed by ⎡Enter⎤.

Ⓓ Choose **Home→Paragraph→ Bullets** from the Ribbon, then type the last three lines.

Format Text Manually

You aren't limited to using styles to format text in Word Online. You can also use manual techniques that you're used to.

8. Change the font color:

Ⓐ Point to the left of the subtitle, then hold down the mouse button and drag right to select it.

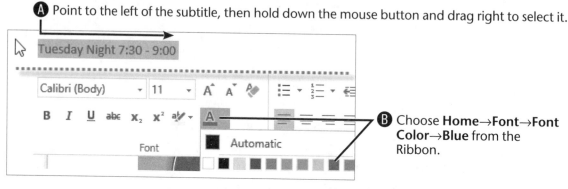

Ⓑ Choose **Home→Font→Font Color→Blue** from the Ribbon.

Ⓒ Point to the left of the location, then drag right to select it.

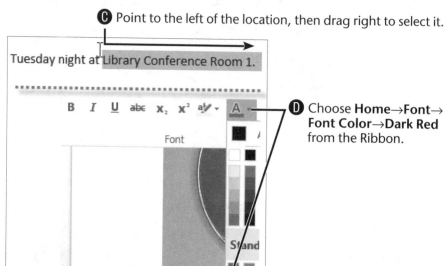

Ⓓ Choose **Home→Font→ Font Color→Dark Red** from the Ribbon.

9. Click once on **Document1** at the top of the document window, type **Flash Fiction Session** as the new name, and tap [Enter].

Normally, you'd have wanted to save the document by now. But Word Online has actually been saving your work with every letter you've typed.

10. **Close** ⊠ the Word Online tab.

OneDrive appears again. Notice that the new document has been added. It's that easy to create a new document entirely online.

11. Click **Back to Course**.

The links to the WebSims on the student resource center reappear.

Concepts Review

To check your knowledge of the key concepts introduced in this lesson, complete the Concepts Review quiz here or on the student resource center.

True/False Questions

Page Number

1. A watched folder automatically uploads files and folders to/from the cloud.   **True**   **False** _____

2. Uploading is the process of moving a file from a remote computer to your local computer.   **True**   **False** _____

3. Word Online is less capable than Word 2013.   **True**   **False** _____

4. You can create new folders within a watched folder.   **True**   **False** _____

5. When you delete a file or folder from OneDrive, it goes into a Recycle Bin.   **True**   **False** _____

6. Files on your OneDrive are always available for viewing.   **True**   **False** _____

Multiple Choice Questions

7. Synchronized storage _____.

   Page Number: _____

   a. uploads files from watched folders to the cloud
   b. downloads files from the cloud to watched folders
   c. makes files available via the web
   d. All of the above

8. The process of copying a file from cloud storage to your local computer is called _____.

   Page Number: _____

   a. uploading
   b. downloading
   c. cloud computing
   d. None of the above

9. A watched folder _____.

   Page Number: _____

   a. syncs files from your local computer to cloud storage
   b. syncs files from cloud storage to your local computer
   c. uploads but never downloads synced files to/from cloud storage
   d. Only a and b

10. A file or folder deleted from OneDrive cloud storage _____.

   Page Number: _____

   a. goes into the cloud storage Recycle Bin only
   b. goes into the local computer's Recycle Bin only
   c. goes into the Recycle Bin of cloud storage and each device you use
   d. Only a and b

Skill Builders

Use Synchronized Storage

On the Web

In this exercise, you will save a file to a watched folder, then view it in cloud storage on the web.

1. Start **Internet Explorer** and navigate to the student resource center by typing `labyrinthelab.com/wtwc5` into the address bar.

2. Click **Lesson 7: Using Cloud File Storage**.

3. Click **Skill Builder 7.1: Use Synchronized Storage**.

    As the WebSim begins, you want to save a file from local storage on your laptop into OneDrive cloud storage.

4. Start **File Explorer** .

5. Display **This PC**, then double-click **Documents**.

6. Double-click **Cloud Storage Intro**.

    This file was created in PowerPoint, a popular presentation program. Now you will save the file into OneDrive.

7. Choose **File→Save As** from the Ribbon.

8. Choose **OneDrive**, then click **Browse**.

9. Double-click **Documents**.

    Although it has the same name, OneDrive's Documents folder is a different location than the one on the PC.

10. Click **Save**.

11. **Close** PowerPoint.

    You are back to viewing File Explorer.

View Synchronized Storage

12. Display **OneDrive**, then double-click **Documents**.

The Cloud Storage Intro file is where you saved it.

13. Start **Internet Explorer**, type **OneDrive.live.com** in the address bar, tap
Enter, and then click **Sign In**.

OneDrive displays your cloud storage because you are signed on to Windows 8.1 using a
Microsoft account.

14. Click **Documents**.

The Cloud Storage Intro file has been synced to your cloud storage as well.

15. Click **Continue to Next WebSim**.

SKILL BUILDER 7.2   **Edit a File in Cloud Storage**

In this exercise, you will download a file from cloud storage, edit it, then upload the edited
file back to cloud storage.

1. Start the WebSim for this exercise if it's not running already.

As the WebSim begins, you are viewing your cloud storage via the web from a computer
that's not your own.

2. Place a checkmark in the **Cloud Storage Intro**, then click **Download**.

3. Click **Save menu** button, then choose **Save and Open**.

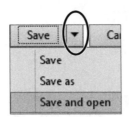

PowerPoint starts to display the file. Notice the Protected View bar. Notice also that the
normal Ribbon commands aren't visible yet.

4. Click **Enable Editing**.

   PowerPoint displays the Ribbon and you can edit the file.

5. Choose **Home→Slides→New Slide** from the Ribbon.

   PowerPoint displays the new slide, ready for you to add content.

6. Type the slide:

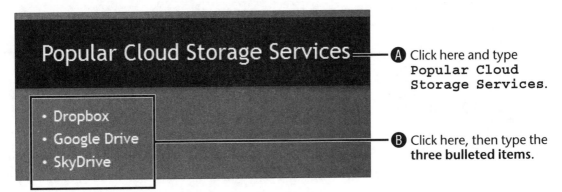

A Click here and type `Popular Cloud Storage Services`.

B Click here, then type the **three bulleted items**.

Save Your Changes

7. Choose **File→Save As**.

   Notice the Current Folder location. The file was originally saved in the Downloads folder. So you'll look for it there when you upload it in the next steps.

8. Choose **Downloads**, then click **Save**.

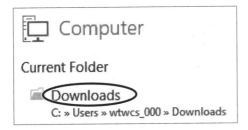

9. Choose **Yes** when asked to overwrite the file.

10. **Close** ☒ PowerPoint.

    You are back to viewing your cloud storage.

Upload the Changed File

11. Click the **Upload** button.

12. Choose the upload location:

Ⓐ Click **Downloads**.

Ⓑ Double-click **Cloud Storage Intro**.

OneDrive starts the upload. Then it sees you have a file by the same name and asks whether you wish to replace it.

13. Choose **Replace**.

OneDrive completes the upload.

14. Click **Cloud Storage Intro**.

OneDrive opens a new tab to display a preview of the presentation.

15. Click **Next Slide**.

The new slide you created comes into view.

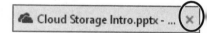

16. Close the presentation tab.

17. Click **Continue to Next WebSim**.

SKILL BUILDER 7.3 ## Edit a File Using a Web App

In this exercise, you will edit the presentation again in online storage. But instead of uploading and downloading it, you will use the PowerPoint Online app.

1. Start the WebSim for this exercise if it's not running already.

As the WebSim begins, you are viewing your cloud storage via the web from a computer that's not your own.

2. Click **Cloud Storage Intro**.

OneDrive opens a new tab to display a preview of the presentation.

3. Open the presentation in the web app:

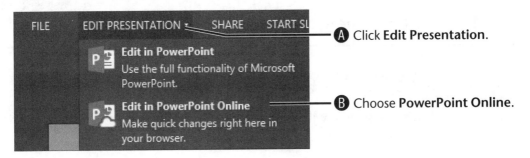

Ⓐ Click **Edit Presentation**.

Ⓑ Choose **PowerPoint Online**.

4. Click **Slide 2**.

5. Choose **Insert→Images→Clipart** from the Ribbon.

6. Find, insert, and resize an image:

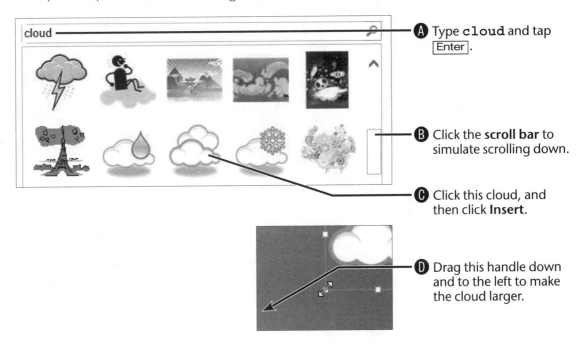

Ⓐ Type **cloud** and tap Enter.

Ⓑ Click the **scroll bar** to simulate scrolling down.

Ⓒ Click this cloud, and then click **Insert**.

Ⓓ Drag this handle down and to the left to make the cloud larger.

Confirm the Changes

PowerPoint Online saved everything as you modified the slide. Let's close the presentation then reopen it to confirm this.

7. Close the presentation tab.

8. Click **Cloud Storage Intro** to reopen it.

9. Click **Next Slide**.

The slide you modified online shows the new clip art. This was much easier than downloading, changing, then uploading the presentation. If you have simple changes to make that an online app can handle, editing a file online makes sense.

10. Close the presentation tab.

11. Click **Continue to Next WebSim**.

SKILL BUILDER 7.4   Set a File for Offline Viewing

In this exercise, you will select files for offline viewing, then access them while not in range of an Internet connection.

1. Start the WebSim for this exercise if it's not running already.

As the WebSim begins, you are using your laptop computer.

2. Start **File Explorer** and display **OneDrive**, and then **Documents**.

3. Right-click **Cloud Storage Intro**, then choose **Make Available Offline**.

You can select multiple files for this command. Let's try it.

4. Make multiple files available offline:

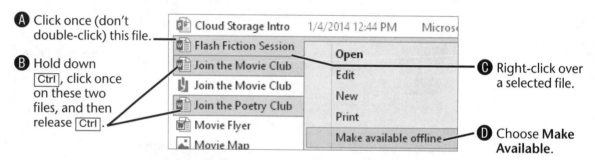

Ⓐ Click once (don't double-click) this file.

Ⓑ Hold down Ctrl, click once on these two files, and then release Ctrl.

Ⓒ Right-click over a selected file.

Ⓓ Choose **Make Available**.

Notice that all the files in the selection are now available offline. The other files in OneDrive won't be available when you don't have an Internet connection.

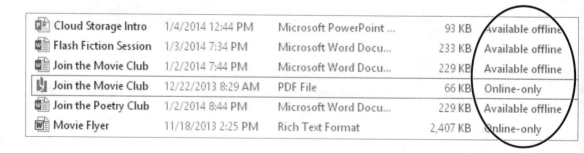

5. Click **Continue to Next WebSim**.

SKILL BUILDER 7.5 Delete a File from Cloud Storage

In this exercise, you will delete a file from cloud storage, then view it in the Recycle Bin on multiple devices.

1. Start the WebSim for this exercise if it's not running already.

As the WebSim begins, you are viewing OneDrive via the web from your laptop.

2. Click **Documents** to view this folder.

3. Right-click **Cloud Storage Intro**, then choose **Delete**.

4. Click **Recycle Bin**.

5. Right-click **Cloud Storage Intro**, then choose **Restore**.

6. Click **OneDrive**.

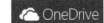

Clicking this logo always returns you to the base level of your cloud storage.

7. Click **Documents**.

The Cloud Storage Intro file has been restored.

8. Click **wtwc's OneDrive**.

Clicking folders in this path display also navigates you back to the base level.

9. Click **Back to Course**.

Sharing Files

Sharing files is a common task in education, whether it's turning in an assignment or collaborating on a project. One method for sharing files is attachments to email messages. A newer but increasingly common method is to share files via links to cloud storage. In this lesson, you will learn various ways to share files via email and cloud storage.

LESSON OBJECTIVES

After studying this lesson, you will be able to:

- Send and receive webmail messages via Outlook.com

- Attach files to email messages

- Open attachments you receive from others

- Share a link to a file in your cloud storage

- Share a folder in your cloud storage

- Use a cloud application to edit a file

Case Study: Online Double-Check

Edward is president of the writer's club on campus. He's a fan of flash fiction, a writing style in which the entire story must fit on one or two sheets of paper. So, when someone proposed a flash-fiction workshop, Edward readily agreed that they should sponsor the event. One member sends him a draft flyer, which Edward saves to his OneDrive cloud storage.

Another club member, Brooke, has offered to review the flyer and make any necessary changes, so Edward sends her a link to the file via his cloud storage service. Now Brooke can preview and edit the flyer. When she's done, Edward simply opens the document from his cloud storage to review the changes.

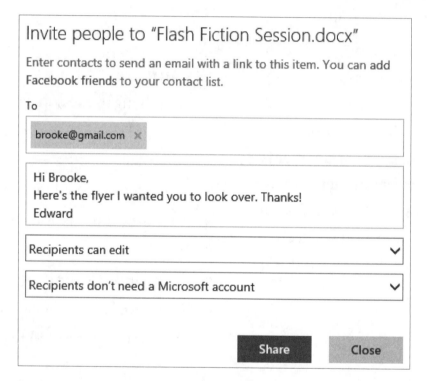

Rather than attaching the file to a message, Edward shares a link to the flyer in his cloud storage.

Using the Outlook Web App

Outlook Web App is a webmail service. There are also colleges, universities, and businesses providing similar accounts to students and workers. Beyond webmail, the Outlook Web App provides calendar and cloud-storage services. You learned about the cloud-storage services in the previous lesson.

> **!NOTE!** For the rest of this lesson the Outlook Web App will simply be called Outlook.

If you're like most students studying with this book, sending and receiving email messages is already familiar to you. This beginner's section contains brief coverage of the basics and details about Outlook's email features.

Composing a Message

Composing and sending a message with the Outlook Web App is like any other webmail service. Outlook's message writing tools are also quite standard.

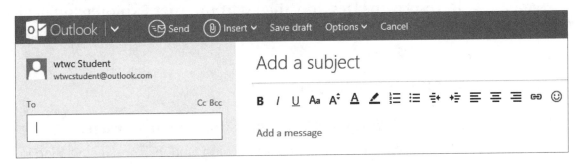

Outlook.com's basic message window.

Multiple Addressees   You can address email messages to more than one addressee. Use a comma or semicolon to separate individual email addresses.

Cc and Bcc Addresses   Cc and Bcc add addressees who aren't the primary recipients. Use each as follows:

- **Cc** – Stands for "carbon copy." Each person Cc'd will appear in the Cc section of the message.

- **Bcc** – Stands for "blind carbon copy." Each person in this list receives the message, but isn't listed as having received it.

Using Email Addresses

All email addresses use the convention shown below. For example, all email addresses always use the "at" (@) symbol to separate the email account name from the domain name.

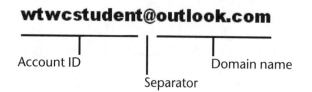

wtwcstudent@outlook.com

Account ID

Separator

Domain name

HANDS-ON 8.1   **Compose an Email Message**

In this exercise, you will compose and send a new email message using Outlook.com.

⚠ **NOTE!** All of the file/folder sharing exercises in this lesson use WebSims.

1. Display the **Desktop**, then start **Internet Explorer** and navigate to the student resource center by typing `labyrinthelab.com/wtwc5` into the address bar.

2. Click **Lesson 8: Sharing Files**.

3. Click **Hands-On 8.1: Compose an Email Message**.

   As the WebSim begins, you are viewing Outlook.com; ready to log in.

4. Sign on to Outlook:

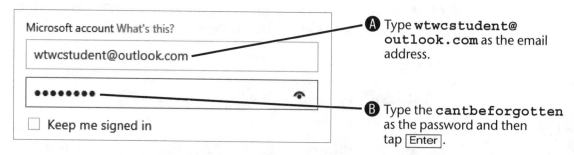

Ⓐ Type `wtwcstudent@ outlook.com` as the email address.

Ⓑ Type the `cantbeforgotten` as the password and then tap Enter .

Internet Explorer asks if you want it to store your password. Let's assume that this is a public computer. It wouldn't be wise to have the password stored here.

5. Choose **Not for This Site**.

6. Click the **New** button. ⊕ New

The new message form appears.

7. Type the message:

Ⓐ Type **brooke@gmail.com**, or click the full address that appears after you start typing.

Ⓑ Type the **Flash Fiction Flyer** as the subject

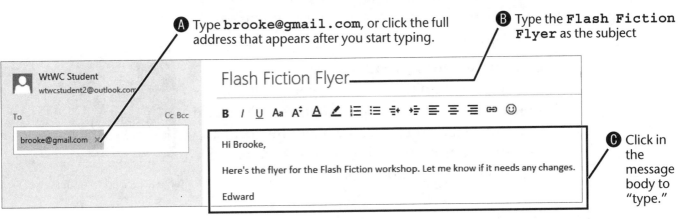

Ⓒ Click in the message body to "type."

Just as with other programs, it's a good idea to save your work from time-to-time.

8. Click **Save Draft**.

Just as with other programs, it's a good idea to save your work from time-to-time. You will return to the message shortly.

9. Click **Continue to Next Exercise**.

The next Websim loads. Read on to the next exercise.

Sharing Files Overview

When you want to share a file, you have two basic choices. Each gets the file to the recipient. Both methods are covered in more detail in the pages that follow.

- **Email Attachment** – This embeds one or more files inside an email message. The recipient can view and save each attachment.

- **Link to the file in Cloud Storage** – This sends the recipient a link to the file in your cloud storage. She or he clicks the link to download and open the file. Or the link may open the file in a web app, such as Word Online, which you used in Lesson 7, Using Cloud File Storage.

A file attached to a message.

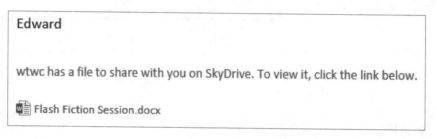

Sending Email Attachments

An attachment is a file sent with an email message. Attachments are useful for sending photos, documents, spreadsheets, and other files. An attachment is usually much more convenient and better formatted than retyping material or copying and pasting it into the body of a message.

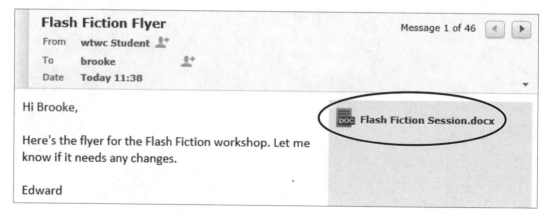

Brooke's webmail program displays an attachment.

Attachment Size

You can attach most types of files to messages. Messages can contain more than one attachment. However, most email services have a maximum attachment file size. So if you attach several full-size digital photos, the message might not go through. (Sharing links to files in cloud storage—as you'll learn to do later in this lesson—avoids this size issue.)

> **!TIP!** There are online services that can send files of almost any size, such as ShareFile.com. These overcome the maximum attachment size limitations of your email service.

Behind the Screen

Avoiding Security Risks

Email attachments and links in messages can be a source of computer viruses. Most antimalware program software automatically scans email messages and any attachments for viruses. Outlook warns you if you attach a file that might contain a virus. In fact, Outlook refuses to open or access some types of files that might contain viruses. For example, Outlook won't let you open any program file (filenames that end with .exe).

> **!WARNING!** *Never* open or view an email attachment or click a link from someone you don't know! There is a high risk the attachment file could contain a virus or a link point to an infected website.

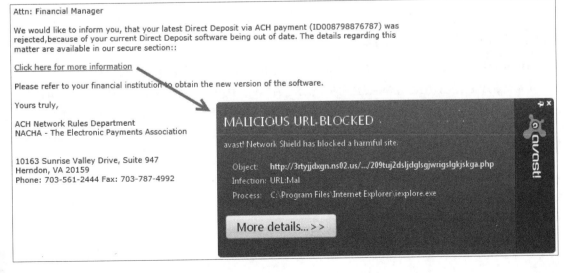

Attn: Financial Manager

We would like to inform you, that your latest Direct Deposit via ACH payment (ID008798876787) was rejected,because of your current Direct Deposit software being out of date. The details regarding this matter are available in our secure section::

Click here for more information

Please refer to your financial institution to obtain the new version of the software.

Yours truly,

ACH Network Rules Department
NACHA - The Electronic Payments Association

10163 Sunrise Valley Drive, Suite 947
Herndon, VA 20159
Phone: 703-561-2444 Fax: 703-787-4992

MALICIOUS URL BLOCKED

avast! Network Shield has blocked a harmful site.

Object: http://3rtyjjdxgn.ns02.us/.../209tuj2dsljdglsgjwrigslgkjskga.php
Infection: URL:Mal
Process: C:\Program Files\Internet Explorer\iexplore.exe

More details... >>

Clicking a message link leads to a malicious website. Fortunately, antimalware software blocked any harmful activity.

HANDS-ON 8.2 Attach a File to a Message

In this exercise, you will attach a Word document to the email message you started.

Before You Begin: If necessary, start the WebSim for this exercise.

1. Attach a file:

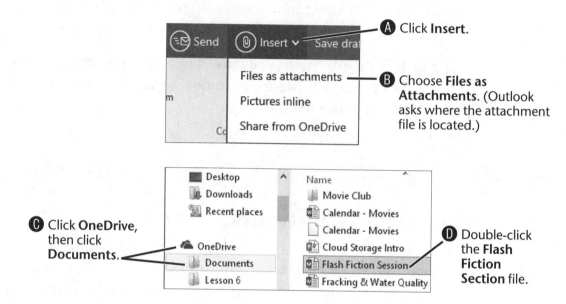

A Click **Insert**.

B Choose **Files as Attachments**. (Outlook asks where the attachment file is located.)

C Click **OneDrive**, then click **Documents**.

D Double-click the **Flash Fiction Section** file.

A large tile for the file appears in the attachments area. You could attach additional files now, but this one will do.

2. Click **Send** ⊟Send.

Outlook sends the message and returns you to the Inbox.

3. Click **Continue to Next Exercise**.

Saving Email Attachments

Attachments remain embedded in email messages until you save them. You can open an attachment when you first view a message, or wait until another time. However, until it is saved, the attachment isn't available to edit. It remains embedded in the message. Saving an attachment to a storage drive allows you to work with it normally.

Attachment Security Risks

Opening an attachment can put your computer at risk. It's rare, but any attachment can contain malware. Internet Security programs typically scan incoming email and all attachments for malware.

Antimalware programs have email and document scanning capabilities.

Example   You receive a message that appears to be from a friend. It tells you to check out the cool message or program attached. You open the attachment and nothing seems to happen. In reality, the attachment might be invisibly infecting your computer.

> **⚠WARNING!** *Never* open an attachment from someone you don't know. Be careful even when opening attachments from people you *do* know.

QUICK REFERENCE: Sending and Receiving Attachments with Outlook.com

Task	Procedure
Send an attachment	• Create the new email message. • Choose Message→Include→Attach File. • Navigate to the attachment file, select it, and click Insert.
Save an attachment	• Click once on the attachment in the message. • Choose Attachments→Actions→Save As.
Save all attachments	• Click once on any attachment in the message. • Choose Attachments→Actions→Save All Attachments. • Click OK, then choose a destination folder for the attachments and click OK again.

 HANDS-ON 8.3   Save an Attachment

In this exercise, you will save an attachment to an email message you've received.

Before You Begin: If necessary, start the WebSim for this exercise.

As the WebSim begins, you are viewing Brooke's reply to your message. She's attached some changes to the flyer. You are ready to download her attachment.

1. Click the **attachment tile**.

   Internet Explorer asks whether you want to open or save the attachment. For now, you'll simply save it. You'll use Save As so you can choose the save location. In this case, you'll save it to your OneDrive.

2. Save the attachment:

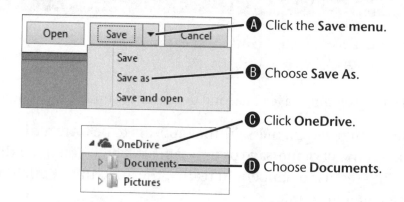

    Ⓐ Click the **Save menu**.

    Ⓑ Choose **Save As**.

    Ⓒ Click **OneDrive**.

    Ⓓ Choose **Documents**.

   Notice the way Brooke changed the name so you can tell her version apart from the original.

3. Click **Save**.

   Internet Explorer saves the attachment. It asks if you wish to open it. Since you know the sender is reliable, you do so.

4. Click **Open**.

   Word 2013 starts and displays the flyer.

5. Click the **scroll bar** to simulate scrolling down the page.

6. **Close** ☒ Word.

7. Start **File Explorer** .

8. Click **OneDrive**, then double-click **Documents**.

   Brooke's edited version is where you saved it. Email attachments are very effective for sending and receiving files. But if you use cloud storage, there's an even more convenient way to share, as you will see in the next topic.

9. Click **Continue to Next WebSim**.

Phishing Scams

Phishing is a technique whereby an unsuspecting victim is duped into giving out personal information to a website that mimics an actual site of a major company. For example, you may receive a message from a bank (possibly your own) that your online account access will be suspended unless you verify your personal information. A link in the message leads to a fake web page that looks just like the actual bank's page. Any information you enter on this page goes directly to the thieves, who can then use this information to access your account.

Account Suspended/Closed   You may receive a message indicating that your online account services have been suspended, closed, etc., or there may be a claim that the online banking system has been recently updated and you need to confirm your account information to resume access.

Dear Customer,

Del Norte Credit Union temporarily suspended your account.
Reason: Billing failure.
We require you to complete an account update so we can unlock your account.

To start the update process *click here*.

Once you have completed the update, we will send you an email notifying that your account is available again. After that you can access your account at any time.

The information provided will be treated in confidence and stored in our secure database.
If you fail to provide information about your account you'll discover that your account has been automatically deleted from DNCU database.

Copyright © Del Norte Credit Union. All Rights Reserved

The link on this email message takes you to a realistic replica of the credit union website. If you were to enter your account information, it does not update your account, but instead gives this information to thieves.

Example of a phishing message.

!TIP! *No* bank will ever ask you to update account information via an email message.

Sharing Cloud Storage Files

Sharing is the ability to give others online access to items in your cloud storage. As digital files grow in volume and number, sharing can be a great convenience. For example, you can share a folder of photos taken during a recent trip. Since most email services limit the size of attachments to messages, sharing can be the best way to distribute large files.

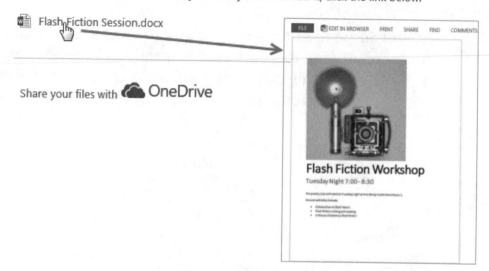

Clicking the link to a share invitation leads directly to a preview of the file. From there, most services let you edit or download the shared file.

Sharing Compared to Attachments

Sharing works by sending a link to a file. Unlike email attachments, the actual file is not embedded in the message. Instead, recipients use the link to view and download the file via your cloud storage service. One advantage of sharing over attachments is that recipients always have access to the latest version of a shared file.

Types of Sharing

Most cloud storage services support multiple types of sharing. Each type has benefits, depending on the type of interactivity you want. Some services require others to log in with an account regardless of the share level. Other services may allow view-only access without a login. By default, OneDrive only allows people you share a file with to view it. But you can change this setting to allow editing too.

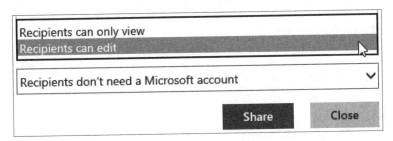

OneDrive displays share options for a file.

NOTE! Shared storage on the cloud is evolving rapidly. New types of permissions may have emerged by the time you read this.

Online Editing of Shared Files

Some cloud storage services, such as OneDrive and Google Drive, support web-based apps for editing common types of files without downloading. Others you share a file with can use the service's apps to edit shared files online. For example, a word processor document can be edited with Word Online or Google Docs.

Editing Shared Files without Web Apps If a cloud storage service doesn't support web apps, shared files must be downloaded for editing using software installed on the computer or tablet. After editing the changed file must be uploaded back to shared storage. This is less convenient, of course. Increasingly, cloud storage services will offer their own web apps to edit files.

QUICK REFERENCE: Sharing Files in Cloud Storage

Task	Procedure
Share a file	• Navigate to the file in File Explorer. • Right-click then choose Share With→OneDrive, or Share Dropbox Link, or a similar command (depending on your cloud-storage service).

HANDS-ON 8.4 **Share a File Link**

In this exercise, you will share the same file with Brooke, but with a link to the file in your OneDrive cloud storage instead.

Before You Begin: If necessary, start the WebSim for this exercise.

1. Start **File Explorer** .

2. Choose **OneDrive**, then choose **Documents**.

3. Give the share command:

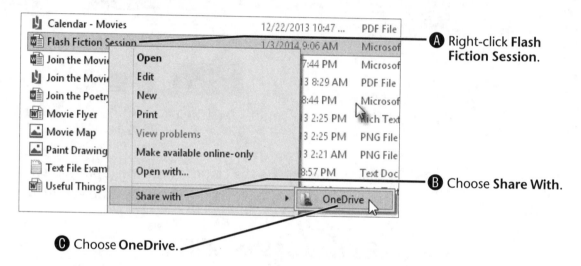

Ⓐ Right-click **Flash Fiction Session**.

Ⓑ Choose **Share With**.

Ⓒ Choose **OneDrive**.

Internet Explorer starts to display a OneDrive Share form. OneDrive has access to your account because you logged in with a Microsoft ID.

4. Fill out the share form:

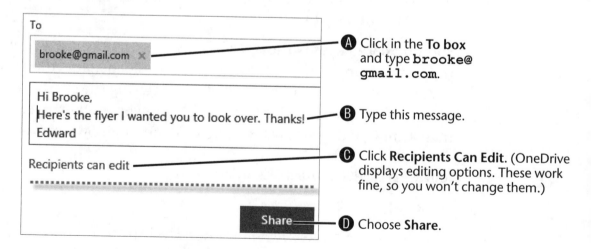

Ⓐ Click in the **To box** and type **brooke@ gmail.com**.

Ⓑ Type this message.

Ⓒ Click **Recipients Can Edit**. (OneDrive displays editing options. These work fine, so you won't change them.)

Ⓓ Choose **Share**.

OneDrive displays the progress of the share, then the file's new share status.

5. Click **Close**.

Open a Linked File Online

6. Click **Switch Chairs**.

You are now at Brooke's computer. She's viewing her webmail and sees the sharing invitation. Notice that the previous message with the attachment has a paper clip icon, but the one with the sharing link doesn't. The share message is also much smaller.

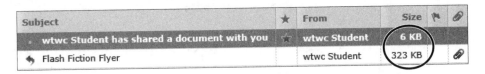

7. Double-click the sharing message.

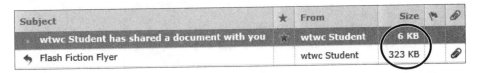

Brooke reads over the message. Notice the brief note at the beginning, then the additional text and link lower down.

8. Click (no need to double-click) the link.

OneDrive displays a preview of the flyer in Word Online in a new tab. Brooke used Word to edit the attachment in a previous exercise. This time, she will use Word Online.

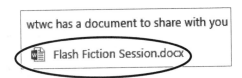

Edit the File Online

9. Click **Edit Document**, then choose **Edit in Word Online**.

Word Online's Ribbon appears with its editing tools; ready for you to make changes.

10. Click the **right scroll bar** to simulate scrolling down.

11. Edit the document:

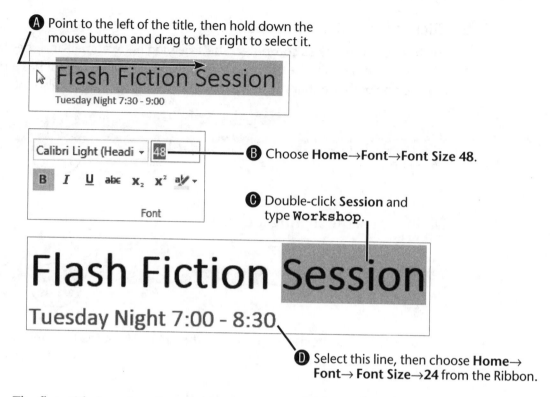

Ⓐ Point to the left of the title, then hold down the mouse button and drag to the right to select it.

Flash Fiction Session

Tuesday Night 7:30 - 9:00

Calibri Light (Headi ▾ 48

B *I* U̲ a̶b̶c̶ x₂ x² a̶ ▾

Font

Ⓑ Choose **Home→Font→Font Size 48**.

Ⓒ Double-click **Session** and type **Workshop**.

Flash Fiction Session

Tuesday Night 7:00 - 8:30

Ⓓ Select this line, then choose **Home→ Font→ Font Size→24** from the Ribbon.

The flyer title is on two lines. Let's adjust the margins to fix that.

12. Choose **Page Layout→Page Setup→Margins→Moderate** from the Ribbon.

Unlike the installed version of Word 2013, Word Online saves everything you do immediately, so there's no Save button. Brooke completes her editing session by simply closing the web page.

13. Close the editing tab.

 (17) Roundcube Webm...   Flash Fiction Sessio... ✕

You are back to viewing the email message. Brooke will send Edward a reply. Let's jump ahead in time to when he receives the message.

Open the Edited File

14. Click **Switch Chairs**.

You are back sitting at Edward's laptop as he views Brooke's reply.

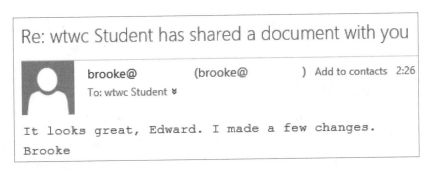

Edward opens OneDrive to check out the changes. He will switch from within Outlook directly to his Cloud storage.

15. Switch from Outlook.com to OneDrive:

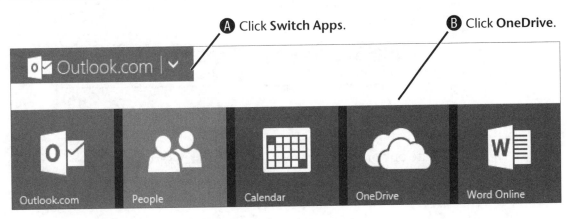

16. Click **Documents**.

Notice that OneDrive marks the Flash Fiction document as *shared*.

17. Click **Flash Fiction Session**.

18. Click the **scroll bar**, to simulate scrolling down the document.

OneDrive displays a preview using Word Online in a new tab. From here, Edward could click Edit Document to make additional changes, just like Brooke did earlier. Or he can close the tab with the preview after he's reviewed the document.

19. Close ⊠ the Word Online tab.

You are back to viewing Edward's OneDrive. He shared a single file easily enough from here. What if he wanted to share an entire folder? That's the next topic.

20. Click Continue to Next WebSim.

Sharing Cloud Folders

You can share entire folders in your cloud storage. This access can be a link, which allows only viewing and downloading. Or access can be granted for the sharer to modify files in the folder. In fact, each person may see the shared folder as part of their personal cloud storage. (These details will vary from one cloud storage service to another.) The process of sharing a folder with others is similar to sharing files.

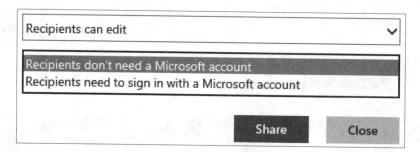

Share options vary between cloud storage services. Some allow non-subscribers to use shared storage, some don't.

Shared Folders and Subscriptions

Many cloud storage services require each person a folder's shared with to have a subscription/account. (OneDrive doesn't, however.) Some cloud storage services feature shared folders that synchronize on each user's computer, just like their personal (unshared) cloud storage. The storage in the shared folder might also count against each user's total free or paid storage.

Dropbox requires you to have a subscription to their service in order to accept a shared folder invitation.

Shared Folder Display

Some services only display shared folders via their web page view. For example, folders shared with you on OneDrive only appear on the web. They don't appear in the OneDrive folder on your computer or tablet.

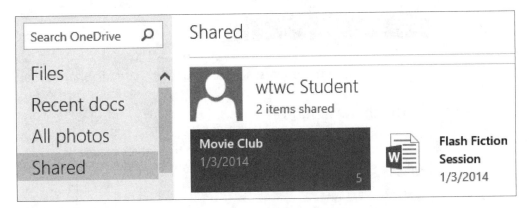

The shared area of OneDrive shows all files and folders shared with you by other users.

NOTE! As suggested in the file-sharing topic, shared storage on the cloud is evolving rapidly. Some limitations mentioned here may be gone by the time you read this.

HANDS-ON 8.5 Share a Folder

In this exercise, you will share your OneDrive lesson folder with others. As the WebSim begins, you are viewing Edward's OneDrive via the web.

Before You Begin: If necessary, start the WebSim for this exercise.

1. Share a folder:

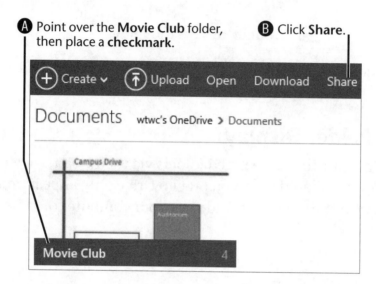

Ⓐ Point over the **Movie Club** folder, then place a **checkmark**.

Ⓑ Click **Share**.

A share invitation form appears, similar to one you used to share a file.

2. Fill in the share invitation:

Ⓐ Click in the **To box** and address the share to these three recipients. Type a comma or semicolon after the first two email addresses.

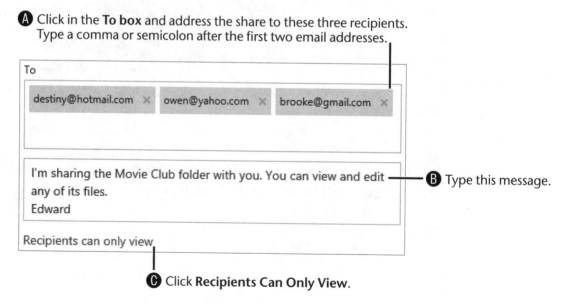

Ⓑ Type this message.

Ⓒ Click **Recipients Can Only View**.

OneDrive displays the available permissions settings so you can change them.

3. Finish the share:

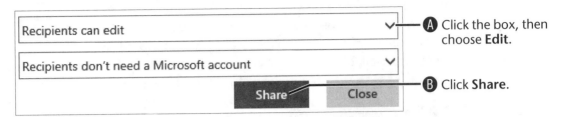

Ⓐ Click the box, then choose **Edit**.

Ⓑ Click **Share**.

OneDrive shows the progress of the share, then the folder's shared status and members.

4. Click **Close**.

OneDrive returns to a view of your cloud storage. Notice that the Movie Club folder now has a *shared* label.

5. Click **Switch Chairs**.

The WebSim switches you to Owen's computer. He too has a OneDrive account. He views the shared folder invitation in his email.

6. Click **Movie Club**.

OneDrive displays the folder in a new browser tab. Notice the address bar, indicating the owner (wtwc) and the folder name.

7. Click the **Join the Movie Club Word** document.

Join the Movie Club
Shared

OneDrive displays a preview. Notice that Owen could open this document for online editing, just as Brooke did with a shared file. In effect, every file Edward saves to this folder becomes available as a shared file. This saves Edward the trouble of sending out a new link for each new file he shares.

8. Click **Back to Course**.

The links to the eLab WebSims reappear.

Back To Course

Concepts Review

To check your knowledge of the key concepts introduced in this lesson, complete the Concepts Review quiz here or on the student resource center.

True/False Questions

		Page Number

1. Word Online is an example of a web-based application. **True False** _____

2. Sharing a file embeds it in the emailed invitation. **True False** _____

3. Outlook.com is a webmail service. **True False** _____

4. An attachment to an email message could be a security risk. **True False** _____

5. OneDrive always includes editing privileges for any file you share. **True False** _____

6. You can share entire folders in cloud storage. **True False** _____

Multiple Choice Questions

7. Email attachments _____.

   Page Number: _____

   a. are embedded inside an email message
   b. must be downloaded in order to make changes
   c. could possibly contain malware
   d. All of the above

8. When you receive an attachment from someone you don't know you should _____.

   Page Number: _____

   a. open it and see if a virus warning appears
   b. scan the message for a virus, if your security software can do this
   c. not open it
   d. None of the above

9. A shared file link _____.

   Page Number: _____

   a. downloads the file to the recipient's computer automatically
   b. takes you back to the previous folder you were browsing
   c. undoes your most recent command
   d. None of above

10. A web app _____.

    Page Number: _____

    a. has to be installed on the computer or tablet to work
    b. can edit compatible files online
    c. can run on any Internet-connected computer
    d. All of the above
    e. Only b and c

Skill Builders

Attach a File to Email

On the Web

In this exercise, you will attach a file to an email message from the Windows 8.1 email app.

1. Start **Internet Explorer** and navigate to the student resource center by typing `labyrinthelab.com/wtwc5` into the address bar.

2. Click **Lesson 8: Sharing Files**.

3. Click **Skill Builder 8.1: Attach a File to Email**.

    As the WebSim begins, you are finishing an email message to a classmate using the Email tablet app built into Windows 8.1. The attachment button on virtually all email programs shows a paper clip.

4. Click **Attach** 📎.

    The tablet email program displays your files and folders in a different fashion than Traditional Desktop programs. It's optimized for touch computing.

5. Choose a location:

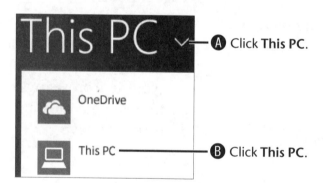

    A Click **This PC**.

    B Click **This PC**.

6. Click **Documents**.

    Folders appear as tiles, files as icons.

7. Click once (don't double-click) **Class Notes**.

    A checkmark appears. You could tap or click other files to add them to the command.

8. Click **Attach**.

    The file appears in the attachment section.

9. Click **Send** .

10. Click **Continue to Next WebSim**.

Save an Attachment

In this exercise, you will save an attachment you've received via email. This makes the file available to work on normally on your computer or tablet.

Before You Begin: If necessary, start the WebSim for this exercise.

As the WebSim begins, you are viewing Edward's email via Outlook.com on the Traditional Desktop.

1. Open an attachment:

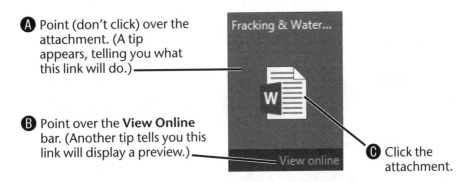

   A Point (don't click) over the attachment. (A tip appears, telling you what this link will do.)

   B Point over the **View Online** bar. (Another tip tells you this link will display a preview.)

   C Click the attachment.

2. Choose **Save menu** ⏷, then **Save As**.

3. Click **OneDrive**, then click **Documents**.

4. Click **Save**.

   Internet Explorer displays an Open option.

5. Click **Open**.

   Word starts to display the document. Notice the Protected View bar. This is to help you avoid malware that might be transmitted via a Word document. Since you know the sender, it's OK to enable editing.

6. Click **Enable Editing**.

   Word's normal Ribbon appears, indicating you can now work with this document normally.

7. Click **Continue to Next WebSim**.

SKILL BUILDER 8.3 Share a Link to a File Using OneDrive

In this exercise, you will share a file from your OneDrive.

Before You Begin: If necessary, start the WebSim for this exercise.

As the WebSim begins, you are viewing Edward's email via Outlook.com on the Traditional Desktop.

1. Start **File Explorer** and display **OneDrive**, then **Documents**.

2. Right-click **Fracking & Water**, then choose **Share With→OneDrive**.
   OneDrive displays a share form.

3. Fill-in the form:
   - Address the message to **Brooke@gmail.com**
   - Type a brief note: **Here's a link to my review of your term paper.**

4. Click **Share**.
   OneDrive displays the progress of the share, then displays the document's status.

5. Click **Close**.

6. Click **Continue to Next WebSim**.

SKILL BUILDER 8.4 Share a OneDrive Folder

In this exercise, you will create a new folder, move files to it, and send a share invitation to a folder.

Before You Begin: If necessary, start the WebSim for this exercise.

As the WebSim begins, you are viewing your OneDrive via the web.

1. Click **Create→Folder**, then name the folder **Writing Groups**.

2. Click **Documents**.

3. Place checkmarks on the following files:
   - Flash Fiction Session
   - Join the Poetry Club (Word doc)

4. Click **Manage→Move To**.

5. Choose **Writing Groups**, then click **Move**.

6. Navigate back to the base level.

   Notice that the new Writing Groups folder now displays a "2".

7. Right-click **Writing Groups**, then choose **Share**.

   Notice that recipients can only view. Let's change the permission level.

8. Click **Recipients Can Only View**, then set the permission to **Recipients Can Edit**.

   After adding email addresses and a short note, the share would be ready to send.

9. Click **Continue to Next WebSim**.

SKILL BUILDER 8.5   # Open a File for Editing Online

In this exercise, you will view a shared folder and open one of its files for editing online.

Before You Begin: If necessary, start the WebSim for this exercise.

As the WebSim begins, you are viewing Brooke's email via webmail on the Traditional Desktop.

1. Click the **2 files** link in the message.

   OneDrive displays the two files in the new shared folder.

2. Click **Flash Fiction Session**.

   A preview of the document appears.

3. Choose **Edit Document→Edit in Word Online**.

   The full Ribbon appears and the document is ready for editing.

4. Click **Back to Course**.

Units of Measure

Units of measure indicate the performance and capacity of a computer system or tablet. A good sense of these measures will help you make better choices when you buy your next computer. For example, the sharpness of the screen is measured by its resolution (not just its size). Measures of storage help you estimate your needs for storage in the computer and on the cloud.

Measures of Volume/Capacity

These terms help you determine the size of a file and the capacity of a disk drive or flash drive to hold those files.

Term	Meaning	Examples
bit	A single on-off switch (transistor) in a byte	0, 1
byte	Eight bits strung together in a specific order to represent a single character of data	A, B, C, &, @
kilobyte (KB)	One thousand bytes (characters) of data	Approximately two paragraphs of single-spaced text
megabyte (MB)	One million bytes of data	About 900 pages of single-spaced text or 3 medium-length novels
gigabyte (GB)	One billion bytes of data	Approximately 200 typical 5 MB digital photos or 250 four-minute songs in high-quality MP3 format
terabyte (TB)	One trillion bytes of data	About 250,000 four-minute songs in MP3 format, 380 hours of DVD-quality video, or about 120 hours of HD-quality video

Measures of Resolution/Sharpness

These terms indicate the size and sharpness of the computer screen.

Term	Meaning	Examples
resolution	The number of pixels (dots of light) arrayed horizontally and vertically on the screen	1366 x 768 (15" laptop screen) 1920 x 1200 (24" monitor) 1920 x 1080 (HDTV monitor)
screen size	A diagonal measurement of the screen's physical dimensions	24" monitor 15" screen (laptop)

Measures of Speed

These terms indicate the speed of a computer's processor or of an Internet connection.

Term	Meaning	Examples
gigahertz (GHz)	One billion cycles per second	1.8 GHz 3.2 GHz
bits per second (bps)	The number of bits (not bytes) that a network connection can transmit or receive	12 Mbps (DSL service) 20 Mbps (cable modem)

Glossary

Aero Snap   Feature that enables a window to be resized by dragging it to the side or top of the Desktop

Aero window commands   Shortcuts to place program windows on the Traditional Desktop
Examples: Aero Snap, Aero Shake

antimalware   Software designed to stop viruses and other uninvited programs from infecting files on the computer
Example: Norton Antivirus

app   Software designed to run on the Tablet Desktop; also a popular term for a small, simple application

application   Software designed to help you get work done
Examples: Microsoft Word, Internet Explorer

bytes   Single characters of data
Examples: A, B, C, etc.

charms   A set of basic commands that appears when you point at the upper-right corner of the screen

click   A tap and release of the mouse button; used to select objects and commands

cloud   Services and storage with an unknown physical location

cloud computing   Relying on cloud-based applications and files to get work done

cloud storage   Files stored in the cloud rather than on a local physical drive

cursor   Blinking indicator where text will appear on the screen when typing; also called the insertion point

domain name   The base electronic address of a location on the Internet
See also About Domains on page 154
Example: amazon.com, google.com, nps.gov

double-click   Two quick clicks in succession; usually used as a shortcut to a commonly used command, such as Open

download   Transferring a file from a remote computer or storage service to your local computer or tablet.

drag   A mouse motion with the mouse button held down as you move an object with the mouse

drive   Permanent storage device

drive letter   Alphabetical designation assigned to storage devices
Example: C:, Removable drive F:

Dropbox   The first popular cloud storage service; similar to OneDrive

email   Short for electronic mail; email messages travel around the world in seconds via the Internet

favorite   Bookmark that makes it easy to return to a specific web page
See also Creating Favorites on page 195

files   Groups of computer data with a common purpose
Example: A paper you have typed, an application program

file sharing   Capability to give access to a files in cloud or network storage to other users

folder   An electronic location in which you store groups of related files

Example: Pictures folder

folder sharing   Capability to give access to an entire folder in cloud or network storage to other users; usually requires that the other users subscribe to the same cloud storage service

gigabytes   Approximately one billion bytes of data

Example: About 3,000 books

gigahertz (GHz)   One billion pulses of electricity in an electrical circuit in a single second; the speed of most processors sold today is measured in gigahertz

Example: Intel 3.2 GHz Core i5

hardware   Physical components of a computer system

Examples: Disk drive, screen, USB flash drive, processor

Internet   The world's largest computer network, used by billions of individuals daily

See also Defining the Internet on page 149

kilobyte (KB)   Approximately one thousand bytes of data

Example: One single-spaced page of text

library   A component of the Windows file storage hierarchy; can contain folders and files from more than one storage drive

Example: The Documents library

malware   Generic term for malicious software viruses that can damage a computer system

megabyte (MB)   Approximately one million bytes of data

Example: three average-length novels

microprocessor   See Processor

monitor   The computer screen on a Desktop computer

Example: 24″ touch screen

mouse pointer   Indicator that moves on the screen in response to the mouse

multitasking   Running more than one program simultaneously so you can switch between them quickly; multitasking can only be performed on the normal Desktop (not the Tablet Desktop)

operating system   Software that manages your system, such as Windows

pin   To add a program icon to the Taskbar for easy access to an application

pixels   Single dots of light on a computer or tablet screen

point   Positioning the mouse pointer on an object without clicking

port   A place (usually at the back of the computer) to plug in a cable

Example: USB port

processor   A single silicon chip containing the complete circuitry of a computer; modern processors now can contain 2 (duo) or 4 (quad) or more processors on a single chip

Example: Intel Core i5, Intel Atom

RAM   Short for random access memory; computer chip designed to temporarily store data to be processed

See also Random Access Memory on page 41

Example: 8 GB RAM

resolution   Measure of the sharpness of a computer screen or a printout

Example: 1680 x 1050 (monitor), 600 DPI (ink-jet printer)

Ribbon   The interface for some Microsoft Office application programs (e.g. Word, Excel); replaces the menu bar and toolbars with one large toolbar

See also How Ribbon Commands Are Organized on page 48

right-click   A click motion using the right rather than the left mouse button; usually used to display a pop-up menu of common commands

scanner   Device that turns photographs and other images into computer files; scanners are also increasingly built into popular all-in-one printers

Example: HP Scanjet G3010c

Sleep   A low-power mode from which the computer or tablet wakes when you click or tap

software   Logical component of a computer system; composed of digital code stored in the form of files; application software helps you get work done; an operating system (e.g. Windows 7 or 8) runs the basic functions of the computer

Examples: Windows, Internet Explorer, a document file

synchronization   Also called sync; the automatic updating of files on a device with the latest versions of the same files on other devices.

tabbed browsing   The capability to open multiple web pages within a single browser window in Internet Explorer and many other web browsers

See also Using Tabbed Browsing on page 189

Tablet Desktop   Place where basic tablet apps run

Taskbar   The bar at the bottom of the Windows Desktop that displays a Start button and icons for pinned and running applications

terabyte (TB)   Approximately one trillion bytes (characters) of data

Example: About 120 hours of HD video

Traditional desktop   Where one or more traditional computer applications run simultaneously; Windows 8.1 also runs limited applications (called apps) on its Tablet Desktop

Undo   Button used to reverse your last action or command

upload   Transmitting a local file to a remote computer or storage service

URL   Short for Uniform Resource Locator; the electronic address of a website

Example: pinterest.com, nps.gov, iaia.edu

USB flash drive   A small file storage device that plugs into a computer's USB port; sometimes called a thumb drive

USB port   Short for Universal Serial Bus port; used to connect devices such as cameras, MP3 players, and external hard drives. USB 3 ports have about 2-3 times the speed capability compared to older USB 2 ports.

Examples: USB flash drive in USB port, portable hard drive with a USB 3 connection

viruses Programs that invisibly "infect" files and disrupt operation of a computer in some way; computer viruses are largely spread via the Internet

Examples: Michelangelo, Love Bug

watched folders Folders that automatically synchronize their content with a cloud storage service

web Short for World Wide Web; the collection of billions of pages accessible via the Internet

web access The ability to view and work with files stored on the cloud via a web browser rather than the service's application program or phone/tablet app.

web browser An application program optimized for viewing web pages

See also Using Internet Explorer on page 150

website A collection of web pages owned by a specific organization or individual

Index

A

Add/Remove Programs on Control
    Panel, 111
address bar, Internet Explorer, 152–153,
    155–156, 177, 185–186
addresses, email, 251–252
ads, online, 219
Aero Peek, 42
Aero Shake, 42
Aero Snap, 42
Aero window commands, 42–45
all-in-one printers, 96
Alt key, 78
antimalware software, 255
application programs (*see* programs,
    application)
Apps screen, 15, 35
ARM processors, 40
attachments, email
    compared to cloud-based file sharing,
        260
    defined, 254
    receiving, 257
    saving, 256–258
    sending, 254–256
    size limitations, 255, 260
AutoComplete, 156–157

B

Back button
    folder window, 123
    web browser, 161–163
bank accounts, phishing scams
    concerning, 259
Bcc address in email, 251
bit, defined, 277
bits per second (bps), defined, 278
bookmarks, web browser (*see* Favorites
    bar)
browsers, web
    (*see also* Internet Explorer (IE);
        searching the web)
    bookmarks (Favorites), 194–200
    printing web pages, 202–205
    tab feature, 189–194
    types, 151
bulleted list characters, 88–90
byte, defined, 277

C

capacity measurements, 277
Cc address in email, 251
charms, 19, 37–38
clicking with mouse, 11, 113–114
Clipboard, 59
closing documents, 106
closing windows, 39

cloud computing
    (*see also* OneDrive)
    defined, 215
    privacy issue, 6, 219
    services based in, 215
    sharing files and folders, 215, 254,
        260–270
    storage options, 118, 216
    synchronizing data, 215, 226–228
    watched folders, 226–230
.com domain, 154
computers
    (*see also* software)
    hardware components, 40–41
    locking, 5, 18
    modes of operation, 18
    networking, 41
    turning on/off, 24–25
Control Panel, 111–114
Copy and Paste commands (*see* Cut,
    Copy, and Paste features)
country-based domains, 154
Ctrl key for keyboard shortcuts, 78
cursor, on-screen, 75
cursor keys, 78, 91
Cut, Copy, and Paste features
    drawings, 58–60
    files and folders, 124, 125–128
    standardization across programs, 87
    text, 91–95

D

Date/Time on Control Panel, 111
default setting, defined, 95, 119
deleting
    data from cloud, 231–232
    favorites in web browser, 200
    files and folders, 131–133, 137,
        231–232
Desktops, 7–9, 47
    (*see also* Tablet Desktop; Traditional
        Desktop)
disk drives (*see* storage devices)
display, computer screen, 58, 111, 278
domains, Internet, 153, 154
double-clicking with mouse, 11,
    113–114
downloading files from web, 220, 223
dragging with mouse, 11
drives (*see* storage devices)
Dropbox, 226, 229, 267

E

.edu domain, 154
email
    attachments to, 254–258, 260
    composing a message, 251–253
    phishing scams, 259
email addresses, 251–252
Esc key, 78

F

Favorites bar, Internet Explorer, 194–199
Favorites Center, Internet Explorer,
    199–200
File Explorer, 115–116
filenames, 21, 54
files
    as attachments to email, 254–258,
        260
    backing up flash drive, 128–130
    browsing through, 115–119
    comparing to folders, 119
    copying, 124, 125–128
    creating on OneDrive, 235–239
    defined, 118
    deleting, 131–133, 137, 231–232
    downloading from web, 220, 223
    libraries, 118
    moving, 124, 125–128
    naming, 21, 54
    opening, 119, 121
    operating system's control of, 21
    organization of, 122–123
    restoring, 131–133
    saving, 134–137
    sharing in cloud, 215, 254, 260–266
    sorting, 116, 117
    storage hierarchy, 118
    uploading to web, 220–223
    viewing options, 116, 117, 233–234
flash drive (*see* USB flash drive)
folders
    comparing to files, 119
    copying, 124, 125–128
    creating new, 122, 123
    defined, 118
    deleting, 131–133, 137
    Favorites in Internet Explorer, 199
    moving, 124, 125–128
    naming, 122
    navigating online, 218
    opening, 122, 123
    organizing, 138
    restoring, 131–133
    selecting multiple, 127
    sharing in cloud, 266–270
    viewing options, 116, 117
    watched, 226–230
formatting text documents, 83–86, 93,
    238–239
Forward button, web browser, 161–163
full screen view for web pages, 166,
    168–169
function keys, 78

G

gestures, touchscreen, 11, 12
gigabyte (GB), defined, 277
gigahertz (GHz), defined, 278
Google.com, 177
Google Drive, 226
.gov domain, 154

H

hand icon for web page links, 159
hardware
    (see also mouse; storage devices)
    basic components, 40–41
    keyboard, 78
    networking, 41
    operating system's control of, 21
    processor, 40, 52
    RAM, 41, 52, 53
    touchpad, 9, 11–12
    touchscreen, 9, 12, 58
    USB port, 41
    video display, 58, 111, 278
highlighting (see selection methods)
History view panel, web browser,
    200–202
Home button, 163
homepage, web browser, 151, 163–166
hyperlinks (see links)
hypertext, defined, 158

I

I-beam symbol (see text pointer)
IE (see Internet Explorer (IE))
images, organizing, 138
Immersive Browser (see Internet
    Explorer (IE))
ink jet printers, 96
Internet
    (see also browsers, web; cloud
        computing)
    definition and scope of, 149
    domains on, 154
    email, 251–260
Internet Explorer (IE)
    address bar, 152–153, 155–156, 177,
        185–186
    Favorites, 194–199
    History view, 200–202
    homepage, 151, 163–166
    links, 158–161
    navigation controls, 161–166
    search suggestions feature, 183
    starting, 150, 151–152
    versions of, 150
    viewing web pages, 166–169
    window features, 152

J

.jp domain, 154

K

keyboard
    overview of features, 78
    special keys, 78
    switching between programs, 45,
        46–47
    web page navigation with, 168
keyboard shortcut, 78
keyword searches, web, 182–183
kilobyte (KB), defined, 277

L

leader, tab, 79–81
libraries, 118
links
    defined, 158
    files in cloud storage, 254, 262–266
    navigating with, 158–161
    sponsored links in search results, 185
    types of, 159
Linux, 20
live tiles, 14
Lock mode, 18
Lock screen, 5

M

Mac OS X, 20
malware, 255, 257
maximizing windows, 39
megabyte (MB), defined, 277
memory (RAM), 41, 52, 53
messages (see email)
metasearch engines, 184
metatags in web pages, 185
microprocessor (see processor)
Microsoft account, 5, 6, 218
Microsoft Office, 216, 229, 235–236,
    251–253
    (see also Word, Microsoft)
minimizing windows, 39
Modern Interface (see Tablet Desktop)
mouse
    buttons and actions, 11, 13
    Control Panel settings, 111, 113
    defined, 9
    scroll wheel, 166
    text pointer, 75

N

naming conventions, 54, 122
native resolution, defined, 58
Nelson, Ted, 158
networking hardware, 41
Notification Area, taskbar, 62
Numeric keypad, 78

O

Office, Microsoft, 216, 229, 235–236,
    251–253
    (see also Word, Microsoft)

OneDrive
    creating files directly on, 235–239
    deleting files from, 231–232
    downloading files from, 220, 223
    folder sharing, 268–270
    lack of shared folder display, 267
    navigating storage in, 216–218
    offline viewing of files, 233–234
    privacy issue, 6
    Recycle Bin, 231
    saving watched folders, 229–230
    as storage option, 216
    subscription-free service, 266
    synchronizing with, 226–228
    types of sharing on, 261
    uploading files to, 220–223
    viewing options, 223–225
opening files and folders, 119, 121, 122,
    123
operating system (OS), 5, 20–21
    (see also Windows 8.1)
.org domain, 154
Outlook web app, 251–253

P

Paint, 48–51
Paste command (see Cut, Copy, and
    Paste features)
PDF file format, saving in, 95, 98–99
phishing scams, 259
photos, organizing, 138
pinning and unpinning programs,
    35–36
pixel, defined, 58
pointing with mouse, 11
printers, 96, 111
printing
    text documents, 95–99
    web pages, 202–205
    wireless, 96
Print Preview, 202–203
privacy issue, 6–7, 219
processor, 40, 52
programs, application
    (see also Internet Explorer (IE); Word,
        Microsoft)
    adding or removing in Control Panel,
        111
    default program for a file type, 119
    multitasking, 45–47
    operating system's control of, 21
    Outlook web app, 251–253
    Paint, 48–51
    pinning and unpinning, 35–36
    Ribbon functions, 48
    running process on computer, 52
    saving data in, 52–55
    searching for, 37–38
    on taskbar, 35–36
    web apps, 235–239, 251–253, 261
    window controls, 39, 42–45
    WordPad, 55–57
protocols, defined, 149

Q

Quick Access toolbar, 125
quick sizing buttons, window, 39, 42

R

Random Access Memory (RAM), 41, 52, 53
receiving email messages, 257
Recent Documents list, 97
Recycle Bin, 131–132, 137, 231
Refresh button, 153
relevance ratings, search engines, 184
resizing windows, 39, 42
resolution, video display, 58, 278
restarting Windows, 24–25
restoring
    files and folders, 131–133
    windows (size), 39
Ribbon
    display options, 39
    File Explorer, 116
    organization of, 48
    Word, 75
    WordPad, 55–56
right-clicking with mouse, 11
rights to cloud content, 219

S

Safely Remove Hardware command, 62
Save vs. Save As commands, 87, 134–137
saving
    attachments to email, 256–258
    automatic save in web apps, 236
    drawings in Paint, 54–55
    file-naming rules, 54
    files in general, 134–137
    PDF file format, 95, 98–99
    standardization across programs, 87
    storage locations, 52–54
    text documents, 81–82
    to watched folders, 229–230
screen size, defined, 278
search bar, Internet Explorer (*see* address bar)
Search charm, 37–38
searching the web
    adding search providers, 178, 179–180
    address bar as search tool, 177, 185–186
    default search provider, 178, 181–182
    interpreting search results, 186–187
    keyword searches, 182–183
    Microsoft's tracking of search, 7
    narrowing search, 187–189
    search engines, 177–182, 184–185
    suggestions while searching, 183
security, online, 255, 257, 259
Select All command, 127
selection methods
    multiple files and folders, 127
    printing web page content, 202–205
    text, 91
server, defined, 215
ShareFile.com, 255

sharing files and folders
    cloud storage, 215, 254, 260–270
    editing, 261, 263–264
    email attachments, 254–258
    overview, 254
shutting down Windows, 24–25
signing on and off, 5–6, 19
Sign Out mode, 18
Sleep mode, 18
software
    (*see also* programs, application; Windows 8.1)
    antimalware, 255
    operating systems, 5, 20–21
    restarting after installing or uninstalling, 24
    standardization of functions, 87
Sounds, Control Panel settings, 111
speed measurements, 278
sponsored links in search results, 185
Start screen (*see* Tablet Desktop)
storage devices
    (*see also* OneDrive)
    drive letters, 120
    flash drives, 61–62, 128–130, 131
    hierarchy in, 118
    operating system's role, 21
    saving information, 52–54
    types of, 53–54
styles in word processing, 83–86, 87
subscriptions to shared folders, 266
symbol fonts, 88
synchronizing data, 5, 6, 215, 226–228

T

tabbed web browsing, 189–194
Tablet Desktop (Start screen)
    Apps screen, 15, 35
    compared to Traditional, 7–9
    Internet Explorer version, 150
    OneDrive app, 217
    overview, 14–18
    pinning apps from, 35
    switching between apps, 45
tab settings, 79–82
Taskbar, 35–36, 45
templates, Word, 74
terabyte (TB), defined, 277
text
    (*see also* Word, Microsoft)
    formatting, 83–86, 93, 238–239
    printing, 95–99
    selection methods, 91
    typing techniques, 75–77
    WordPad, 55–57
text pointer, 75
themes, Word, 83–86
This PC file storage option, 118
tiles on Start screen, 14–18
top-level Internet domains, 154
touchpad, 9, 11–12
touchscreen, 9, 12, 58

Traditional Desktop
    clearing of open windows, 45
    compared to Tablet, 7–9
    controlling windows, 39, 42–45
    copy and paste functions, 58–60
    Internet Explorer version, 150
    multitasking, 45–47
    removing flash drives safely, 61–62
    Ribbon, 48
    saving data, 52–55
    searching for programs, 37–38
    taskbar, 35–36
    word processing with WordPad, 55–57
turning on/off computer, 24–25
typing techniques, 75–77

U

Undo command, 124–125, 126
units of measure, 277–278
uploading files to web, 220–223
URLs (uniform resource locators), 152–153
USB flash drive, 61–62, 128–130, 131
USB port, 41

V

video display, 58, 111, 278
viruses, computer (*see* malware)
volume measurements, 277

W

watched folders, 226–230
web, defined, 147
    (*see also* browsers, web; cloud computing)
web access, and cloud storage, 216
web apps, 235–239, 251–253, 261
webmail, 251–253
WebSims, 159
windows
    Back button, 123
    clearing screen of open, 45
    closing, 39
    controlling, 39, 42–45
    sizing, 39, 42
    switching between, 45–47
Windows, versions of, 21
Windows 8.1
    (*see also* Tablet Desktop; Traditional Desktop)
    charms feature, 19
    Control Panel, 111–114
    Desktops comparison, 7–9
    disruption of changes in, 10
    input controls (mouse, touchpad), 9–13
    modes of operation, 18, 22–23
    Recycle Bin, 131–132, 137, 231
    restarting, 24–25
    shutting down, 24–25
    signing on and off, 5–6, 19
    Sleep mode, 18
    starting, 5–6
Windows 8.1 RT, 40

Windows key, 78
wireless printing, 96
Word, Microsoft
    bulleted list characters, 88–90
    closing documents, 106
    Cut, Copy, and Paste commands,
        91–95
    formatting, 83–86
    new document, creating, 73–75
    printing documents, 95–99
    Ribbon, 75
    saving documents, 81–82
    tab settings, 79–82
    templates, 74
    themes, 83–86
    typing text, 75–77
    viewing options, 76
    web app version, 236–239
WordPad, 55–57
word processing, 55–57, 73

Z
zooming the view on web page, 167, 168